T0339600

Practical Financial Modelling

Practical Financial Modelling

The Development and Audit of Cash Flow Models

Third Edition

Jonathan Swan

AMSTERDAM • BOSTON • CAMBRIDGE • HEIDELBERG
LONDON • NEW YORK • OXFORD • PARIS • SAN DIEGO
SAN FRANCISCO • SINGAPORE • SYDNEY • TOKYO

Butterworth-Heinemann is an imprint of Elsevier

ISBN: 978-0-08-100587-3

British Library Cataloguing-in-Publication Data
A catalogue record for this book is available from the British Library

Library of Congress Cataloging-in-Publication Data
A catalog record for this book is available from the Library of Congress

For information on all Butterworth-Heinemann publications
visit our website at http://store.elsevier.com/

Working together
to grow libraries in
developing countries

www.elsevier.com • www.bookaid.org

Publisher: Nikki Levy
Acquisition Editor: J. Scott Bentley
Editorial Project Manager: Susan Ikeda
Production Project Manager: Nicky Carter
Designer: Mark Rogers

Typeset by TNQ Books and Journals
www.tnq.co.in

Printed and bound in the UK

Dedication

To Rebecca, Jack, and Jeremy:
Modelling is nothing to do with catwalks.

Contents

About the Author   xvii
Preface to the Third Edition   xix
Preface to the Second Edition   xxi
Preface to the First Edition   xxiii
Acknowledgements   xxv
About Operis Group   xxvii
Introduction   xxix

Part I
The Modelling Environment

1. Quality Assurance   3

    The Modelling Environment   3
    The Project Finance Sector   4
    The Regulatory Environment   5
    It Doesn't Affect Us, Does It?   6
    Case Study: The Macpherson Report   7
    Case Study: ICAEW's 20 Principles   8
    Modelling Standards   9
    Quality Assurance   10
    Senior Responsible Owner   12
    Modelling Compliance Officer   12
    Modelling Environment   13
    Model Audit and Model Review   13
    Risk Assessment   16
    Risk Controls   16
    Access Control   16
    Input Control   17
    Change Control   17
    Version Control   17
    Quality Assurance and the Modelling Methodology   17

2. Quality Control   19

    Introduction   19
    Understanding Error   19

Pointing Errors   19
Input Errors   20
Omission Errors   20
Commission Errors   20
Alteration Errors   21
Calculation Errors   21
Timing Errors   21
Competence Errors   21
Domain Errors   22
Error Recognition   22
Audit Tools and Techniques   22
F2 Edit Cell   23
F9   23
Trace Precedents   23
Ctrl+[and F5 Combination   24
F2 and F5 Combination   24
View Formulas   24
Formula Auditing Ribbon Group   24
Evaluate Formula   25
The Watch Window   26
Error Checking   26
Error Values   27
#VALUE!   27
#REF!   28
#NAME?   28
#DIV/0!   28
#NUM!   29
#N/A   29
Debugging Error Values   29
Printing without Errors   29
The 'Break-and-Make' Technique   30
The Model Reviewer and the Review Plan   30
Printing   31
Issues Reporting   31
The Audit Sheet   32
The Purpose   32
The MUT   33
Layout   33
Environmental Checks   35
Time Stamping   35
Iteration Status   36
File Links   37
R1C1 Reference Style   38
Structural Checks   39
Location of Inputs   39
Hard-Coded Values   39
References to Blank Cells   41
Left-to-Right Consistency   41

3-D or Cross-Sheet Calculations   42
Errors   43
Hidden Columns and Rows   44
Hidden Sheets   44
Merged Cells   44
Array Formulas   45
Arithmetical Checks   46
The Audit Check Formula   47
Financial Checks   49
Principle   49
Balance Sheet   49
Cash Flow   50
Income Statement   50
Other Financial Checks   51
Ratios   51
Internal Rate of Return   52
The Audit Chart   53
Change Checks   53
Model Comparison   53
Model Map   54
Using the Audit Sheet   56
The Audit Workbook   56
Layout   57
Alignment of Timelines   57
Key Results   59
Reconstruction   59
Sensitivities and Deltas   62
Third Party Model Audit Tools   64

3.   **Model Structure**   **67**

Introduction   67
Choosing the Right Tool   67
The Three Principles   68
Two Approaches   68
Purpose   69
Structure   70
Version Control   71
Periodicity   71
Accuracy   72
Colour   72
Workbook Structure   73
The Inputs or Assumptions Sheet   74
Absence of Calculations   74
The Workings or Calculations Sheet   74
Logic Cascade   75
The Size of the Sheet   75
No Numbers   75

Outputs	76
Rationale	76
Audit or Control Sheet	77
Variations	77
Documentation	80
Inputs	80
Comments and Text Boxes	80
Key Information	81
Microsoft Backstage	81
File Properties	83
General	84
Summary	84
Statistics	84
Contents	85
Custom	85
Printing and Reporting	86
Print Area	86
Group Mode	87
Page Setup	87
Fit to Page	87
Headers and Footers	87
Print Titles	88
Reports and Custom Views	88
Model Development	89
New File	90
Saving	90
Grouping	90
Layout	90
Units and Base Columns	91
Number Formatting	91
AutoComplete	91
Printing	92
Data Entry	92
Cell Comments	92
Fill Right	92
Sign Conventions	93
Navigation	93
Ctrl+PgUp/Ctrl+PgDn	93
Alt+PgUp/Alt+PgDn	93
Right-Click Scroll Tab Buttons	94
Home/Ctrl+Home	94
Ctrl+End	94
Ctrl+arrow	95
F6	95
Go To	95
Name Box	95
Ctrl+[	96
Hyperlinks	97

Part II
The Modelling Process

4.   Referencing and Range Names   **101**

Relative and Absolute References   101
R1C1 Referencing   102
Range Names   104
Natural Language Formulas   104
Geographical Precision   105
Speed   105
Poor Teaching   105
A Rule of Thumb   106
The FAST Viewpoint   106
The Principle   107
Name Conventions   107
Benefits   109
Reusable Code   109
The Certainty of Names   110
One Dimension versus Two Dimension   110
Creating Names   110
Defining Names   112
Name Manager   112
Using Names   113
Individually Named Cells   114
Paste Name   115
Formula AutoComplete   115
Applying Names   115
Editing Range Names   116
Deleting Names   117
Removing Names   117
Extending Ranges   119
Moving Named Ranges   119
Names and Functions   120
Additional Name Functionality   121
Combination Names   121
Intersection Formulas   121
Sheet Level or Local Names   122
Three-Dimensional or Cross-Sheet Names   123
Relative Names   124
Mixed Absolute and Relative Names   125
Naming Values and Formulas   126
Dynamic Range Names   127
Listing Names   128
Empty Ranges   129
Multiple Names   129
External Name References   130
Phantom File Links   130

5. Mainly Formulas — **131**

Introduction — 131
Bodmas or Pemdas — 132
Timing — 132
Time Dependency and Time Independency — 133
Left-to-Right Consistency — 133
Base Column — 134
Corkscrew — 135
Technical Formulas — 137
Masks — 137
Flags — 138
Switches — 138
Coercion — 139
Counters — 139
Changing Periodicity — 140
Quarterly to Annual — 140
Rolling Total — 141
Relative Totals — 143
Circularities and Iteration — 144
Debugging Circularities — 145
Trial and Error — 146
Error Tracking — 147
Handling Circular Code — 149
Advanced Formulas — 154
Array Formulas — 154

6. Mainly Functions — **157**

Introduction — 157
Late Binding Functions — 157
Error Handling — 158
IFERROR and IFNA — 159
IFERROR Problem — 159
Good Old IF — 159
Using AND and OR — 161
A MAX/MIN Solution — 161
Starting Again — 162
The Logical Mask — 162
Putting it into Practice — 165
Revolving Credit — 172
Lookup — 175
Good Old VLOOKUP and HLOOKUP — 175
Lookup Without Using LOOKUPs — 178
INDEX — 180
MATCH — 182
MATCH and INDEX — 182

The Concept of the Pool   184
Fixed Schedules   188
OFFSET   189
Dates   193
NOW()   193
DATE (Year, Month, Day)   194
Financial   196
NPV   196
XNPV   197
Other Useful Functions   200
LARGE and SMALL   200
RAND   201
ISTEXT   201
N   203
Concatenation   203
TEXT   204
INT and MOD   204

7.   **Model Use**   **207**

Introduction   207
Risk Controls   207
Access Control   207
Input Control   207
Change Control   208
Version Control   208
Protection   208
Sheet Protection   208
Workbook Protection   210
Password Protection   210
Grouping and Outlining   211
Data Inputs   213
Data Validation   214
Custom Validation   214
Problems with Validation   215
Drop-Down Lists   215
List and Combo Boxes   216
Conditional Formatting   219
Problems with Conditional Formatting   222
Custom Formatting   223
Styles   227
Reporting   228
Currency   228
A Type of Conditional Format   228
Charting   229
F11 and Alt+F1   229
Updating Charts   230

8.   Sensitivity Analysis and Scenarios   **231**

Introduction   231
Model Interrogation   231
Sensitivities   233
Goal Seek   233
Data Tables   235
The One-Way Data Table   235
The Two-Way Data Table   236
Observations   236
Table Recalculation   236
Scenarios   238
Scenario Manager   239
CHOOSE   240
LOOKUP   242
INDEX   243
Issues with the Function Approach   243
Multiple Input Sheets   244
The Cell Reference Method   244
The Range Name Method   245
Using Multiple Inputs Sheets   246
Printing Scenarios   247
Delta Sheets   248
Solver   250
Risk   250
Monte Carlo Simulation   252
Risk Analysis Using Data Tables   254

9.   Automation   **255**

Introduction   255
Macro Security Settings   256
Personal.xlsb   257
Recorded Macros   257
Recorded Macro Options   257
Iteration Macro   258
Assigning Macros   261
Keyboard Shortcuts   261
Workbook Buttons   262
Adding Macros to the Ribbon   263
Written Macros   264
Branching Macros   265
Writing the Macro   266
Quarterly/Annual Macro   267
Error Handling   268
Debt Sculpting   269
Workbook Formulas   270
Debt Sculpting Macro   274

Debugging   275
Step Mode   276
Breakpoints   276
Locals Window   277
The Immediate Window   277
User-Defined Functions   278
Tax Calculator   279
Local Range Names   281
Managing UDFs   282

Appendix 1 Good Modelling Practice   283
Appendix 2 Keyboard Shortcuts   289
Index   291

About the Author

Jonathan is the director of training at Operis TRG Ltd, the training division of Operis Group plc. He has extensive experience of skills and knowledge transfer in this field and has been involved in delivering modelling training since the early 1990s. He has since developed the Operis portfolio of financial modelling courses, which he has delivered to finance and management professionals around the world. He is a member of the European Spreadsheet Risks Interest Group (EuSpRIG), the international financial modelling thought leaders' forum. Jonathan holds an MBA from the East London Business School, and a Bachelor of Education degree. He was appointed as a Visiting Fellow at the Lord Ashcroft International Business School in 2011.

Preface to the Third Edition

There are far more books on the subject of financial modelling now than when the first edition of this book appeared back in 2005. Ranging from academic tomes full of financial algorithms, to books on company valuation, modelling risk, cash flow forecasting, corporate finance, through to applied Excel techniques and VBA programming, the financial analyst now has a good chance of finding a book relating directly to their modelling needs.

The financial modelling environment has also matured: a range of methodologies are now available, such as the Operis method as set out in this book, and the very similar FAST, SMART and BPM systems, amongst others. These methodologies are used by the increasing number of specialist financial modelling firms, such as Operis, Financial Mechanics, F1F9 and Corality, as well as by the large accounting and consulting firms. Although the financial regulators are still unwilling to provide guidance, here in the United Kingdom we have recently seen the publication of the 'Review of Quality Assurance of Government Analytical Models' (the Macpherson report, HM Treasury 2013) with guidelines for spreadsheet modelling practice across the whole of the UK public sector. The Institute of Chartered Accountants of England and Wales is promoting its *Twenty Principles for Good Spreadsheet Practice*.

Financial modelling practitioners are generally better trained and have greater experience than before. Industry groups and forums such as the European Spreadsheet Risks Interest Group (EuSpRIG) have reinforced the message that modelling is an inherently error-prone activity and good modellers routinely employ a range of checks and controls in their work. The focus has shifted away from model development and much more into model audit and review. The question posed in the preface of the first edition of this book remains the same: is this model right? Previously we answered this question by exploring and understanding the modelling methodology needed to develop our own model. This time we work more on the assumption that someone else has produced the model. It may or may not conform to a standard methodology, but now we need the tools and techniques to provide the assurance to the model owners or sponsors.

Preface to the Second Edition

There have been two main incentives to produce a second edition of this book. The first and perhaps most obvious reason is the introduction of Microsoft Excel 2007, with its radical new appearance. Microsoft's market research suggested that the vast majority of Excel users appear to treat the software as a gloried tool for producing tables, and the new 'results-oriented user interface' is designed to make them far more efficient at doing so. Unfortunately for anyone with a reasonable level of competence in Excel there is a substantial learning curve, and some of the most straightforward commands have become frustratingly obscure. Although the underlying Excel functionality remains largely unchanged, the new command sequences and shortcuts have entailed a substantial revision of many of the command sequences used in this book.

The second reason for a new edition is rather less obvious but I believe of greater significance. I have previously been critical of the way in which organisations and individuals are able to generate financial spreadsheets and models in an uncontrolled way and it would now seem that there is a growing recognition of this problem by the regulatory authorities. In the United States, the Sarbanes–Oxley Act (2002) sets out a legal framework for financial reporting and the use of risk controls and this is having a major impact on the way organisations manage their spreadsheets. Historically, European regulators operate by principles rather than by rules but there are already signs that the Financial Services Authority and its European Union equivalents are being influenced by this legislation. It has been gratifying to note that the modelling methodology set out in this book is effectively a compliance process, and that the risk controls can be mapped directly to the model structure discussed in Chapter 3.

I am grateful for the very positive feedback that I have received from a number of readers and I have taken account of several suggestions for improvements. I have revised and updated a number of examples, including a cash cascade treatment. I have included self-test exercises to help readers apply and extend the techniques covered in each chapter (these are now on the Elsevier website). I am delighted that my publishers have decided to use full colour for the illustrations and examples.

Preface to the First Edition

Most of the books on financial modelling that I have read tend to go long on the financial and short on the modelling. Most of them are full of genuinely useful financial calculations and algorithms but they offer little insight into setting up and working with robust and reliable models, in much the same way that a dictionary helps you with your spelling but does not help you write good prose. To stay with this analogy for a moment, I would describe this book as a grammar that will provide you a structural and conceptual basis for your financial modelling. I shall assume that you have a good working vocabulary, or the ability to refer to the appropriate dictionary, as needed. This book is not a financial text book, nor is it an Excel manual – it sits between the two on your bookshelf.

My intended reader is the financial analyst – a catch-all term covering the wide range of people like you who are involved, in some way, in the preparation and use of financial models and spreadsheets. You may be preparing cash flow forecasts, project evaluations or financial statements. You may be working on your own, or in a finance department, or in an investment bank or multinational financial institution. You may be a student, or a part-qualified accountant, or a practitioner, or you may be in a position where you don't actually to modelling yourself anymore but you want to keep up with developments.

I should state at the outset that there is no agreed 'best practice' in financial modelling – the methodology and techniques are those best suited to the task in hand. In this book, we will examine some of the common, generic, approaches that you will encounter in financial models today, with a view to understanding the technical background. You will appreciate that the same problem can be often solved in several ways, some of which appear better or more reliable than others, and some of which appear counterintuitive and less satisfactory. The intention is to encourage you to reflect on your own practice in the light of these suggestions and examples, and I am confident that you will be able to generate your own solutions to the problems and issues that follow. Even if you are not convinced by my arguments, by engaging with them you will have greater confidence in your own modelling abilities. You have picked this book from the shelf because at some point you asked yourself the fundamental question – is this model right?

Acknowledgements

I would like to express my gratitude to my colleague and mentor, David Colver, from whom I have learnt so much over the two decades we have worked together. Thanks also to my many colleagues who contributed to my thinking about the subject, and of course to my many students, who, through their questions and enthusiasm, continue to stimulate and challenge me every step of the way.

About Operis Group

Over the last 25 years, Operis has established itself as a leading advisor in project finance, specialising in the analytical aspects of financial transactions. The firm was established in 1990 and now has a headcount of over 40, making it one of the largest teams devoted to its particular discipline. As a financial advisory firm, our key activities fall into three areas and they are explained below.

CONSULTING AND ADVICE

Operis has significant experience in model auditing, modelling and other advisory work for project and transaction funders in respect of financial models, associated legal documentation, taxation and accounting matters.

We are one of the market leaders in this field and, internationally, the only firm outside the leading accountancy firms to hold a reputation for world-class model assurance.

We have been mandated by most of the leading banks and bond arrangers around the world. We are well known by the key funding guarantor bodies and have been mandated and approved by major export credit agencies, multilateral and supranational bodies and monoline insurers.

FINANCIAL MODELLING TRAINING

Operis offers financial modelling training to analysts and finance professionals from the banking and finance industry and many other sectors from the City of London and internationally.

We teach a robust and transparent modelling methodology which we use ourselves in developing some of the most complex financial models used by lenders and investors in projects around the world. Course delegates benefit from our wide-ranging perspective on state-of-the-art modelling in the financial sector.

Our portfolio of courses covers project finance, PPP/P3, company valuation, cash flow forecasting, model analysis and financial model audit. In addition, we have written and delivered financial modelling courses on solar energy, wind farms, waste and other client-specific operations.

OPERIS ANALYSIS KIT

Operis Analysis Kit (OAK) is a set of spreadsheet analysis, audit, review and reporting tools developed by our analysts for developing and checking large spreadsheet models. It is an Excel add-in and works with all versions of Excel.

It is used by almost all of the large accounting firms and by major financial institutions around the world and is under continual development to ensure that it remains relevant and compatible with current versions of Excel.

For more information see www.operis.com.

Introduction

THE CONTEXT OF FINANCIAL MODELLING

The big passion of my life, outside financial modelling, is the Great Highland Bagpipe. I've been playing for about 15 years, primarily for my own pleasure but on occasion for others. The aspiring bagpiper begins their piping career not directly on the bagpipes but on a smaller instrument called a practice chanter – it is like a large recorder but with a much less melodic sound. This is used to develop competence in playing; there are only nine notes but there is a whole series of small note sequences called grace notes, which include combinations such as the doubling, the grip, the taorluath and the crunluath. The beginner must not only master these embellishments, but must also memorise the tunes, for the simple reason that the bagpipe is so loud that any mistakes will be heard right across the neighbourhood. And not only as pipers do we have to buy the practice chanter along with a set of bagpipes, we are also expected to wear a kilt, with a sporran and a glengarry and all the gear that goes with the popular image of the bagpiper.

Figure 1.1 shows an old favourite: Scotland the Brave.

Or is it? It is a musical score, and it has Scotland the Brave in the title. But how do we know that this is the correct tune, with the correct grace notes and timing? Unless you can read music you will have to take this on trust, and you

FIGURE 1.1 Scotland the Brave.

must accept my word as a reasonably proficient, experienced piper that this is indeed the sheet music for this tune.

Now consider a management spreadsheet. It has been prepared by a reasonably proficient, experienced analyst, looking the part in a nice expensive suit. There are lots of numbers on the printout, and there are underlying calculations in the workbook, but how do we assure ourselves that the model is correct?

I hope the analogy between music and modelling makes sense. Both activities require a high level of technical knowledge and skill, both allow for a reasonable amount of creativity within the rules, and the output may (or may not) be readily understood or appreciated by the audience. The big difference between the two is that if my pipes are out of tune, or I play the wrong notes, we will know about it straight away. Not so with the spreadsheet.

The European Spreadsheet Risks Interest Group (EuSpRIG) was founded in 1999 to 'address the ever-increasing problem of spreadsheet integrity'[1] and membership is drawn from industry and academia, comprising some of the leading financial modelling thought leaders in the world today. A highlight of the year is our annual conference, at which many of these practitioners and researchers gather to listen to seminars and presentations on aspects of spreadsheet modelling. This two-day event usually concludes with an open floor plenary session, at which current issues and topics relating to modelling practice can be discussed. At some point someone will mention modelling standards and then perhaps unwisely use the phrase 'best practice'; as can be imagined, this causes immense and intense debate as there is no overall agreement as to what this term might mean. We are certainly agreed on what constitutes good practice, and we are very clear about bad practice, but even after all these years we cannot define 'best practice'.

Making mistakes is part of human nature, and human error has been the subject of academic and operational research for many years. There is a rich literature which includes the psychological analysis of error, various taxonomies of error and models of human performance. Financial modelling has been investigated in this context for over three decades and the published research, although somewhat limited and circumscribed, is remarkably consistent. In order to understand the causes of error the researchers have attempted to investigate the modelling process and those carrying out the modelling activity. Unfortunately investment banks and large corporations seem reluctant to allow their analysts and managers to be used as subjects, and given that most researchers are based in the business schools, the research guinea pigs are typically MBA or undergraduate business studies students.

A consequence is the difficulty in setting a meaningful modelling exercise for research purposes – most tend to be fairly limited, with a small number of inputs leading to a relatively simple set of calculations. Given these constraints, however, the results highlight both inconsistencies in the way in which subjects

---

1. www.eusprig.com

develop models, and perhaps more importantly, a general lack of diligence in checking through completed work.

It might be assumed that the business school student is not representative of the financial analyst of the investment bank, but in fact there is one key similarity: it is highly unlikely that either of them have ever received formal training in financial modelling. Indeed, many organisations (and individuals) equate 'competency with Microsoft Excel' with 'competency in financial modelling', which reveals a fundamental lack of understanding of the skills and knowledge required.

THREE PRINCIPLES

I have taught practical financial modelling for nearly two decades. The methodology I teach is based on that used by my colleagues, who have worked on some of the most complex financial modelling assignments in the industry worldwide. This methodology is not unique, it certainly is not rocket science, and I would never suggest that it is the only or 'best' methodology. It is my intention to introduce the methodology in this book, and in doing so, compare and contrast it with alternative approaches which are in common use and might be described as current practice, such as FAST, SMART and BPM.

The individuals attending my courses are highly motivated finance, banking or management professionals who bring a range of modelling experience with them, and my exposition of our methodology is often the stimulus for robust debate. However, although we may disagree on the finer points, I am usually able to convince them of the validity of our approach because it is based on my three interlinked principles: the 'principle of error reduction', the 'feedback principle' and the 'top-down principle'. These principles will be seen again as we go through each stage of this book.

The Principle of Error Reduction

The principle of error reduction is a simple concept based on our own experience and that of others in the business, where we recognise that certain modelling operations are more error-prone than others. Going back to the research referred to above, it seems that humans have a natural error rate to the order of 1% (for every 100 notes I play on the bagpipes, I will get one wrong). Some of the research recognises that financial model development is an activity similar to computer programming which has been extensively studied. It seems that computer programmers anticipate an error rate of around 3% and spend up to 40% of their time checking and reviewing to reduce this rate even further. Is it worth asking how much time the average financial analyst spends on model review and audit? And yet I still come across very intelligent people who claim that their work is error free. I believe in adopting a pragmatic approach which accepts that errors are inevitable but then seeks to minimise their occurrence and to enhance their detection.

The Principle of Error Reduction accepts that errors are inevitable. Some techniques are more prone to errors than others. We reduce the risk of error by using alternative techniques and a consistent methodology that serves to enhance the detection of errors should they occur. This principle is not unique to spreadsheet modelling; it is the rationale behind many management and industrial methodologies, such as Six Sigma and total quality management. The difficulty of error reduction is that it is both inherently negative and requires some knowledge: I worked with a bank that had an in-house modelling manual, and one of the rules was 'avoid bad practice'. Clearly error reduction in practice, but how does a junior analyst know what constitutes 'bad practice', unless they have a very clear understanding of 'good practice'?

The Principle of Error Reduction equates to quality assurance, as it forces us to recognise the inherent limitations of the spreadsheet model (and perhaps the modellers themselves), and to implement a framework which provides the resources and controls to minimise or mitigate the whole process of model specification, development, testing and use.

The Feedback Principle

As I write this paragraph I have a model in front of me from a former student. It is for the investment evaluation and analysis of power generation projects. She is the only modeller in her firm, and wrote the model entirely by herself. She has had no feedback at any stage during the 10 months she has been working on this project. The feedback principle is based on precisely this sort of experience: error reduction is about being sensitive to, or aware of, potential errors, but if nothing appears to be wrong then the modeller can develop a false sense of security. The feedback principle means that we *actively* seek to test and validate our work continuously throughout the modelling process. I further describe positive feedback and negative feedback – the former is the system of checks and controls we impose in order to detect and remedy problems in our models; the latter, negative feedback, is that received from others who have found errors in our work. Positive feedback is good – we can learn from it, and because we seek it throughout the process it enhances both the quality and the value of our work. Negative feedback is bad and represents a breakdown in the assurance process, such that an external party (the auditor or the client) is the first to detect that something is wrong.

Positive Feedback	Negative Feedback
Problems anticipated	Problems not detected
Methods and controls for checking and testing	False confidence
Review processes	Errors detected late in the process (if at all)
Early detection of errors	Errors detected by 'outsiders'
Errors detected and resolved internally	The 'blame game'
Useful lessons learned	Lack of trust/confidence
Greater confidence	

To obtain feedback we implement a number of feedback controls, which can be elements such as the audit workbook and report, the internal audit sheet and the various checks and tests carried out during model development and use. The feedback principle, and its associated feedback controls, is a fundamental part of the quality control framework.

The Top-Down Principle

The top-down principle helps us make sense of the complexities of the modelling environment. Rather than becoming immersed in immense amounts of detail (bottom-up), we retain a view of the model's overall purpose and results. The audit profession refers to two approaches to audit: 'controls testing' and 'substantive testing', and this is essentially what the top-down principle provides – the key results are the controls; if they look reasonable then we can be selective in our choice of substantive tests to run, rather than analyse each formula in turn (the substantive approach). In reviewing a 50 Mb spreadsheet our immediate concern is that the key results are correct; we are less concerned with layout, hidden content or bizarre formulas.

There is no methodology for error-proofing; there is no way of ensuring a plus is typed instead of a minus. These principles enable us to recognise potential sources of error and to either substitute them with a more reliable technique, or to implement an audit check or control which can be used to test the validity of the routine. Note that my three principles are overarching: they do not specify, nor are linked to, any particular modelling methodology, but are fundamental elements of the quality assurance and control processes in which the modelling takes place.

In the early days of financial modelling, users and sponsors were willing to accept a certain element of ambiguity; that the model was, of course, only an approximation of the transaction. The accountants use the idea of 'materiality' to give them a legitimate margin of error. In recent years, there has been a trend to see the model as the ultimate reality with generalised assumptions taking on the guise of hard fact. It might be helpful to remind ourselves of the old adage: is it better to be vaguely right, or precisely wrong?

THIS BOOK

The overall structure of this book reflects the theme of quality assurance which begins in Part 1 with the modelling environment – the external and internal influences on the modelling activity. Quality control at one level is the audit and review of the model; and is also the selection and application of the modelling process and methodologies, including risk controls. We consider how model purpose can dictate model structure, and follow this with an exploration of various layouts which are designed in consultation with the users or model sponsors. Part 2 leads into the techniques used in model building, the formulas and functions used for the calculations, as well as the techniques which enhance the usability of the model but at the same time protect the model from unwanted or inadvertent amendments. The primary use of any model is to test the effects of changes to the inputs and we examine sensitivity and scenario management. We conclude with a review of the use of VisualBasic for Applications (macros and user-defined functions) in financial modelling.

PART 1: THE MODELLING ENVIRONMENT

Chapter 1: Quality Assurance

The financial model plays a central and highly visible rôle in the project finance sector. As the link between the raft of contracts, agreements, covenants and operational forecasts these models are examined and reviewed by bankers, accountants, lawyers and project sponsors in a way not seen in corporate modelling. With such a heavy reliance on models this sector has been at the frontline in the development of modelling standards and practices and the implementation of quality assurance systems. This chapter examines the external factors that have influenced quality assurance in spreadsheet modelling and describes the principles of spreadsheet governance and risk controls in the modelling environment that provide a framework for modelling quality control.

Chapter 2: Quality Control

Unlike a manufacturing process where defects can be quickly identified and remedied, errors in spreadsheets can be extremely difficult to detect. This chapter begins with a consideration of human error in the context of the spreadsheet and introduces a number of simple techniques to interrogate formulas. The quality control framework is developed using firstly the audit sheet, with a standard battery of checks, and extended with the introduction of the audit workbook and more advanced techniques for formula reconstruction and analysis.

Chapter 3: Model Structure and Methodology

The quality control and assurance environment is designed to minimise, if not eliminate, errors during the model development process. The key to good modelling is a sound and robust modelling methodology. This chapter explores a model structure which separates out the inputs, workings and outputs. The model development process from the blank workbook to the printing of the outputs, incorporating appropriate documentation and audit controls from the outset.

PART 2: THE MODELLING PROCESS

Chapter 4: Referencing and Range Names

Cell references are the traditional elements of Excel formulas but become increasingly difficult to work with as the workbook increases in size and complexity. Range names are the spreadsheet implementation of the concept of the 'natural language formulas', which I argue is a key application of the error reduction and feedback principles. They allow modellers to construct formulas using descriptive language, rather than cell references. This is a deeply contentious issue and the arguments on both sides are fully explored. The creation and management of names, including naming conventions, is discussed, along with their use in formulas, functions and Visual Basic for Applications.

Chapter 5: Mainly Formulas

This chapter explains a number of key modelling techniques, such as left-to-right consistency, the base column, and corkscrews, masks, counters, flags and switches, which are used to simplify potentially complex formulas and in particular the handling of timing problems and time-dependent and time-independent inputs and formulas. Techniques for managing changing time periods are explored. The problem of accidental and deliberate circular formulas and their management is considered, along with the pros and cons of using Excel's iteration functionality. The chapter concludes with the use of array formulas.

Chapter 6: Mainly Functions

Excel has over 400 functions of which only a handful are required in general financial modelling. The techniques for avoiding IFs introduced in the previous chapter are now extended with the use of MAX, MIN, AND and OR. The timing of events in the forecast period is resolved by introducing INDEX and MATCH to replace the restrictions of the Lookup family of functions, and various date functions are explained. Recognising that most financial institutions do not allow the use of Excel financial functions the issues are identified and the arithmetical solutions are shown. The chapter concludes with a handful of less common but still useful functions.

Chapter 7: Model Use

The completed model is an analytical tool for the users but before we look at techniques for sensitivity analysis and scenario management we need to ensure the finished model is robust and usable. In this chapter, we are less concerned about calculations and more about managing inputs and results. We review the elements of risk control discussed in earlier chapters and consider techniques to prevent changes to the model contents and structure. Input or data entry control is explored through the use of data validation and list and combo boxes. Conditional formatting is used to flag up key issues in the results, conditional formatting helps make results more readable, and we conclude with charting techniques for the graphical display of results.

Chapter 8: Sensitivity Analysis and Scenarios

The reason we build financial models is to examine financial performance in response to the financial assumptions. Sensitivity analysis is a term used to describe the techniques for testing the model's reaction to the effects of changing a small number of model inputs, often independently of each other; scenario analysis is concerned with multiple, simultaneous changes to economic or operational assumptions. There are three aspects to modelling sensitivities and scenarios: firstly that the changing inputs can be clearly identified and that there is reproducibility – that a test can be run, and rerun, as required. Secondly, that the model formulas are able to handle the input changes without requiring intervention from the user. Thirdly, that the effects of input changes on the output results can be clearly seen.

Chapter 9: Automation

This chapter examines the use of Visual Basic for Applications as a tool for the development of macros and user-defined functions (UDFs) to perform tasks in Excel. We look at macro security settings, and then introduce the Visual Basic Editor by recording a simple Iteration macro. These macros are assigned to keyboard shortcuts, worksheet and Ribbon buttons. We then look at written macros, and use the If...Then...Else, For...Next and Do...Loop methods. Techniques for debugging and error handling are introduced, leading to a debt sculpting macro. Finally we look at writing UDFs to perform complex calculations.

MICROSOFT EXCEL CONVENTIONS

I have tested all the exercises and examples in this book with all versions of Excel from 2003 through to Excel 2013, but not with Lotus 1-2-3 or Quattro Pro. We shall be using Microsoft Excel 2013 throughout, and I have endeavoured to use native Excel functionality without resorting to macros, add-ins or third-party software.

I travel very widely in the course of my teaching and I am well aware of the international differences in formulas, functions and formatting, and most of all in keyboard shortcuts. With a view to my international readership I have tried to anticipate possible problems when working on the exercises and examples in this book, and in several cases I point out where specific shortcuts do not work. In this book, I will use UK/US settings for my routine work. I use the following formula conventions:

    =IF(E25>1,000.00,E25,0)

Elsewhere I would write this as:

    =WENN(E25>1.000,00;E25;0) or =SI(E25>1 000,00;E25;0), that is, using the local name for the function and the local argument separators and number formatting.

Anticipating that readers may wish to copy formulas directly from the page, I have elected to show them exactly as they should be written. This may be at the cost of clarity, but entering spaces into calculations can cause problems. For example, = SUM(E24:K24) generates a #NAME? error, because the spaces are treated as text and Excel does not recognise the SUM.

All formulas shown in this book are written using Microsoft's standard Calibri font to match what you will see in your spreadsheet if you work on the examples.

KEYBOARD SHORTCUTS

I encourage the use of keyboard shortcuts to make your work more accurate and efficient. Learn the shortcuts most relevant to the work you carry out routinely. A full list of the keyboard shortcuts used in this book is included in the appendix. Keyboard shortcuts may have a direct effect in the workbook, such as Ctrl+B for bold, or indirect, where they bring up a dialog box, for example, Ctrl+1 for Format Cells.

Control Key Combination Shortcuts

Control key shortcuts are used in combination with other keys without activating the Ribbon command sequences. For example, Ctrl+C copies the selection, and Ctrl+V is used to paste. Many of these are now listed within the Ribbon tool tips which are shown when you hover your mouse pointer over a button. A large number of these shortcuts appear to be version and language independent, so that Ctrl+S (Save) or Ctrl+Shift+F3 (Create Names) will work on most versions of Excel around the world. An example is Ctrl+[(open square bracket) which serves to select precedent cells on an English language installation of Excel. Although the [character exists on other keyboards it may not work as a shortcut.

Function Key Shortcuts

A number of shortcuts are based on the functions keys, such as F12 (Save As).

Ribbon Shortcuts

With the introduction of the Ribbon in Excel 2007 there are now shortcuts for everything. The secret is the Alt key – when this is pressed, a letter is shown for each tab, and then for each command on that ribbon. For example, the width of a column can now be changed by using the Home tab, Format, Column Width and then typing a number in the Column Width dialog box; as a shortcut this is Alt+H, O, W, number, Enter.

Note that the tab letter has to be pressed even if the tab is currently active; for example, if the Home tab is on display we can't simply type the O, W sequence.

There are also some double-key shortcuts. If we want to change the fill colour of a cell, Al+H shows the fill colour tool as FC. The letter F is used for 13 other buttons, including the format painter, font size and find & select, so we type FC in quick succession. Excel is now better at handling rapid keystroke sequences as your expertise improves!

Dialog Box Commands

The general principle for navigating dialog boxes is to use either the Tab key or to press Alt+underlined letter. Tab can be combined with Shift to reverse the direction of movement. In larger dialog boxes, such as Format Cells, we can move from one tab to another using PgUp/PgDn or by pressing the first letter of the tab name. To select commands within the dialog box, use the Tab key (or Shift+Tab), or better, press Alt+the underlined letter in the command. Check boxes and items in lists can be selected using the Spacebar.

The full keystroke sequence for File, Options, Formulas, Enable iterative calculation is:

Alt+F, T, F, Alt+I.

If you are using Excel in a language other than English, substitute the appropriate command and shortcut sequences.

In most dialog boxes the OK button is the default, which means that we can simply press Enter to confirm the command. Esc will cancel the operation.

Shortcut Menu and Toolbar Shortcuts

An alternative method of activating the main menu bar is to press F10. The context-sensitive shortcut menu – the equivalent of right-clicking on a cell or object – is shown by pressing Shift+F10.

Keyboard Shortcuts Conventions

For the purposes of this book we will use the convention of writing out the command sequence in full but marking the shortcuts, as in:

Data, What-If Analysis, Data Table
This can be read as Alt+A, W, T.
If there is a direct shortcut we will show it as:
Home, Find & Select, Replace (or Ctrl+H)
This can be read as Alt+H, FD, R (or Ctrl+H). In this example note the double-key shortcut.

FURTHER INFORMATION

A list of keyboard shortcuts used in this book is provided in the Appendix. For more information about these and other shortcuts use Excel Help (F1) and simply search for 'keyboard shortcuts'.

Part I

The Modelling Environment

Chapter 1

Quality Assurance

THE MODELLING ENVIRONMENT

When I wrote the first edition of this book my opinion was that most financial analysts and managers had no idea what a good financial model looked like, nor did they have the relevant skills to prepare one. I was also of the opinion that this was through no fault of their own; most of the time the models, forecasts and budgets they prepared seemed to do the job, and there seemed little incentive to progress. I raised the issues of good practice, quality control and modelling standards, and I hoped that these would be as equally relevant to the realities of life and work in the busy finance department as they would to the glamorous worlds of project and corporate finance. There has been a great deal of progress since and my current view is far less negative: modelling standards and training have received much attention, with the outcome that models and modellers generally are of a much higher standard; but there is still a huge challenge when we provide these models to a nonmodelling audience. There is an increasing recognition on the part of management and others that they simply don't understand what the model does, and they possess few of the skills required to examine a spreadsheet in a meaningful way. One of our commonest course requests over the last couple of years has been for training on 'how to understand financial models'.

We have also seen the global financial crisis and many people have attempted to attribute at least some of the blame to the financial models used by the banks and financial institutions. This is clearly wrong: a model is only ever going to be a representation of reality, subject both to the limitations of the inputs supplied to the model, and the calculation rules being used for the analysis. The quantitative modellers learned that lesson with Black-Scholes, and we cash flow modellers followed behind. The model is a tool; potentially a highly sophisticated one, and it is the poor worker who would seek to blame the tool. But we return to the theme of good models being incorrectly used or interpreted: there continues to be a constant flow of stories in the financial press concerning corporate disasters involving financial models. There is also anecdotal evidence to suggest that many cases never appear in the open. But one very public story has had a major impact in the United Kingdom.

The railway system in Britain was broken up and privatised in the 1990s. One route, the InterCity West Coast franchise, was awarded to Sir Richard Branson's Virgin Trains. In 2012, the British Department for Transport (DfT) put the franchise out to the market in a competitive tendering exercise. To Virgin's immense surprise they lost to the First Group, and Sir Richard promptly obtained a judicial review to examine the way in which the bids were assessed by the DfT, which subsequently led to the cancellation of the competition. The Laidlaw Enquiry (2012) and the Public Accounts Committee report (2013) made it very clear that modelling, and in particular the interpretation of the modelling, was at the heart of this very public fiasco. The eventual outcome was the Macpherson report[1], an ambitious and overarching approach to modelling standards in the UK public sector, and which will be discussed in some detail in this chapter.

Part of the significance of Macpherson is that in the United Kingdom historically there has been little in the way of imposing a regulatory structure on the development, use and control of models and spreadsheets; and within the financial services industry there is a long tradition of the self-taught amateur, lacking any formal training in the disciplines of financial model development but seemingly capable of doing the job. The National Audit Office (NAO) produces frequent reports into public–private partnership (PPP) projects and often comments on the nature of the models used, but it seems reluctant to suggest that there might be a standard way of producing the complex financial models seen in the sector. This is despite the basic similarity within some of the initiatives and there has long been a feeling in the private sector that some form of standardisation may be appropriate.

The Project Finance Sector

The PPP concept is a public sector approach to government procurement by engaging the private sector in the provision of facilities and services. Developed in the UK originally as the private finance initiative it has evolved into PF2; and this model has been adopted elsewhere in the world where it is known as PPP, or in North America as P3 (and in Canada as alternative finance procurement or AFP). The process is heavily dependent on financial modelling and because of this project finance modelling has in many ways influenced the discussion and debate about modelling standards. The distinctive feature is that the model is used by so many parties – the project bidders, the banks, investors, lawyers, government advisers and the project sponsors, amongst others. Unlike corporate models which stay within the organisation, these models are exposed to considerable external attention. It could be argued that this open and active environment has led to project finance modelling becoming the benchmark for modelling standards generally, in terms of model specification and development, documentation and audit methodologies.

The expectations of PPP models may have improved with increased NAO experience and the maturation of the PPP sector and it would seem that this top-down pressure has fed down through the supply chain, as both private and public sector organisations now clearly realise the critical importance of the financial model. The last decade has seen a growth in the number of firms which

---

1. Review of quality assurance of government analytical models, HM Treasury, 2013.

can provide the specialist independent financial model audit services that NAO now requires of models submitted in the PPP bid process, but this is extremely unusual outside this particular sector.

The Regulatory Environment

The UK regulatory environment is set out in company law and by the Financial Conduct Authority. At the moment spreadsheets and models might loosely be covered by the various reporting requirements, which would include record keeping, but no formal risk controls have yet been imposed. The Institute of Chartered Accountants of England and Wales (ICAEW) has recently published its *Twenty Principles for Good Spreadsheet Practice*[2], an ambitious if slightly anodyne list of good practices for the accounting profession.

The story around the rest of the world is similar. The Basel II requirements concerning operational risk controls, introduced in 2006, were aimed at banks and international financial institutions, and the latest implementation (Basel III, 2010) addresses further risks in the banking sector such as capital adequacy and the stress testing. These may not appear to relate to other areas of the financial sector but as I have previously noted financial models and spreadsheets are being identified as potential risks and the regulatory authorities will become increasingly interested in the controls used in managing the use of such models. These controls can be expected to filter down from the financial sector to other areas of business. I believe that the day of ad hoc spreadsheet development in the financial sector has drawn to a close.

Across the Atlantic the situation changed with the implementation of the Sarbanes–Oxley Act (2002) (SOX). Stringent controls have been imposed on firms in the production of statutory financial statements and reports. Section 404 of SOX relates directly to the controls on the development and maintenance of spreadsheets, and senior management in US organisations had to face up to the fact that the development and use of financial models and spreadsheets had to be properly controlled. This development highlighted the main problem that there had been an historic lack of discipline or rigour involved in preparing and using models and that those involved lack the skills and experience to impose the standards required.

The effects of Basel II and III and SOX are being seen in the UK and in Europe and it would make sense for financial managers to anticipate the cost in time and additional staff resources to their organisations of any regulatory framework that might eventually be imposed on the use of financial models and spreadsheets. Professor Ray Panko[3], a noted researcher and commentator on financial modelling issues, has coined the term 'spreadsheet governance' to reflect new approach. The objective of SOX (and indeed of senior management)

---

2. *Twenty principles for good spreadsheet practice*, ICAEW 2014.
3. Professor Ray Panko, Shidler College of Business, University of Hawaii www.panko.shidler.hawaii.edu.

is to focus attention on those spreadsheets which are used in the preparation of public financial statements. The internal and external audit functions have an important role to play as the emphasis is shifting towards the way in which the financial information is handled in the first place, and the quality of the models used to record results and prepare forecasts, and indeed the people who use the spreadsheets in the decision making and reporting.

Fifteen years ago our concern was that those carrying the modelling function in the organisation lacked training or modelling standards, with the focus on the modellers themselves; this subsequently evolved into recognising the need for the organisation to impose some form of standards, to be led by those managing the modelling team. We are now seeing the reverse process: organisations are defining what they require from their models and modellers.

It Doesn't Affect Us, Does It?

Given that not all spreadsheets and models actually support significant financial processes, organisations need to decide on their priorities in order to direct resources to the areas of greater concern. Risk management is a familiar theme in both the private and public sectors and it is prudent to adopt a risk-based assessment of the importance or otherwise of the spreadsheets in the organisation. Organisations should recognise that responsibility for compliance lies ultimately with the board of directors, and it may be appropriate to assign oversight for the systematic review of spreadsheets to the audit committee, if there is one. From my own experience as chair of several audit committees, the problem here is that few, if any, internal audit firms have the expertise to provide assurance about the development and use of financial models. This isn't a criticism of these firms, indeed Operis has been engaged by them in the past to provide forensic financial modelling advice.

The European Spreadsheet Risks Interest Group (EuSpRIG[4]) draws its membership from financial modelling thought leaders and practitioners in industry and academia. For well over a decade it has been advocating the importance of modelling standards and a particular focus has been on 'end-user computing': the development of business critical models by individuals lacking the necessary skills or processes, and the inherent risks of using such models. A regular theme is the uncontrolled proliferation of spreadsheets within organisations, where it is not uncommon to find hundreds of thousands of Excel workbooks on the company server. A trite response would be that we would probably find far more Word documents, and perhaps millions of emails, so on the grand scheme of things surely it doesn't really matter?

Although most firms would profess to have modelling standards and procedures, the reality is that responsibility for the financial modelling function is often diffused, and individual analysts apply their own interpretation of quality control. I have even heard directors claiming that 'we only recruit the best

---

4. EuSpRIG is the European Spreadsheet Risks Interest Group www.eusprig.org.

MBAs from the most prestigious business schools' as if this mantra somehow protects them from poor modelling and its consequences.

Case Study: The Macpherson Report

In some 20 years of working in the financial modelling industry I have seen many initiatives and attempts at promoting some form of generic or corporate standards and it is worth examining the Macpherson report[5] as a case study in spreadsheet governance. The report sets out eight recommendations:

1. All business critical models should have appropriate quality assurance of their inputs, methodology and outputs in the context of the risks their use represents. If unavoidable time constraints prevent this from happening then this should be explicitly acknowledged and reported;
2. All business critical models should be managed within a framework that ensures appropriately specialist staff are responsible for developing and using the models as well as quality assurance;
3. There should be a single responsible owner (SRO) for each model through its life cycle, and clarity from the outset on how quality assurance is to be maintained. Key submissions using results from the model should summarise the quality assurance that has been undertaken, including the extent of expert scrutiny and challenge. They should also confirm that the SRO is content that the quality assurance process is compliant and appropriate, that model risks, limitations and major assumptions are understood by users of the model, and the use of the model outputs is appropriate;
4. The accounting officer's governance statement within the annual report should include confirmation that an appropriate quality assurance framework is in place and is used for all business critical models. As part of this process, and to provide effective risk management, the accounting officer may wish to confirm that there is an up-to-date list of business critical models and that this is publicly available;
5. All departments should have a plan for how they create the right environment for quality assurance, including how they address issues of culture, capacity and capability and control;
6. All departments should have in place a plan for how they ensure they have effective processes – including guidance and model documentation – to underpin appropriate quality assurance across their organisation;
7. A cross-departmental working group will share best practice and embed this across government;
8. HM Treasury will organise an assessment of this process.[6]

The ambition inherent in these recommendations becomes clear when we consider what the government means by spreadsheet modelling: the spectrum

---

5. Review of quality assurance of government analytical models: final report, HM Treasury 2013.
6. Review of quality assurance of government analytical models: final report, HM Treasury 2013.

ranges from the largest model in the UK public sector, the Meteorological Office weather forecasting model (the Unified Model, or MetUM), which runs on a Cray XC40 supercomputer, right down to simple cash flow forecasts prepared by managers in the National Health Service, or in local authorities, using Excel. The recommendations are therefore about overarching quality assurance principles, rather than specific details of policy, procedure or practice. Although it is possible to criticise the report because of the absence of specific guidance, there is the deliberate intention that each department develops its own modelling standards based on the type of modelling activity undertaken, and the relevance of the recommendations to the private sector is immediately apparent.

The standout feature of Macpherson is the attention the report gives to the modelling environment and quality assurance, rather than to modelling practice and quality control. This is the framework of controls and responsibilities around the modelling function, and right there in the first recommendation is the pragmatic acceptance that the modelling activity requires time and resources, both of which are finite. This, then, is not simply a line management function, but something which crosses departmental and team boundaries. No longer is the development and use of models seen as an isolated function, but it now becomes embedded in the organisational culture.

Case Study: ICAEW's 20 Principles

The ICAEW has long been interested in spreadsheet governance and modelling practice, publishing the Accountant's Digest 473 back in 1993 and my report into financial modelling[7] in 2007. With over 144,000 members worldwide, however, it has found it difficult to reach consensus in establishing a definition of good modelling practice, but has now contributed to the quality assurance discussion with its publication of its 20 Principles.[8] The principles are as follows:

1. Determine what rôle spreadsheets play in your business, and plan your spreadsheet standards and processes accordingly.
2. Adopt a standard for your organisation and stick to it.
3. Ensure that everyone involved in the creation or use of spreadsheets has an appropriate level of knowledge and competence.
4. Work collaboratively, share ownership, peer review.
5. Before starting, satisfy yourself that a spreadsheet is the appropriate tool for the job.
6. Identify the audience. If a spreadsheet is intended to be understood and used by others, the design should facilitate this.
7. Include an 'About' or 'Welcome' sheet to document the spreadsheet.
8. Design for longevity.

---

7. Special Report in Financial Modelling, Swan, ICAEW 2007.
8. *Twenty Principles for Good Spreadsheet Practice*, ICAEW 2014.

9. Focus on the required outputs.

10. Separate and clearly identify inputs, workings and outputs.

11. Be consistent in structure.

12. Be consistent in the use of formulae.

13. Keep formulae short and simple.

14. Never embed in a formula anything that might change or need to be changed.

15. Perform a calculation once and then refer back to that calculation.

16. Avoid using advanced features where simpler features could achieve the same result.

17. Have a system of backup and version control, which should be applied consistently within an organisation.

18. Rigorously test the workbook.

19. Build in checks, controls and alerts from the outset and during the course of spreadsheet design.

20. Protect parts of the workbook that are not supposed to be changed by users.

The Macpherson recommendations are deliberately vague as they cover all aspects of modelling in the public sector; the ICAEW principles are aimed at spreadsheet users and are more focussed on quality control.

Modelling Standards

The objective of this book has always been to close the gap between the grand, overarching quality assurance statements and the frontline practice of spreadsheet modelling. This is achieved by describing a robust and reliable modelling methodology that has been used by my firm for over 25 years. It isn't an 'in-house' methodology, in the sense that we build models for our clients, not just for ourselves. But we aren't alone in establishing a modelling methodology: the FAST Standard[9] has been developed over the last decade by a number of individuals and organisations. The FAST ('flexible, appropriate, structured and transparent') document can be freely downloaded and consists of some 134 rather prescriptive modelling rules covering workbook and worksheet design, line items and Excel features used in modelling. It is promoted heavily as *the* standard, and its 'adherents' (sic) have an almost evangelical zeal to spread the good word. There is also the SMART methodology and the BPM standard, with their own proprietary handbooks of modelling rules. But despite the extensive list of do's and don'ts, the vast majority of the rules are accepted across the modelling community as plain common sense, and as the FAST Alliance, SMART and BPM are fellow members of EuSpRIG this point is regularly discussed at conference. Medieval theologians are often caricatured

---

9. The FAST Standard Version 2a 29.05.14 http://www.fast-standard.org/document/FastStandard_02a.pdf.

for long meaningless debates about the number of angels who could dance on the head of a pin, and in many ways the 'compare and contrast' approach to the Operis and FAST methodologies is equally unproductive: readers with FAST, SMART or BPM backgrounds will probably be astonished by the overlap between these methodologies. We are all fully committed to the principle of error reduction, and the feedback principle and the top-down principle, as described in the Introduction.

In 2010, Thomas Grossman and Özgür Özlük reviewed three modelling methodologies and presented their findings to the EuSpRIG conference:

> *Many large financial planning models are written in a spreadsheet programming language (usually Microsoft Excel) and deployed as a spreadsheet application. Three groups, FAST Alliance, Operis Group, and BPM Analytics (under the name 'Spreadsheet Standards Review Board') have independently promulgated standardized processes for efficiently building such models. These spreadsheet engineering methodologies provide detailed guidance on design, construction process, and quality control... They share many design practices, and standardized, mechanistic procedures to construct spreadsheets. We learned that a written book or standards document is by itself insufficient to understand a methodology. These methodologies represent a professionalization of spreadsheet programming, and can provide a means to debug a spreadsheet that contains errors. We find credible the assertion that these spreadsheet engineering methodologies provide enhanced productivity, accuracy and maintainability for large financial planning models.*[10]

Grossman made the distinction that these methodologies – disciplines – based as they are on experience, research, practice and a shared commitment to quality assurance and control, put us in a very different space to that occupied by the average spreadsheet hack. A three-way comparison of SMART, FAST and BPM[11] failed to demonstrate any significant or meaningful difference between the methodologies; indeed the only issue of contention is the use of range names (see Chapter 4).

It is clear that merely subscribing to a methodology or standard does not in itself offer any real assurance. It should also be apparent that the quality assurance framework requires a controlled modelling methodology but should be indifferent as to which standard is actually employed.

Quality Assurance

Quality assurance is defined by ISO 9000 as 'a part of quality management focused on providing confidence that quality requirements will be

---

10. Spreadsheets Grow Up: Three Spreadsheet Engineering Methodologies for Large Financial Planning Models, Grossman and Ozluk, Proc. European Spreadsheet Risks Int. Group 2010.
11. www.bpmglobal.com/download_content/PDFs/BPM-Standards%20Comparison.pdf, 2014.

fulfilled'.[12] This describes the modelling environment; at this level we are not concerned about the modelling methodology itself, but more about the checks, tests and controls in specifying, developing, testing and subsequently using the model.

Referring to our case study, Macpherson describes a number of sources of quality assurance:

1. Developer testing: using a range of developer tools including parallel build and analytical review or sense check;
2. Internal peer review: obtaining a critical evaluation from a third party independent of the development of the model, but from within the same organisation;
3. External peer review: formal or information engagement with a third party to conduct a critical evaluation, from outside the organisation in which the model is being developed;
4. Internal model audit: formal audit of a model within an organisation, perhaps involving the internal audit function;
5. Quality assurance guidelines and checklists: model development refers to departments' guidance or other documented quality assurance processes;
6. External model audit: formal engagement of external professionals to conduct a critical evaluation of the model, perhaps involving audit professionals;
7. Governance: at least one of planning, design and/or sign-off of model for use is referred to a more senior person. There is a clear line of responsibility for the model;
8. Transparency: model is placed in the wider domain for scrutiny, and/or results are published;
9. Periodic review: model is reviewed at intervals to ensure that it remains fit for the intended purpose, if used on an on-going basis.

The details of developer testing and internal/external peer review, and internal/external model audit, will be explored in the next chapter as quality control procedures; but clearly the fact that such procedures are undertaken contributes to the quality assurance environment. Guidelines and checklists are important but less common: within the public sector there are publications such as the HM Treasury *Green Book*[13] or the *JSP 507* [14], and in the private sector BP has its economic evaluation methodology (EEM). Such guidelines tend to be very large documents and can go into great detail, with specific descriptions of calculations. Governance both contributes to, and receives assurance from, the quality procedures. Transparency is a good idea and seems to work well in the public sector but is subject of course to the demands of commercial sensitivity, which would exclude this principle entirely from the private sector.

---

12. ISO 9000 clause 3.2.11, 2008.
13. *The Green Book: Appraisal and Evaluation in Central Government*, HM Treasury 2014.
14. *Joint Service Publication 507: Guide to Investment and Appraisal*, MoD 2014.

Senior Responsible Owner

The identification of the rôle of the SRO is as welcome as it is crucial: the model sits in the middle of a vast range of project specifications and agreements, bank covenants, contracts and subcontracts, macroeconomic assumptions and operational parameters. The SRO is working with lawyers, accountants, bankers, investors, operations management, suppliers and contractors, local and national authorities and regulators, and must therefore be satisfied that the modelling function is working to the same professional standards and that the model is fit for purpose.

Having worked with financial institutions in the past I have often noticed that there is rarely an individual who might be described as an SRO or even having such responsibilities; instead 'model ownership' is unclear and quite often is synonymous with the individual modeller.

Developing the SRO concept further, I would describe it as a vertical rôle, in that the SRO has ownership of the financial model in the context of ownership and governance of the project itself, as opposed to all of the models produced by the team or the organisation. This removes any requirement, or assumption, of modelling expertise from this individual and instead emphasises the ownership of the quality assurance process; although the SRO must be knowledgeable about the model and its risks and limitations.

Modelling Compliance Officer

One of the risks with the SRO approach is that, by definition, this individual has responsibility for the one model, but not for others, and depending on the nature of the job itself may only hold this position for a limited time. To provide continuity I would add a further rôle within the modelling quality assurance environment: that of the modelling compliance officer. This is a horizontal rôle, in which the individual oversees the modelling function across the organisation. The individual may be an expert, but more importantly they:

1. determine and safeguard the modelling methodology (the 'modelling champion');
2. manage the modelling resource;
3. identify training needs;
4. select and apply the appropriate review/audit procedures;
5. liaise with developers/users/customers/auditors; and
6. provide assurance to the various SROs.

The modelling compliance officer is charged with quality control, for which the ISO definition is 'a part of quality management focused on fulfilling quality requirements'.[15] This rôle is actually quite common, but it is normally taken on by individuals as part of their overall responsibilities, rather than as the specific

---

15. ISO 9000 clause 2.2.10, 2008.

remit, and the quality of their work therefore is subject to pressure from other work commitments. The modelling compliance officer is the link between the modelling environment and the modelling process.

Modelling Environment

Both the SRO and the modelling compliance officer determine the modelling environment, which covers the way in which models are used in the organisation. This will identify the existing demand for, and reliance upon, and indeed confidence in, spreadsheet models. The process of model specification and development should be clearly defined, along with the identification of those who have the appropriate levels of skills and experience to be assigned to the modelling task. There are also various groups who help define the modelling culture and environment:

- Model commissioners: the management or operational function that determines the business requirement for a spreadsheet model and which then develops the model specifications (in consultation with the intended model users or customers);
- Model developers: the analysts or specialists who build, test and review the model;
- Model users: run the model;
- Model customers: use the results from the model as part of their decision-making process. Need to be aware of model limitations and confident that the results are robust for the use they are making of them.

Model Audit and Model Review

The quality assurance framework requires those charged with (spreadsheet) governance to seek assurance that the model is fit for purpose. This can be obtained from various sources as already discussed, but the terms 'audit' and 'review' can prove difficult to define. As a model audit firm, we find that most of our clients will think the terms synonymous but, they describe different processes which vary in rigour, the level of assurance provided, and more importantly, cost. A simple framework is illustrated in Figure 1.1.

Model review, rather than audit, is usually an informal process, and the peer review is one of the most common quality assurance procedures. It can cover the following:

- Code review by colleagues ('two pairs of eyes')
- Review by colleague (same team or different team) and/or manager review
- Conformance with internal modelling standards and procedures
- Standard battery of checks, tests and controls
- Limited testing (including stress testing)
- Limited sensitivity and/or scenario analysis

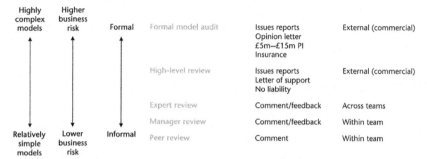

FIGURE 1.1   Model audit and review.

- Sign-off by management
- Presentation to management committee (or equivalent)

The apparent informality of the peer review process can also bring its own problems:

- Lack of expertise amongst colleagues (the 'avoiding bad practice' paradox)
- Lack of time/resource
- Lack of consistency
- Conflicts of interest (Chinese walls)
- Lack of training/standards
- 'group think'
- 'blame game'

For many organisations the peer review will be the only form of model scrutiny; due to cost and other resource constraints, and is therefore a combined quality control and assurance process.

The formal model audit, at the highest level, is a full analysis of the client's model, usually of the base case and including a handful of sensitivities. It follows the accounting auditor's procedures of the review of high level controls testing, followed, where indicated, by substantive tests. The opinion letter is a legal document, and is often a condition precedent to any loan agreement, or in PPP work the award of any contract. To quote from my firm's description of services:

Approach: the Operis approach to formal model audit is not based on defined physical portions of a model or a line-by-line code review (approaches take by some of our competitors) but is aligned more with the concepts the model is representing – whether the key outputs (typically financial statements, banking ratios, and investors' returns) are consistent with the intended treatment and the inputs provided. We combine certain specific tests on given items with selected reconstructions of items such as operating cash flows to ensure we arrive at the same answer from a different route. Common examples are tests to ensure a cover ratio has not omitted any relevant cash flows, or checks to ensure the out-turn interest paid on a given financing instrument reconciles with the rate as input.

Issues: issues found during the review are collated in issues reports, and graded according to severity. Our reports are written in plain language, rather than as a technical spreadsheet, deliberately so that the broader audience can easily read and make sense of the issues, not just the modeller.

Review: as the audit progresses additional issues reports are prepared as further revised models or documents are received. Issues reports are typically addressed to the sponsors and the modeller, and lenders if they are involved in the review at this stage. Some clients require only a high level review (which sits below a full model audit), the end deliverable being a Letter of Support.

Final Opinion Letter: the final Audit Opinion letter is the ultimate deliverable produced upon completion of a formal model audit. This letter describes the models and associated documents that have been reviewed, any outstanding issues which the client is prepared to have listed as caveats, and a sign-off on the agreed level of liability. This is a legally-binding document and usually a condition precedent to lending.

We use the following protocol:

1. Plan and design the audit approach.
2. Perform tests of controls (methodology and documentation).
3. Perform substantive tests of key results and financial instruments.
4. Perform analytical procedures of cash flow drivers.
5. Complete audit and issue audit report (see Chapter 2).

A typical model audit will cost, in 2015, around €35,000. There is no specific timeframe; we usually have a busy week or so setting up the audit working papers and we normally aim to get the first issues report out within five to seven working days. The project documentation may not be available or the project timeline might be such that the audit is then put on hold for a few weeks. There is also usually a delay when the issues reports are sent out, as we await the client's response. As will be emphasised throughout the next chapter, the model auditor will never change the model under test, as this is the responsibility of the owner. For bid models, or projects reaching financial close, there is often an intense period of activity as the model is updated and amended. As will also be seen, the spreadsheet model is a representation of a whole series of legal agreements and contracts, and the relationship between the model and the documentation is the focus of a great deal of expert attention. A good model audit firm will also offer cover through professional indemnity insurance.

We would expect that a model submitted for model audit has already been subject to extensive peer review by the client. As described above, the review forms the quality control, and the audit provides the quality assurance.

The high-level review and its corresponding letter of support (also known as a comfort letter) reflects a simpler and cheaper process which suits some clients.

One practice to avoid is that of 'code review' which is offered by some firms. This is a visual inspection of every formula in the workbook and, as might be expected, is both tedious in the extreme and generally of very little consequence. A code review is about the technical aspects of the model, whereas we believe the client is more interested in the project the model represents.

RISK ASSESSMENT

The modelling process should be subject to a cost/benefit analysis. The methodologies and techniques set out in this book are really geared towards spreadsheets and models which will be used for critical, significant or important transactions. The definition of what is 'critical', 'significant' or 'important' is the first step in risk control, and this is down to each organisation and it is essential that the terms are agreed. This may be around a risk register scoring system (impact × likelihood), or it could be an economic measure (transaction value greater than €1 million), or audience (external stakeholders vs internal management). Within an organisation it should be possible to develop some firm understanding of these concepts: the accountants provide us with the useful expression of 'materiality'. We could define this in terms of the value of the transaction or the overall value of the balances, or the impact on published financial statements (the objective of the Sarbanes–Oxley Act). Nonfinancial factors include the size and/or complexity of the model, intended use and users and one that is too frequently overlooked, the capabilities of the model author (modelling experience, knowledge of the business). It becomes apparent that some, if not all, of the risk assessment will involve high-level management, and that internal and external auditors may need to be involved. This is certainly a new way of thinking, due to the historical absence of any risk controls in the development and use of financial models.

RISK CONTROLS

Once the risk assessment has been carried out, and assuming that the proposed model is classed as critical, significant or important, the appropriate controls should be implemented.

Access Control

This would be the lowest level of control, allowing or restricting access to the model and its results by end users. At its simplest this could be through the use of passwords to open the file (as noted in Chapter 3, it is also possible to implement a further level of password control to allow users to access a model but not to save it). Sheet protection would further restrict the ability of users to interfere with the content or structure of the model.

Input Control

This level of user would be allowed to enter/amend/delete values in specific inputs cells only, which by definition do not contain formulas. Further control would be through the use of data validation, drop-down lists, combo and list boxes and protected/unprotected cells.

Change Control

This is the basic level of access for the model developers, in which calculations can be written and edited in the workings sheet. Sheet-level password protection could be applied. This should allow access to the audit sheet; although, significantly, the model auditor may not need change control rights.

Version Control

This is for the manager of the model development team, responsible for model testing, validation and auditing, with full access to all components of the model. Version control is a key task of the model SRO.

QUALITY ASSURANCE AND THE MODELLING METHODOLOGY

We have established a robust case for the implementation of quality assurance procedures from the outset. We have to recognise that for most organisations, resource constraints make it difficult, if not impossible, to implement a model development procedure which would allow the model to be tested, reviewed or audited by anyone other than the model author, with peer review being the highest level of assurance. However, if a standard approach to modelling is used across the team or department, and in particular if there is a standard battery of audit checks as set out in the next chapter then it should be feasible for a colleague to be able to review and comment upon our model in a reasonable amount of time. Ideally we should have a known and documented modelling methodology, such as Operis, FAST, SMART, or BPM, to avoid idiosyncrasies and persistent errors, but the quality assurance framework and the review/audit procedures should be unaffected by the modelling methodology actually used.

Other control-related issues include the development life cycle itself, documentation, and back-ups and archiving, and which are covered at various points in this book. The implementation of controls, if they do not already exist, is likely to prove difficult given the ease with which spreadsheets can be developed and used by individuals at all levels throughout the organisation. However it is possible to build in risk control features as part of the design and specification phase such that these controls are included from the outset.

We have described the rôle and sources of quality assurance in the modelling process. The next chapter discusses the implementation of quality control procedures.

Chapter 2

Quality Control

INTRODUCTION

Following on from the discussion on quality assurance and the modelling environment, we now consider the modelling and the quality control processes and risk controls we should employ. With the principle of error reduction, we want to anticipate potential errors and, using the feedback principle, to incorporate a system of model checks and controls. This chapter sets out the requirement for us to incorporate quality control into the model development process, recognising that, if left too late, minor errors have a habit of compounding themselves and they become very difficult to untangle. Along with a basic understanding of the various types of errors and their possible causes, we will look at formalising the quality control regime with the implementation of audit sheets and audit workbooks.

A point of language arises: I have generally referred to 'errors' in spreadsheets, and this word has very negative connotations. If we are working in a quality assurance environment and applying quality control processes and methodologies, 'errors' should be managed out of the system; but we may be left with inconsistencies, exceptions or what at my firm we call 'issues'. Given the minefield of corporate and individual egos and reputations we have found it so much easier to speak to the analyst about an 'issue' with the model, than to upset them by describing it as an 'error'.

UNDERSTANDING ERROR

Spreadsheet error is not simply a matter of getting the sums wrong. Research findings and long experience show that there are many different types of mistakes and many causes for them. Errors are grouped into classes, and collectively these are described as taxonomies. There is no clear agreement about a definitive classification but I would start with the following and refer you to the research if you would like to look further into this fascinating subject. You will see that many of the modelling ideas in this book are influenced by this important area of error research.

Pointing Errors

By far and away, the commonest error in all the research exercises and seen in general practice is the discrepancy in the cell reference. There is a simple rule – never type a cell reference. To put a reference into a formula, either click on the cell with the mouse, or better, use the arrow keys to select the cell (the keyboard is slower – pointing errors are normally caused when working at speed). Alternatively, consider the use of range names instead of cell references (Chapter 4). It is quite difficult, although not impossible, to put the wrong name into a formula, but it is much easier to spot such errors if they have occurred. Pointing errors increase in frequency the greater the distance between the formula cell and the reference cell, and especially if the reference is to another sheet.

Input Errors

You know it is 5000, I know it is 5000, but somehow it ended up in the model as 5 and the numbers are a factor of a 1000 out somewhere. Input errors can be incredibly difficult to spot, especially when the natural assumption is that a formula must be at fault. A general rule is that the numbers on the inputs sheet are expressed in the same units as in the project or transaction documentation. A further rule is to include a units column for every item, or a declaration that 'all numbers in £000s unless expressed otherwise'. Remember the old expression, Garbage In, Garbage Out (GIGO).

Omission Errors

Naturally, the most difficult type of error to spot, and the one that is most frequently noted after the event is an omission error. If the analyst has not been told to include a particular set of costs or fees, for example, who is responsible for the error? This is best avoided by adopting the top-down approach to model building, outlined in the next chapter. By preparing the model outputs first, and by engaging in an iterative process with the model sponsors, many such omission errors are trapped at the very outset of the modelling process. A good familiarity with the model documentation is very helpful in avoiding omission errors, as is a standard approach to calculation rules.

Commission Errors

These occur when the analyst does something that they are not required to do, such as adding extra detail or including calculations that are not needed but which affect the model's results. A common issue at the moment is the transition from UK GAAP (generally accepted accounting principles) to the International Financial Reporting Standards (not just a UK problem). This can also involve the subjective interpretation of definitions – using a project finance example, the elements of the cash flow are usually clearly specified, but little attention is given to earnings. Again, the top-down approach to model design helps prevent this: agreeing the model inputs and outputs in advance reduces the scope for creative modelling; and again the model documentation can provide assurance.

Alteration Errors

A variation of the commission error, where perhaps a flaw or mistake has been identified and corrected by the modeller, but the model sponsors were not told of the update. If the model reviewer finds a formula which should be corrected, I would recommend that, as part of the audit process, this is reported to the modeller but the reviewer should make no changes to the code. All such suggestions and amendments should be logged on the audit sheet or model documentation as part of the ongoing version control.

Calculation Errors

A general description for the largest category of error, and many such errors can be hard to track down. A particular problem is the long formula, containing several sets of brackets, lots of sheet names and wrapping around the formula bar. Not only do such formulas look unpleasant, but research shows that they are rarely checked or tested in detail, and quite often even the analyst who created them is unsure of their exact function. The BODMAS issue (the rules of arithmetic priority or order of operations) is a common source of error in long formulas: the order in which the elements of a calculation are worked out may be in a different order to that intended when written. One of the themes of the formulas and functions in chapters is to break formulas into short sections over several cells, which may appear less intellectually rigorous but is far more reliable in the long term. A criticism of the short formula argument is that if we have more formula cells then statistically there is a greater risk of error, but the point is that the formulas are shorter and simpler and inherently less error prone.

Timing Errors

Calculations involving the timing of an event, or the duration of a process such as depreciation, are often some of the most difficult to set up reliably. Workarounds include such dodges as simply writing the formula in a fixed number of cells, such that if the asset life, for example, is changed, the calculations do not reflect this unless they are copied to the new cells. This category also includes errors such as using the annual interest rate when calculating interest on a quarterly basis. Chapters 5 and 6 set out a number of reliable techniques which address this type of problem.

Competence Errors

This is a category of my own devising and borne out more by experience than research. A warning sign is the extensive use of functions such as INDIRECT and OFFSET, or IF functions that test for, or return, "" (empty quotes), or

SUMs that contain calculations; or a perception that the model is heavily over-engineered. These issues reflect more on the mind-set of the analyst and give an early indication that there may be other modelling issues which suggest not bad practice but confused or less clear thinking.

Domain Errors

Domain knowledge refers to professional knowledge – finance, accounting, management or operations. The researchers reassuringly note that this is the least common type of error – we all know that cash is not profit, that we should depreciate our assets, pay tax, use real discount rates on real cash flows, even if we are not sure how to perform the calculations. However, in-depth domain knowledge or experience does not necessarily translate to good modelling skills and returning to the modelling environment we would expect such experts to inform the model development but perhaps not to attempt to build it themselves.

ERROR RECOGNITION

My financial modelling courses are based on extended case studies and the principle is that I guide my delegates through a series of activities and exercises which produce specific results. At each stage, we have check numbers to confirm that the calculations are correct, and this process will usually highlight any errors. However, I would estimate that around 3% of these analysts fail to demonstrate an ability either to recognise errors or that they then exhibit no strategy for error resolution when an error has been identified. Whether they have the wrong results, error values or even circularities, they seem to carry on regardless, and on being challenged will often inspect random parts of the model. If this is a true example of their behaviour in a straightforward training exercise under the watchful eyes of an instructor, what would happen in the workplace, with a real model? It is this observation, more than anything else, that gave rise to the feedback principle, where we actively seek confirmation that the model is error free.

AUDIT TOOLS AND TECHNIQUES

Excel contains a surprising amount of formula auditing functionality without recourse to expensive third party auditing software. In addition to a range of error checking features, it has a number of tools to assist in the model audit process. To get the most out of these tools, as with any diagnostic procedure, it is important to be able to understand the significance of the tests, and the meaning and implications of the results. Be aware that some features of the auditing toolbar and several of the audit shortcuts may be disabled if Excel's protection, group or objects features have been set.

F2 Edit Cell

We know about using F2 to edit the contents of a cell directly in the worksheet, rather than using the Formula Bar. If this does not seem to work, run File, Options, Advanced and check that the Allow editing directly in cells has been selected. In passing, note that the Formula Bar can be resized by clicking and dragging its lower border. Use Ctrl+Shift+U to resize it using the keyboard.

We can use the Home, End and Shift and arrow key combinations to correct or amend the formula. If the wrong cell references have been entered, we can use the trick of pressing F2 again, then using the arrow keys to select the correct cells in the worksheet (Point mode, shown on the status bar). Press F2 once more to carry on editing the formula.

This same technique can be used in some dialog boxes which require range or cell references. Any attempt to use the arrow keys will cause the references to change, which can be annoying if you are simply trying to edit part of a cell address, for example. Press F2 to change from Point to back to Edit mode.

Remember, F2 is your primary diagnostic tool for inspecting Excel formulas.

F9

Sometimes we want to get some information about a cell without actually wanting to see it. Press F2 to inspect the formula of interest and select one of the cell references. Then press F9. The address converts to the value in the precedent cell. Repeat for each part of the formula, until all references are converted to values. Do not press Enter otherwise the references will be permanently converted to values (Figure 2.1).

If you use this technique with range names, Excel will treat the name as an array reference and on pressing F9 it will return every value in the array. Not helpful.

Trace Precedents

One of the most useful shortcuts in Excel is the Ctrl+[(open square bracket). Select a cell containing a calculation and press Ctrl+[to select (highlight) the formula's precedent cells. Press Enter to then cycle through these cells (or Shift+Enter to cycle through in reverse). Pressing Ctrl+[repeatedly will select the precedents for the active cell each time. As a general rule of thumb, I would expect to find myself on the inputs sheet (or equivalent) within five keystrokes. The Ctrl+[is not very reliable if formulas refer to multiple sheets but works best on the workings sheet system described in the next chapter.

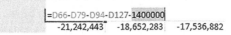

FIGURE 2.1   Select the cell reference and press F9.

Ctrl+[and F5 Combination

Note that Excel does not highlight the original formula under inspection; the trick here is to press F5 (Go To). Excel automatically provides the address of this cell, so we simply press Enter to return. The Ctrl+[/ F5 combination is one of the most powerful audit shortcuts available. It will work across sheets and across workbooks. However the square brackets do not work the same way on all keyboards, but the command can be carried out using F5, Go To, Special, Precedents.

F2 and F5 Combination

F2 simply points to the precedents of a formula, where Ctrl+[actively selects them for inspection. F9 allows us to convert references to values. To examine a precedent cell but without dropping out of the formula under inspection, we can press F2 to edit the cell, select a reference and press F5 – Excel will put the address directly in the Go To reference box. Press Enter and we can see the precedent cell and its value; press Enter again to return to the original cell. With this technique there is no risk of inadvertently converting a reference to a hard-coded value, nor of losing sight of the cell under inspection.

View Formulas

We can click on individual cells to inspect their contents on the formula bar. Sometimes, however, we want to get a bigger picture of the type and structure of the formulas used in a workbook, and a neat trick here is to use Formulas, Show Formulas (Figure 2.2).

Alternatively, use the keyboard shortcut Ctrl+' (left apostrophe) – unfortunately this does not work on most European keyboards. This doubles the width of the worksheet columns and exposes the underlying formulas. This can be very useful to get an overall impression of the workbook, and it is worth noting that this is a printable view. By hiding appropriate columns and adjusting column widths as required we can print out a hard copy of the sheet for future reference. To restore the view, repeat the command sequence/shortcut.

Formula Auditing Ribbon Group

The Formula Auditing tools group can be found on the Formula tab. It contains buttons for tracing precedents and dependents, tracing errors and for locating invalid entries when using data validation (Chapter 7). I am not particularly keen to see blue arrows drawn all over my workbook, but the toolbar does have some uses, particularly for off-sheet formulas. In this example, the revenue calculation feeds into a cash flow calculation further down the workings sheet, as well as to the revenue line on the Cash Flow report. On clicking Trace Dependents, Excel points to both. The workbook icon indicates that the dependent formula is off-sheet, and we can double-click the dashed arrow to

=Inputs!D23	=Inputs!E23	=Inputs!F23
=D72*D43	=E72*E43	=F72*F43
=Inputs!D24	=Inputs!E24	=Inputs!F24
=D76*D39	=E76*E39	=F76*F39
=D73+D77	=E73+E77	=F73+F77
=Inputs!D27	=Inputs!E27	=Inputs!F27
=((D66*D84)/91)*(1+$C$133)	=((E66*E84)/91)*(1+$C$133)	=((F66*F84)/91)*(1+$C$133)
=Inputs!D28	=Inputs!E28	=Inputs!F28
=D73	=E73	=F73
=((D89*D88)/91)*(1+$C$133)	=((E89*E88)/91)*(1+$C$133)	=((F89*F88)/91)*(1+$C$133)
=C95	=D95	=E95
=D95-D93	=E95-E93	=F95-F93
=D85-D90	=E85-E90	=F85-F90

FIGURE 2.2   View formulas.

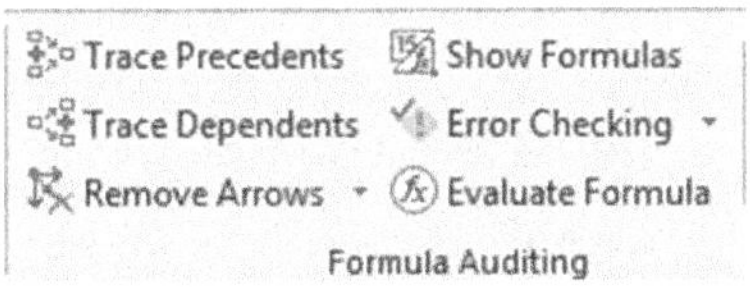

FIGURE 2.3   Formula Auditing ribbon group.

see the Go To dialog box which lists the off-sheet references. Generally I find the Ctrl+[(Select Precedents) and Ctrl+] (Select Dependents) shortcuts more useful (Figure 2.3).

Trace Error is used for auditing cells which contain error values, which in themselves are relatively easy to audit anyway, as we shall see.

Evaluate Formula

This tool extends the F9 functionality by launching a dialog box which allows the individual components of the selected formula to be evaluated, using the rules of arithmetic priority. Each click on the Evaluate button returns the result of a calculation within the formula. The Step In/Step Out buttons can be used to return the cell references of any range names used in the calculation. As this is done within the dialog box there is no risk of converting the cell references to hard-coded values (Figure 2.4).

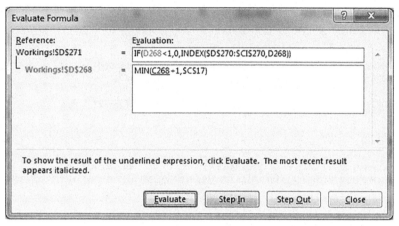

FIGURE 2.4   Evaluate formula dialog box.

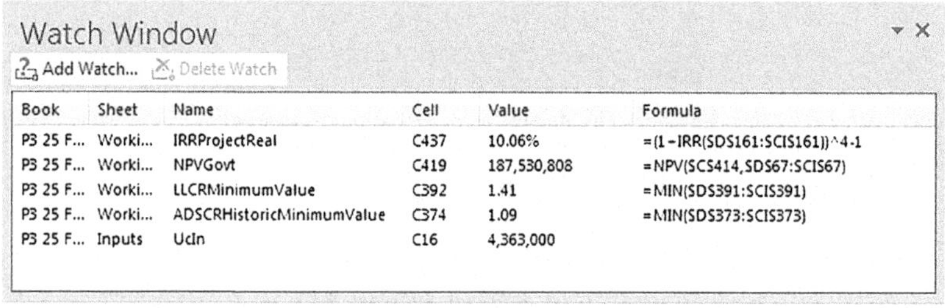

FIGURE 2.5   A Watch window.

The Watch Window

This little known feature in Excel is rather useful. It is found on the Formulas tab, Watch window. A small window is displayed from which we can monitor a formula and its value.

To use it, select a cell or range (which can contain either values or formulas) and choose Add Watch in the Watch window (Figure 2.5). The Watch window works across sheets, so that the effect of changing an input value or precedent formula can be seen on the dependent formula or result. The headings (Book, Sheet, Name, etc.) can be clicked to sort into alphabetical or numerical order. The list of references included in a Watch window is persistent, which means that if the workbook is saved, the Watch window will bring up the same list when the book is reopened.

Error Checking

Excel's error checking tools have not proved a major success, primarily because most users do not understand what Excel is telling them, and I normally find that the Error checking feature has been switched off. It isn't merely a glorified spell checking tool, and it is worth knowing what Excel is trying to tell us. First check to see if error checking is enabled by using File, Options, Formulas, Enable background formula checking.

Excel can check for the following errors, each of which can be enabled or disabled.

- Cells containing formulas that result in an error
- Inconsistent calculated column formula in tables
- Cells containing years represented as two digits
- Numbers formatted as text or preceded by an apostrophe
- Formulas inconsistent with other formulas in the region
- Formulas which omit cells in a region
- Unlocked cells containing formulas
- Formulas referring to empty cells
- Data entered in table is invalid

When Excel identifies an error a green error indicator triangle appears in the top left corner of the cell, and an error checking button appears when the cell is selected. Clicking the button will give options, which are different according to the nature of the error. Note that one option is to ignore the error – if this is done, the error indicator disappears and Excel will not mark the error again. The commonest error I encounter is the 'Formulas inconsistent with other formulas in the region' because I've written a mixture of cell reference and range name formulas. Not very helpful.

A sheet-level error check can be run at any time, if Error checking is enabled (Run Formulas, Error Checking, Error Checking).

ERROR VALUES

Error values signify Excel's inability to understand a formula or function and in themselves can be helpful diagnostic tools. Regardless of the specific layout, we tend to see that formulas cascade through the model, and on encountering an error value we simply work back to locate the first occurrence of the error. If we understand the error value it is usually fairly simple to resolve the problem. I describe some of the common error values and their causes below, but refer to Excel Help for more detailed explanations and for less common causes and to Chapters 5 and 6 for error handling formulas and functions.

#VALUE!

This error has two common causes:

1. Referencing a cell that contains text. Select the cell with the error and press F2 or Ctrl+[. Inspect the precedent cells and correct as necessary. If the cell looks empty, the problem could be that a user has pressed the Spacebar to clear the contents of the cell, so press the Delete key to make sure.

2. Referencing a range instead of a single cell, for example, =E10+(E12:E20). In this case, we have missed out the required SUM. A similar problem arises with range names if the reference to the range name is outside the columns included in the name range, for example, in column D the formula reads =EBITDA, but the range EBITDA is defined as E42:K42 (see Chapter 4 for further information).

#REF!

This error is commonly found when rows or columns are deleted from the model, such that a formula refers to a cell which no longer exists. The unpleasant feature of the #REF! error is that Excel will substitute it into the formula in place of the original cell reference. If several rows or columns have been deleted it can be difficult to rebuild the formula, or to work out what the formula was originally referring to =(#REF!-E66-#REF!-E117). If it is possible, undo the deletions and instead select and delete the contents of the unwanted cells (not the rows or columns themselves). Then, with the cells still selected, type some text and press Ctrl+Enter. This should fill the range with text and the dependent formulas now return the #VALUE! error. Locate these formulas and make the appropriate amendments whilst the cell references are still available; or at least put in a cell comment to provide instructions on what to do with the formulas after the unwanted rows (or columns) are finally deleted. Do not simply delete the original cell contents as you may end up with formulas that refer to blank cells, a cardinal modelling error.

#NAME?

This error clearly indicates that Excel does not recognise the range name you have entered into a formula. Normally this is easy to fix: on pressing F2, the range names and references in the formula that Excel recognises should appear in colour; if a name remains black it is likely to be the unknown name, although it is possible that it could refer to a range on another sheet. Alternatively, use the F9 technique from the previous chapter: click and drag over each range name and press F9. If Excel recognises the name, it displays the values from the range (usually all of them, as an array). If a name evaluates to #NAME?, it has not been recognised. The corrections are equally simple. Check the spelling of the name and type the correction, or press F3 or Formulas, Use in Formula, Paste Names and select the name from the list. If neither of these work, check that the name exists in the first place by using Ctrl+F (Home, Find & Select, Find), typing in the unknown name (as spelled in the formula), and seeing if Excel can find the original name in the worksheet. If the row is located, use the Name Manager (Ctrl+F3) on the Formulas tab as required. Range names are explained in much more detail in Chapter 4.

#DIV/0!

This error often occurs either when precedent values have been deleted from a model, or when formulas are being written in advance of the relevant information being provided. The denominator is missing from a division formula, so once the information or precedent calculation is provided, the error will disappear. If the information is genuinely unavailable, use unit values (1) instead, as a temporary workaround. Document your work accordingly. Clearly if the formula was written, deliberately the analyst would have anticipated that the denominator could be 0, and should have included an appropriate error trap.

#NUM!

Not a common error, this usually occurs with the IRR function. Excel uses an iterative technique to calculate the IRR and if it cannot generate an answer within 20 iterations, it returns the #NUM! error. This typically happens if all the values in the cash flow have the same sign.

#N/A

This is often generated by the VLOOKUP, HLOOKUP and MATCH type functions explained in Chapter 6, usually because there is no exact match for the item being looked for. Each of these functions contains an argument to specify if an exact match is required for the lookup item. If the argument has been omitted, Excel assumes that it has been sorted and if there is no exact match the error is produced. If you encounter this problem, refer to Chapter 6 and make sure that the function contains a FALSE or 0 argument or an error-handling mechanism.

Debugging Error Values

Once a formula generates an error value, all dependent formulas do the same, unless there is a circularity or calculation has been set to manual (press F9 to force a recalculation anyway). To locate the source of the error browse down the left-hand column of the calculations area until you find the first occurrence of the error, or alternatively use the Trace Error tool to locate error values (Formulas, Error Checking, Trace Error). Find and fix.

Printing without Errors

During model development, it is not uncommon to have error values simply because formulas are being written for test or other temporary purposes – for example, the debt service cover ratio calculations may return the #DIV/0! error before the debt routine is complete. To avoid printing errors, we can use the Page Layout, Page setup launcher command and select the Sheet tab in the Page Setup dialog box. We can then click the Cell errors as list, to show errors either as displayed, <blank>, -- or #N/A.

The 'Break-and-Make' Technique

When adding a new section to an existing model it is sometimes difficult to confirm that the new content is correctly recognised by the rest of the model – a key part of the feedback principle. The danger lies in failing to link the new logic to the old formulas in the right places. I like to use what I call the 'break-and-make' approach: I introduce a deliberate error value into the new code, either by using a nonexistent range name (generating the #NAME? error) or dividing the formula by zero (#DIV/0). As I update the model, the error should start spreading. Corrections to the new code should resolve the problem.

As a more aggressive approach, I might introduce an error into the original model. As the new code is linked to the old code, the error spreads into the new section. When I am ready, I revisit the broken formula (and I know where it is!) and correct it both and if necessary amend it with the appropriate references to the new routine. The error values disappear and I am confident that the model has been thoroughly updated.

THE MODEL REVIEWER AND THE REVIEW PLAN

By this stage it should be apparent that the model reviewer, whether as colleague offering a second pair of eyes or as a manager, doesn't need to be a modelling expert but does need to be reasonably competent in navigating spreadsheets and auditing formulas. In describing the formal attributes of a peer reviewer, I would suggest the following:

- appropriate technical skills,
- appropriate project knowledge,
- appropriate domain knowledge,
- access to project and ancillary documentation,
- access to the model developer,
- appropriate time and resources,
- authority and willingness to challenge,
- confidence to provide meaningful feedback,
- awareness of own limitations,
- willingness to seek specialist advice (e.g. tax) if required.

As discussed in Chapter 1 there are various interpretations used for the terms 'model audit' and 'model review', and as mentioned I tend to find that most people actually mean the latter. It is important that the objectives of any review process are stated explicitly so that both the modeller and the reviewer have reasonable expectations. A general plan might be as follows:

1. Agree timescales.
2. Receive the model for review (and make read-only).
3. Receive relevant documentation.
4. Prepare audit sheet/audit workbook.

5. Inspect and record model results (consider version control).
6. Run first analysis using review software tools (if available).
7. Examine the model for Excel/technical/structural issues.
8. Inspect model results and check calculation methodology against documentation.
9. Examine model inputs and check against documentation.
10. Write first issues report/feedback and return model to developer.
11. Repeat from step 2 as required.

We should recognise from the outset that the management of time and resources are fundamental to this process; both the reviewer and the modeller will have other work in hand and neither may be able to provide immediate responses. Step 1 should give both sides a reasonable time frame in which it is expected to be completed.

Printing

One of the very first actions we take when we receive a model is to print the reports. There is some simple thinking behind this: the absence of print settings (headers, footers, print titles, etc.) indicates that the model has never been printed. If the reports have never been printed, it is unlikely that anyone senior has ever seen the model. Is it reasonable to expect the SRO or director to examine a 25-year-forecast period on screen? At least one of the 'magic circle' law firms has a policy of banning the on screen review of legal documents and insisting that all such papers are printed, for much the same reason. As we will see in the next chapter, the model reports are the key deliverable, and the investment or credit committee want to see an attractively bound report bundle, not a spreadsheet beamed on to a wall.

Issues Reporting

In both the audit sheet and audit workbook processes, we should consider how we will deal with issues as they are detected. As we have resolved not to use language such as 'error' or 'problem', the issues report is a positive communication tool that helps the reviewer explain their concerns and for the modeller to provide a response. Unlike the audit sheet approach which is used in the context of peer review and is usually rather informal, the audit workbook is far more formal and there may be some distance between the reviewer and the analyst, which underlines the importance of recording these discussions. As previously emphasised, the reviewer is under no circumstance permitted to alter ('correct') the model under test (MUT) as ownership is retained by the modelling team.

As model reviewers or auditors we are not particularly concerned about the modelling methodology nor about the calculations themselves. We will not add value to the review process if we simply feedback our dissatisfaction with the number of IFs, or the use of range names, or any breaches of 'best practice', provided we are satisfied that the model is fit for purpose. A scoring or grading system will help us provide useful feedback to the analyst from the outset, and at Operis, we use the following system:

A: matters which have a large material impact on the viability of the transaction and which would require attention in order for a formal audit opinion to be released;

B: matters of significance which would be mentioned in a formal audit opinion letter but the correction of which is not essential for the release of such a letter;

C: matters or points of note which would either be covered by general caveats or would not affect a formal opinion;

Q (query): matters which require clarification to further the audit process.

THE AUDIT SHEET

The Purpose

The audit sheet is an additional sheet in the model in which we carry out and record our quality checks. Models have different purposes and uses, so the audit sheet can be as simple or as complex as required. A further, more compelling reason, to include the audit sheet is to demonstrate compliance with risk controls and to assist in the risk assessment exercise required to establish conformance with Macpherson principles or Sarbanes–Oxley regulatory requirements. An organisation may wish to impose a standard battery of tests which may go beyond the model audit checks described in this chapter; for example, a statement of materiality, or a report of the magnitude of the cash flows, or of the relationship of the model to the strategic business plan. Additionally we may use the audit sheet to record the testing regime applied to the model, such as the stress or sensitivity tests described in Chapter 8; for example, are the lending ratios still satisfied if the forecast revenues fall by 10%?

In the previous chapter we briefly considered the various proprietary modelling methodologies such as Operis, FAST, SMART and BPM. At this stage, however, we are still concerned with the modelling environment, and it is important to recognise that model review and audit *must* be independent of, and indeed indifferent to, the specific modelling approach used in the model under review. The audit sheet and audit workbook can be used in any type of model, whether financial or operational.

One of the commonest model inspection and validation regimes is that of peer review, which can become a rather informal process. The audit sheet techniques help introduce an element of formality and will provide assurance to those outside the modelling function.

We will consider five types of check which we can perform within or of the model:

- environmental;
- structural;
- arithmetical;

- financial; and
- change checks.

Many of these could also be described as risk factors, and I have included a list of these in Appendix 1. The results of these checks should be recorded and we should recognise that these checks do not necessarily indicate errors or problems, merely 'issues' for resolution; there may be a perfectly valid reason why the analyst has hidden a column, or used a hard-coded value in a calculation. The purpose of audit is to better understand the model and its operation, and to satisfy ourselves that it does what it is supposed to do. If we are auditing our own work, we can make corrections as necessary, but when checking someone else's work the primary rule is that we never make changes to the MUT: we should find out who has the responsibility for making changes.

The MUT

As we begin the process of model review we introduce the expression 'model under test' or MUT. The primary rule to be followed is that we, as reviewers, must not make any changes to the MUT, instead we refer any findings or discrepancies to the modeller or modelling team, for their comment or correction. This principle establishes clear boundaries between the reviewer and the modeller so that individual responsibilities are understood and accepted. This is particularly important if the reviewer is not a modelling expert but is acting as a second pair of eyes or is the manager of the modelling function.

To ensure that we can't change the MUT we make it read-only, by using F12 (Save As), Tools, General options and clicking in the Read-only recommended box (Figure 2.30).

The audit sheet approach potentially introduces an immediate breach to this rule, in that the introduction of an audit sheet is clearly a structural change to the MUT. There are two responses to this: the modeller could add the audit sheet during the model design stage; or the introduction of the audit sheet is the first stage in the review process and accepted as such.

We will look at the audit workbook concept later in the chapter. This is a separate spreadsheet, linked to the MUT but not a part of it.

Layout

To set up an audit sheet in an existing model, simply copy an existing output sheet (try Ctrl+click and drag a sheet tab). Delete any existing sheet content, and any number/text formatting, but retain the column headings. Name the sheet as Audit. This sheet should conform to the same layout as used in the rest of the workbook. Each audit check is then listed.

Here is a basic audit sheet layout (Figure 2.6). At the outset, before the checks are carried out, the result of each test is a fail, and we enter the logical

AuditCheck		▼	:	✕	✓	*fx*	=AND(D:D)		

	A	B	C	D	E	F	G	H
1	Period from				01 Apr 17	01 Apr 17	01 Jul 17	01 Oct 17
2	Period to				30 Jun 17	30 Jun 17	30 Sep 17	31 Dec 17
3								
4	AUDIT							
5								
6					FALSE	AuditCheck		
7								
8	Environmental checks							
9								
10	Calculation mode							
11	setting							
12	check			FALSE				
13								
14	Iteration							
15	setting							
16	check			FALSE				
17								
18	Links to other documents							
19	setting							
20	check			FALSE				
21								
22	Workbook macros							
23	setting							
24	check			FALSE				
25								

FIGURE 2.6 The start of the audit sheet.

operator FALSE. As there may be a substantial number of checks, it is helpful to have an audit summary, which reads TRUE if all checks have been passed, and FALSE if any one or more has failed. In the example below, the results of each test are recorded in the base column, in this case column D. I have entered the following formula in a cell in column E: =AND(D:D).

The AND function is explained in detail in Chapter 6, and the D:D notation in Chapter 5. The effect of the formula is that Excel scans all the results in column D. If any one (or more) reads FALSE, the function returns FALSE. Only if every single test is TRUE does the function return TRUE. We get a problem if a test returns an error message, because the audit check will simply repeat the error. We will return to this particular problem later. Also, jumping slightly ahead of ourselves, we can give the cell the name AuditCheck (Formulas, Create from Selection – range names are discussed in Chapter 4).

On each output sheet we can put in a link to AuditCheck, so that the current audit status is recorded on any printouts that we generate.

It would also be helpful if we could list the number of audit tests, and to count those that currently evaluate to FALSE. In a cell below AuditCheck, write the following formula:

```
=COUNTIF(D:D,FALSE)
```

This returns the number of tests that read FALSE.
In the cell below, enter the following formula:

```
=COUNTA(D:D)
```

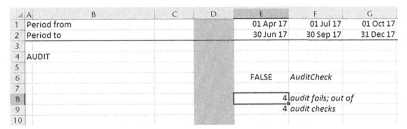

	A	B	C	D	E	F	G
1	Period from				01 Apr 17	01 Jul 17	01 Oct 17
2	Period to				30 Jun 17	30 Sep 17	31 Dec 17
3							
4	AUDIT						
5							
6					FALSE	AuditCheck	
7							
8						4	audit fails; out of
9						4	audit checks
10							

FIGURE 2.7   Counting errors.

This returns the total number of audit tests. This approach is expanded in the Balance Sheet section below (Figure 2.7).

ENVIRONMENTAL CHECKS

The first audit checks relate to the Excel environment and simply identify if Excel itself is working as it should. It wouldn't look too good if we hadn't picked up that the model was using manual recalculation, for example, or was using iteration (Chapter 5). Technical settings such as the 1904 date system or the Set precision as displayed option should be noted (Figure 2.8).

This is really just a simple list of things to look for, which can be found in the File, Options dialog box in the Formulas and Advanced sections. There is no requirement to change anything but we should record the current settings. Set the audit check to TRUE to show the check has been performed, regardless of the setting. Finally document any findings of concern, to follow up with the modeller.

Many people are thrown by changes to the Excel screen, so display options such as scroll bars and row and column headers might need to be checked, and explanations sought if the modeller has decided to change the appearance or environment of the workbook. Excel's worksheet protection features can affect the availability of commands and functionality, as well as the ability to inspect or review formulas. Protection can be disabled using Home, Format, Unprotect sheet.

Time Stamping

Both the environmental and the structural checks are manual, in that we inspect components of the spreadsheet and Excel. If the model is complete it may be sufficient to run these tests once and to record our findings. However, if the model is still under development, or there are issues requiring attention later, we may need to repeat the tests with each iteration of the model. In this case it can be helpful to time stamp the audit sheet. As each audit result is entered, in the adjacent cells we can use Ctrl+Shift+: to insert the time, and Ctrl+; to insert the date, as hard-coded values.

We could also enter this information as a cell comment, using Shift+F2 and then the same shortcuts for the date and time; the benefit is that your user name, as reviewer, is recorded at the same time (Figure 2.9).

11	Environmental checks		
12			
13	Calculation mode		
14	setting	Manual	
15	check		TRUE
16			
17	Iteration		
18	setting	Off	
19	check		TRUE
20			
21	Links to other documents		
22	setting	None	
23	check		TRUE
24			
25	Workbook macros		
26	setting	None	
27	check		TRUE
28			
29	Precision as displayed		
30	setting	Off	
31	check		TRUE
32			
33	1904 date system		
34	setting	Off	
35	check		TRUE
36			

FIGURE 2.8   Examples of environmental checks.

5			
6	Left-to-right consistency		Jonathan Swan:
7	check	TRUE	13:39 25/03/2015
8			
9			
10			
11			

FIGURE 2.9   Time stamping a cell comment.

Iteration Status

Iteration is a powerful feature and is explained in much more detail in Chapter 5 but for the moment we should note that it is used to solve circular calculations. The problem with this is that the majority of circularities are accidental and iteration will happily calculate both deliberate circular code and simple slips. We should always check that either iteration is off and that the model is non-circular, or that iteration is on and that the circular code is controlled with a switch (Chapter 5). Inspect this setting in File, Options, Formulas, Enable iterative calculation.

One of the reasons for running this check in particular is that Excel has a habit of saving the iteration status as a file attribute. When the workbook is reopened, Excel will switch on iteration without any other warning, and so it is not safe to assume that the iteration status is always off by default.

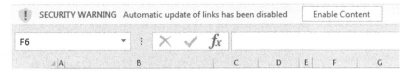

FIGURE 2.10   The file links notification.

During model build, the iteration should always be off, as it is during the development phase that circular errors are most likely to arise.

Record the iteration status on the audit sheet.

File Links

Generally, file links should be avoided at all costs. Your model may be unusable if Excel cannot establish or refresh links to precedent files. I recommended that if file links are to be used, the link formulas are entered on a single sheet per linked file for easy reference and management. Excel will normally warn you if there are external links in your workbook when you attempt to open the file, although in Excel 2013 this is now a security warning strip across the top of the workbook (Figure 2.10).

The Data, Edit Links command simply lists the files which are linked to your workbook, but it does not tell you where the link formulas are. However, as with three-dimensional (3-D) calculations, they are easy to locate because the unique feature of such formulas is the use of the [or] (square brackets) around the filename. Use Ctrl+F (Find) and enter either the [or] as the search string. Amend as required, and update the audit sheet with an entry to confirm the absence of file links.

File links can be manually broken. If the Data, Edit Links, Break Link command is used, the link formula is replaced by the current value shown in the cell. The same dialog box allows the Startup options to be changed, so that users may or may not see the prompt to update links, and links may or may not be updated automatically, without user intervention. It is also possible to check the status of the linked file: amongst other things it may be open, not found, not updated or not recalculated (Figure 2.11).

There are occasions when, having eliminated all link formulas from the entire workbook, you may still find Excel offering the file link security warning when you open the file. The trick here is to check if the model contains range names, and if so, if any of them are links to other files. This can be tested by moving the active cell to a blank part of the workbook and then:

1. Use Formulas, Use in Formula, Paste Names (or press F3) and click on Paste List (see Chapter 4).
2. Excel produces a list of all range names in the model.
3. Press Ctrl+* to select this list (Select Current Region).
4. Use the Ctrl+F (Find) command to search for the [or], as before.

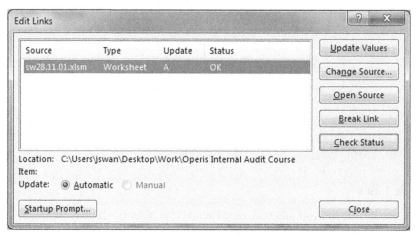

FIGURE 2.11   The Edit Links dialog box.

5. Note the name containing the file link reference, and use Formulas, Define Name, Define Name (Ctrl+F3).
6. Locate the errant name in the list and click the Delete button.
7. Repeat steps 3–5 as required.

To confirm that all file links have now been removed, check the Data, Edit Links command. If it is greyed out, then there are no file links in the workbook. Having done this, we then need to locate any formulas which contain the now deleted range name, using the audit check to locate errors, below.

R1C1 Reference Style

This is another feature that can be used as a security setting; it can either be tested in the environment settings section of the audit sheet or in the structural section. The familiar cell references are replaced with an obscure and, to many users, meaningless reference system based on rows and columns. A formula such as =SUM(A5:D5) in cell E5 appears as =SUM(RC[-4]:RC[-1]). This translates as 'sum the cells from A (which is -4 columns from the formula cell) to D (which is -1 columns) on this row (no row number given)'. Negative row and column numbers are to the left and above the formula cell, positive row and column numbers are to the right and below.

The R1C1 style is enabled or disabled using File, Options, Formulas, R1C1 reference style. The use of this style should be noted and perhaps explained on the audit sheet. Needless to say, the combination of R1C1 and array formulas can be a very powerful security setting. Interestingly, range names in formulas are unaffected by this style.

STRUCTURAL CHECKS

Having identified that Excel is working as it should, or with explanations for any exceptions, we can now examine the structure of the spreadsheet – are things where they should be? Structural checks are manual checks, in that we must carry out particular command sequences each time we wish to run a particular audit test. The results must then be recorded on the audit sheet.

Location of Inputs

Whatever methodology is being used in the model, we should always be able to locate and identify the input values in the workbook. Although some users suggest using colour, I have recommended that inputs should be located only on the inputs sheet(s). What if they are not?

1. Select the columns containing the calculations.
2. Press F5 and the Special button (or Home, Find & Select, Go To Special).
3. Choose the Constants option. You can then deselect Text, Logicals and Errors.
4. Choose OK (Figure 2.12).

Excel now highlights all cells containing input values. I suggest that we apply a fill colour at this point, to prevent us losing the selection and having to repeat the Go To sequence. When running audit checks I use a nonstandard fill colour (one that I wouldn't use in normal work). Now browse the worksheet to find any coloured cells. Make any corrections or notes and then put in a line on the audit sheet to record that the test has been carried out successfully.

Hard-Coded Values

These are input values which have been written directly into calculations (`=E117*1.175`) and can be harder to locate. It would be logical to expect the Go To Special, Formulas, Numbers command to select formulas which contain numbers. But it doesn't.

An alternative is available, if you feel bold enough. We recognise that all the numbers in the workings and outputs are ultimately derived from the inputs. If there are no inputs, there should be no results.

1. Back up (save) the file.
2. Select all the inputs and delete them (assuming you can locate the inputs in the first place, if not, use the F5 Special command to select them).
3. Check the results and workings. If any numbers are visible, they must be hardcoded. Do not rely on this step, because your inputs currently have a value of zero. Dependent formulas, particularly multiplications, will mask any hard-coded values. Also you may have a rash of #DIV/0! errors, which further serve to cover up any values.

FIGURE 2.12   Using Go To Special to locate input values.

35	INFLATION							
36								
37	CPI							
38	rate (% pa)			100%	100%	100%	100%	100%	100%
39	index		1	2.00	4.00	8.00	16.00	32.00	64.00
40								
41	Building Materials Index							
42	rate (% pa)			100%	100%	100%	100%
43	index		1	=C43*(1+D42)^0.25	1.68	2.00	2.38	2.83
44								

FIGURE 2.13   Using predictive values: the first index is working correctly. The second index produces an unexpected sequence of values, on inspection we find a hard-coded value.

4. With the original input cells selected, remove any number formatting (File, Format Number) or Ctrl+Shift+~.

5. Type 1 and press Ctrl+Enter to fill the selected range. All input cells should have a value of 1 (Figure 2.13).

Now inspect your workings and outputs. You are looking for unusual number sequences. Growth or inflation, for example, are now compounding at 100% and should be generating the exponential sequence 1, 2, 4, 8, 16, 32,… You should be able to recognise this in its various permutations in the workings. Anything with a different sequence must be driven by different values. Check and locate any hard-coded numbers. Make any corrections, and then put in a line on the audit sheet to record that the test has been carried out successfully.

References to Blank Cells

It is a cardinal rule in modelling that formulas must never refer to blank cells, and to do so is to invite disaster. This problem often arises when people decide to delete routines from their models, without realising that there are dependent formulas. In this case, I always recommend that we could delete the rows containing the redundant formulas in their entirety, as dependent formulas will then return the #REF! error and can be easily located (the break-and-make technique mentioned previously). In reality, I would run a Trace Dependents check before deleting anything.

So how do we find references to blank cells?

1. Select the columns containing the calculations.
2. Press F5 and click the Special button.
3. Choose the Precedents option (note that the Ctrl+[shortcut does not work for this technique).
4. Choose OK. Excel should have selected every formula on the sheet.
5. Immediately press F5, and click the Special button again.
6. This time, choose the Blanks option.
7. Click OK.
8. Run the F5 Special command again and select Dependents to trace the formulas which refer to these blank cells.

Hopefully Excel will tell you that no cells were found. If it does not, apply a fill colour and search for the selected cells. When you find them, it may be apparent as to which formula is reading that cell, if it is not, select the blank cell and press Ctrl+] (Select Dependents). This should then reveal the formula with the reference to the blank cell. You should decide what to do about the problem, such as substituting in zero or unit values, or rewriting the formula. Put a line on the audit sheet to record your findings.

You can also do this test in reverse:

1. Select the whole sheet.
2. Use F5 Special and choose Blanks. This selects all blank cells in the worksheet.
3. Press Ctrl+] (Trace Dependents).
4. Apply a background colour.
5. Any selected or coloured cells will refer to a blank cell.

Left-to-Right Consistency

An important modelling rule relating to our calculations is that there should only be one formula on each row; that is, the formula in the first cell of the row must be the same as that in the last cell in the row. There are instances where it might be considered appropriate to have two or more formulas, for example, in some projects we might have a development or construction phase, followed by an operational phase. There are differences in the accounting treatments used in each phase, in that, for example, assets are not depreciated until they are put into use, or that interest is capitalised during development and expensed during operations. It is not appropriate to have different calculations on the same row, because the transition from one phase to the next is indicated by input information such as the start of production or the generation of revenues. If the project slips or is brought forward, the user simply changes the inputs sheet. If the left-to-right consistency rule has not been followed, any such alteration to inputs will require the user to then locate and change the dependent formulas on the workings, and this should be avoided at all costs. If the formula is not updated, the model is wrong. The technicalities of this important issue are considered in more detail in Chapters 5 and 6, but for the moment we are considering audit checks, and so we need to be able to confirm that the left-to-right consistency rule has been followed. This uses another of the Edit, Go To, Special commands.

1. Select the columns containing the calculations. Make sure that the active cell is in the left-hand column.
2. Press F5 and click the Special button.
3. Choose the Row differences option.
4. Choose OK.

Excel now compares every cell on every row with its neighbours, and highlights any that differs from the first cell in the row. Again, I would normally recommend using a fill colour at this stage, so that you can browse through the worksheet at leisure. There are two common sources of error which we can trap at this stage: first, a formula has been corrected or updated, but has not then been copied across the row; and second, where a formula has not been copied to the end of the row, but not copied the row – this typically happens with mouse users who use the AutoFill click-and-drag technique to copy formulas across the row. These can be easily corrected. The shortcut for Row differences is Ctrl+\ (with the range selected first).

If we locate a genuine difference in formulas in one row which is based on an assumption about the timing of an event, we need then to consider what steps we then need to take – are we able to correct the formula or write a revised routine ourselves, or does the problem need referring back to the model's author or owner for clarification? Make sure the audit sheet is updated accordingly, and the model documentation is updated to reflect your findings and actions, if any.

3-D or Cross-Sheet Calculations

3-D calculations are calculations which refer to cells on different sheets, for example,

```
='Balance Sheet'!F27-'Balance Sheet'!E27-'Income Statement'!E24
```

I would suggest that this is not the best way to write formulas, not least because even this little formula looks rather more complex than it actually is, simply because each of the references is prefixed with a sheet name. The difficulties of auditing such formulas are notorious – even with F5 Go To/Go Back techniques, it can be time-consuming to locate each reference. We also remember that the operational researchers point out that the use of multiple sheets increases the risk of error in itself; as we check each reference on each sheet, we need to verify that the reference itself is correct in the context of that sheet. It induces a certain amount of gloom when reviewing an apparently straightforward model, in which virtually every formula takes up two or more lines on the formula bar (my colleagues refer to this as 'spaghetti modelling'). I would suggest that we work with two-dimensional formulas – calculations that are based on references on the same sheet (this is a key part of the inputs–workings–outputs methodology). And I know that you are going to point out that you know where everything is in your model, and that you don't have a problem with 3-D calculations, but I would suggest that your colleagues are not so familiar with your work, so the less clutter the better.

We can easily locate 3-D calculations because they all have a unique feature – the exclamation mark. All we need to do is Ctrl+F (Find) using ! as the search string. Unlike the Go To, Special commands, we need to repeat the Find command after locating each 3-D calculation. Having confirmed the absence of 3-D calculations, put a line on the audit sheet to record the result.

In Chapter 3, I will recommend that input values are linked through to the workings sheet, for example,

```
=Inputs!E5
```

I would suggest, pedantically, that this is an example of a 3-D *formula*, in contrast to

```
='Balance Sheet'!F27-'Balance Sheet'!E27-'Profit and Loss'!E24,
```

which is a 3-D *calculation*. The rule is that we avoid the latter, but 3-D links are perfectly acceptable.

Errors

In any model, there is a possibility that some cells contain error values, and that these messages are not causing any output problems, perhaps because they occur in some calculations used for a particular scenario. On first inspection, all seems to be well, but following further work the errors suddenly manifest themselves. We can use another Go To, Special command:

1. Select the columns containing the calculations.
2. Press F5 (Go To), and click the Special button.
3. Choose the Formulas option, and uncheck the Numbers, Text and Logicals boxes.
4. Choose OK.

Apply fill colour to the selection, and browse through the model. Locate and repair formulas, as required. Record your results on the audit sheet.

The Name Manager (Formulas, Name Manager or Ctrl+F3) has the ability to filter range names to show those containing error values (Names with Errors) and the formulas are shown in the Name Manager dialog box. If a name does contain error values, the reference can be double clicked to view the Edit Names dialog box, and clicking in the Refers To box highlights the cells in the worksheet. This feature is explored in more detail in Chapter 4.

Hidden Columns and Rows

It is quite common to use the Group and Outline techniques (Chapter 7) to make large models easier to handle. In this case, rows and columns are hidden in a structured and systematic way and can be expanded or collapsed as required. At other times, columns and rows may be hidden for aesthetic purposes or to simplify printing, and later on we will look at issues concerning quarterly and annual modelling which will require us to hide columns. But there are instances when the analyst has concealed key drivers or formulas and we should be able to locate and explain such hidden detail. The audit check is simple:

1. Press F5 (Go To), and click the Special button.
2. Choose Visible cells only.
3. Apply a fill colour to the cells selected by Excel.
4. Select the whole sheet (Ctrl+A).
5. Use the Home, Format, Hide and Unhide, Unhide Rows/Unhide Columns commands.

Any hidden rows or columns are now exposed. Inspect their contents and if appropriate, hide the rows or columns again. Record your results on the audit sheet.

Hidden Sheets

Sheets are often hidden to prevent users from accessing calculations or key inputs (Figure 2.14).

Use Home, Format, Hide & Unhide, Unhide Sheet to see the list of hidden sheets. Identify why they have been hidden, and hide again if necessary.

If the Visual Basic property of xlSheetVeryHidden has been used, it will not be possible to unhide the sheet without the appropriate access to the macro or VB code.

Merged Cells

When centring a heading over a range of cells, Excel now creates merged cells. These are a little dangerous in that the grid or matrix structure of the

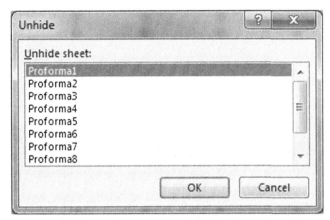

FIGURE 2.14   Hidden sheets.

spreadsheet is now compromised. The merged cell is referenced by the cell at the top left of the range, and the contents of the cell can be referred to in formulas. On setting up a merged cell, any existing data in the source cells is lost other than that in the top-left cell. Formulas which refer to other cells included in the merge will return zero values regardless of the content of the merged cell and the audit techniques of F2 and Ctrl+[point to the original locations of the cells even though they no longer exist. There is no simple audit check for merged cells; the only method of which I am aware is to start in column A and press Ctrl+Spacebar to select the column. I then move the active cell and repeat this action in column B, and so on. The presence of merged cells is revealed if Excel highlights two or more columns when you attempt to select one. They are not easy to spot, and it may be helpful to apply a fill colour and then to move down through the column pressing Shift+Spacebar to select the row. Once you have found the merged cell, decide whether it is worth unmerging – if it is a title or heading you may be able to accept it. Unmerge using Home, Merge & Center, Unmerge Cells command. Always press Ctrl+] (Trace Dependents) to make sure that there are no formulas linking to the cell. Record your findings on the audit sheet.

Array Formulas

Array formulas are discussed in Chapter 5. They are a particular type of calculation which because of their advanced nature tend to be written only by competent analysts and as such tend not to be a major source of error. Most of the examples I have found have been set up for security purposes, as they are difficult to edit and so are reasonably tamper-proof. They come in two flavours: single cell array calculations and multiple cell array calculations. They can be difficult to understand and as such their presence in a model should be recorded on the audit sheet. Having looked at how we can find 3-D (cross sheet) formulas

FIGURE 2.15   Excel doesn't like changes to arrays or data tables.

and file link formulas, it is tempting to assume that we could simply run Ctrl+F (Find), using the unique feature of the array formula which is the curly bracket { or } as the search string. Unfortunately, Excel cannot identify that these brackets exist in the formula, so we have to resort to a cumbersome method similar to that used for locating merged cells. If we select a column in the sheet and press Ctrl+Plus to insert a column, Excel will complain that we are attempting to change part of an array. This technique will locate data tables, which are of course one of the commonest forms of the array calculation. Once an array has been located, press Ctrl+/ to select all the cells in the array (Figure 2.15).

If this action is repeated over the width of the workings area and no such error messages are seen, then there are no multiple cell array formulas.

The curly brackets also disappear if we use Ctrl+' (Formulas, Show Formulas), or if we attempt to use techniques such as replacing the = with ^, or prefixing the = with an apostrophe. This means that it is not possible to easily locate single cell array formulas without using a macro.

Remember to record your findings on the audit sheet.

ARITHMETICAL CHECKS

Up to this point the environmental and structural checks have been manual: some form of inspection has been required. The next set of checks are calculations based on the model's content and include the financial checks.

Some auditors use the expression WYSIWYT or 'what you see is what you test'. The Operis approach generally results in one check for every four lines of code in the model under test, and this includes our own internal tests of the direct audit checks. The accountants teach us that if we can calculate the same thing using different methods and get the same result, then we can be confident about our work. As the model is being developed, the values generated by our calculations will change, and so these audit checks must be dynamic. The arithmetical checks are designed to check that things add up. Even a simple model can merit a quick crosscheck. Assuming a reasonably mature modelling methodology, such as Operis or FAST, it is unlikely that results have been calculated directly on the output sheets themselves. If the inputs–workings–outputs structure has been used, with or without variations

11	Arithmetical checks				
12					
13	Project cash flow				
14	on workings		-21400000	-18930000	-17930000
15	on cash flow		-21400000	-18930000	-17930000
16	check		0	0	0
17					

FIGURE 2.16   The project cash flow check.

as described in the next chapter, it is likely that the reports contain totals and subtotals which duplicate calculations in the workings. We can turn this to our advantage by comparing the results. If a discrepancy is found, it will usually be due to one of four common errors:

1. a calculation has been updated to reflect a new element on the workings sheet, but the relevant output sheet has not been updated to show this new element;
2. a calculation has been updated to reflect a new element on the workings sheet *but not then copied across the row*, and the output has been updated;
3. the output has been updated but with no changes made to the workings sheet;
4. there has been a mix-up with signing.

For example, the project cash flow on the workings sheet should have the same values as the project cash flow summary formula on the Cash Flow report. On the audit sheet, we link the two lines and subtract one from the other. The result should be zero (Figure 2.16).

This example is a little unsatisfactory – the numbers look OK in the screen shot, but what about in future periods? We will now develop a further audit routine used on calculated checks.

The Audit Check Formula

We could begin with a simple SUM in the audit column; if it reads 0 then the check is satisfied, and if it returns a value then there is a problem. However, this is a little simplistic. Rather than show zero it would be better if we returned TRUE, consistent with the other audit checks. We could write this as:

```
=SUM(E18:CJ18)=0
```

But the accountants teach us about a type of error called the 'compensating error'; simply put, if we have an imbalance of −10 in one period and +10 in another, the result is zero and would not be detected arithmetically. To avoid this, we can nest each of the project cash flow check formulas in the ABS function:

```
=ABS(E16-E17)
```

The ABS function returns the absolute value, that is, without the sign. This should allow the SUM function to flag up any errors.

But we might also have very minor rounding errors floating around. If the check row reads 2.32831E-10 (this is Excel's exponential number format, used for very large or, in this case, very small numbers) in a particular period the logical SUM check returns FALSE. On inspection, however, it might be difficult to locate the rounding error, particularly if the audit sheet has been formatted. We could agree a particular level of tolerance or rounding, say, 0.0001, and enter this into a cell at the top of the audit sheet (and perhaps give it a range name such as Tolerance). We then return to the SUM function and update it:

```
=SUM(E18:CJ18)<Tolerance
```

This is still not completely satisfactory as, over an extended period, a number of trivial rounding errors might in total exceed this threshold. Although we could use Excel's ROUND function to resolve this, a simpler alternative is to use a MAX in place of the SUM:

```
=MAX(E18:CJ18)<Tolerance
```

This will flag up if any individual imbalances exceed the threshold. However, ensure that the individual imbalance results are still covered by the ABS function – a negative number is, of course, less than the Tolerance.

Rather than having separate arithmetical and logical checks, we could combine the ABS and the MAX into one substantial audit formula. The formula might look something like this:

```
=MAX(ABS(E18:CJ18))<Tolerance
```

Unfortunately this won't work, because the ABS function won't work on ranges; the result is the #VALUE! error. But there is a trick (and in anticipation of the full explanation in Chapter 5): we write the formula as shown and press Ctrl+Shift+Enter. This creates an array formula which appears in the cell as:

```
{=MAX(ABS(E18:CJ18))<Tolerance}
```

This is the complete audit check formula (Figure 2.17).

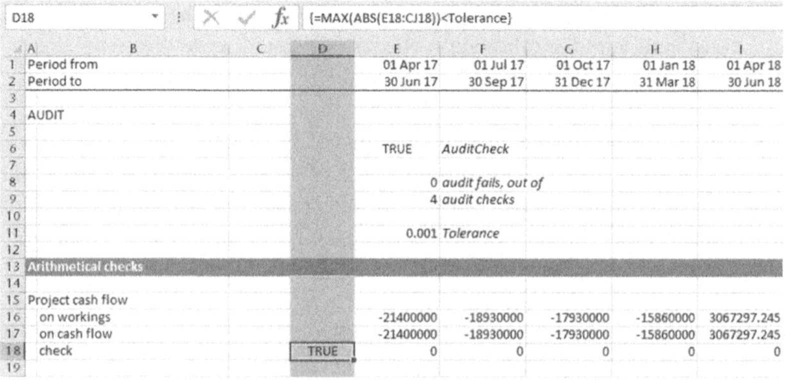

FIGURE 2.17   The audit check formula.

Other such arithmetical checks might include the financing cash flow, earnings before and after tax, increases or moves in cash balances and retained earnings.

Another form of arithmetical check is to test that the assumptions reported in the outputs match the original assumptions on the inputs sheet. This serves to ensure that the same units are used throughout. Link the input values from the inputs sheet, and the output values from the reports, and set up a logical sum as the audit check.

We will develop further ideas about arithmetical checks in the audit workbook section.

FINANCIAL CHECKS

Principle

The arithmetical checks simply prove that things add up. If they do not, the underlying problem is usually fairly easy to identify, using the navigation shortcuts. Financial checks test the underlying financial and accounting policies used in the model, and can be much more difficult to remedy if errors are found.

The researchers point out that as financial professionals, finance is described as our 'domain knowledge' and as such the evidence is that there are markedly fewer errors in this area: it is unlikely that we would use an incorrect depreciation treatment or an out-of-date tax calculation. Whether they are modelled correctly is another story, and thus the need for financial checks. These should include verification that the appropriate accounting and financial rules have been applied – the notes to a company's audited accounts provide a conceptual guide. We also need to recognise that individuals and organisations may have different definitions of the metrics being used in the model: is your understanding of 'cash flow available for debt service' the same as mine? How many different ways do you know to calculate Return on Capital Employed/Return on Investment? Whether you choose to provide definitions here in the audit section or to set them out in the reports is a decision you need to make soon.

Balance Sheet

The first, classic, financial check is that of the balance sheet. A lot of modelling is based on cash flow analysis and balance sheets are not created routinely; some analysts never use them. However, it is worth noting that a lot of people involved in financial modelling hold financial rather than accounting qualifications, and so are not too familiar with the concept of double entry accounting and the basic accounting equation that:

```
ASSETS = LIABILITIES + EQUITY
```

22						
23	**Financial checks**					
24						
25	Financial position statement					
26	total assets		21400000	40330000	60663000	78905324.03
27	total liabilities + equity		21400000	40330000	60663000	78905324.03
28	check	TRUE	0	0	0	0
29						
30	Income statement					
31	earnings		-339500	-676716.25	-1044386.284	-1179300.635
32	partners equity		1660500	983783.75	-60602.53438	-1239903.17
33	partners cash flow		2000000	0	0	0
34	check	TRUE	0	0	0	0
35						
36	Cash flow					
37	cash balances		0	0	607.2864768	1046.830001
38	overdraft balances		0	0	0	0
39	net cash flow		0	0	607.2864768	439.5435242
40	check	TRUE	0	0	0	0
41						

FIGURE 2.18   Financial checks.

For example, any tax we incur is paid from our cash flow and also deducted from our profits. Interest payments reduce our cash, and (in most jurisdictions) is charged to our profits, which will reduce our tax liability. Accounting for one part of the transaction and not the other is quickly highlighted if even the simplest of balance sheets is included in the outputs, whether or not it is formally required. Alternatively, set up an abbreviated balance sheet on the audit sheet. We can then test that movements in the cash flow report are reflected in the cash balances, and that movements in the profit and loss or income statement are mirrored in the retained earnings on the balance sheet (Figure 2.18).

Cash Flow

The second of the classic financial checks is the reconciliation of cash flow movements with the cash balance on the balance sheet. My own preference is that the net cash increase and the cash carried forward (closing or ending balance) are linked through to the audit sheet as two identifiable lines, rather than running the test as a single, 3-D calculation. The test is that this period's cash carried forward balance less the last period's cash carried forward balance is the same as the net cash increase (decrease) from the cash flow statement. Put in an appropriate logical sum in the audit column.

Income Statement

The third classic financial check is the reconciliation of movements on the income statement with changes in the retained earnings on the balance sheet. This should prove that the retained earnings carried forward balance for this period, less the retained earnings balance for the last period, should be the same as the increase (decrease) in retained earnings from the profit and loss/income statement.

Other Financial Checks

It should be borne in mind that the majority of calculations seen in the model are derived from the project documentation. This particularly applies to the financial instruments such as the loans and their fees, interest and repayment calculations, and even to items such as revenues which may have a timing component. The reviewer must have access to the various contracts, agreements and convenants that specify the methods to be used; the model must conform to the documentation and exceptions must be recorded as issues in the audit sheet or workbook. Each financial instrument in the model should have its own audit check or checks. For example, a bank loan should be repaid, so at some stage the balance reaches zero. The repayments (excluding interest and fees) should equal the original amount borrowed. Reserve accounts, such as Major Maintenance and Debt Service, will usually have specific target amounts, and the model should show that these are achieved.

If we have balances for any items, such as debt or fixed assets or tax, generally speaking they should never go negative, so this can be tested for (using =MIN(balance)>=0). In project finance, we often see that the project company, or special purpose vehicle, is wound up at the end of operations, so we should see that there are zero balances in the final period.

Ratios

One of the common reasons we build models is to carry out ratio analysis on cash flows for a variety of purposes. I would suggest that such analysis can be used during model development as what I would describe as a rationality check. If you have some experience of working with ratios, and you have an understanding of the entity you are modelling, you may have a gut feeling for what sort of values you might expect to see. If these expectations are set out formally, you and your colleagues are able to monitor them as the model is developed. The liquidity ratios (current assets, acid test), efficiency ratios (stock turnover, debtors and creditors, etc.) and profitability ratios (return on capital employed, gross profit, net profit, etc.) are very helpful. As this list is fairly extensive, I will defer to your own professional knowledge and experience to select the ratios of most relevance to your own requirements. On the audit sheet, list the ratios to be tested, along with your expected threshold values. As with the profit and loss and cash flow checks, link through the source information on a line by line basis, and write the appropriate calculations. These could either be as one-offs, for example, an overall return on capital employed, or on a periodic basis copied across the row. In either case we are concerned that the ratio passes or fails the test, rather than its numerical outcome, so the formula should be a logical test. The audit column cell should then return TRUE if the ratio test is satisfied in all periods, and FALSE if any one (or more) fails. This is a simple AND function, as above.

It is important to document the method for calculating the ratio, as for example, return on capital employed has many flavours. We should also document our assumptions about the threshold values, remembering that they will depend on the circumstances of the model and the company, industry or country. From your experience you will know that not even the textbooks agree on the expected values of particular ratios, but even if you are not that familiar with using ratios I would recommend using them as an audit check, as they can rapidly point out flaws in assumptions or calculations that might be otherwise difficult to spot. Just to give one example, in setting up the receivables (debtors) and payables (creditors) inputs in a model, the values for the debtor days and creditor days were transposed – instead of expecting the company's customers to pay within 30 days, and the company to pay its bills within 90 days, the figures were reversed. The subsequent working capital results did not merit attention, nor was the effect noticed on the cash flow. However, the current assets ratio (current assets/current liabilities) was in excess of 4 to 1, where we would expect this type of company to have a ratio to the order of 2.5 to 1 or less. If this ratio had been set up as an audit check early on, this error would have been detected and resolved at the time, rather than at the late stage of development that it actually reached.

Internal Rate of Return

The internal rate of return (IRR) is directly related to the net present value (NPV) of an investment and its cash flows. Ignoring interest and inflation, if we invest 1000 today, and receive four annual payments of 250, the NPV is 0 and the IRR is 0%. We can use this as an audit check if we recognise different types of elements in the model as being cash flows. As a simple example, we could consider calculating the IRR of a debt. The debt cash flow is made up of the amount drawdown, the repayments and the interest charged by the bank. From this it may be obvious that the IRR of a debt cash flow must be equal to the interest rate, although this does depend on the interest calculation being used and that the interest rate remains constant. If, for audit purposes, we charge interest on the opening balance and calculate the debt cash flow as the debt drawdown less the repayments less the interest, the IRR equals the interest rate. We could also recognise that the NPV of the debt cash flow, discounted at the interest rate, should be 0 (Figure 2.19).

D68			f_x	=ABS(D60-D67)<Tolerance		
A	B	C	D	E	F	G
59 Senior debt						
60 interest rate			0.0175	0.0175	0.0175	0.0175
61 interest				0	339500	670775
62 bf				0	19400000	38330000
63 drawdown				19400000	18930000	20333000
64 repayment				0	0	0
65 cf			0	19400000	38330000	58663000
66						
67 Senior debt cash flow		IRR	0.0175	19400000	18590500	19662225
68 check			TRUE			
69						

FIGURE 2.19   A simple IRR check.

The Audit Chart

Although not strictly an audit check as such, in large models it can be hard to form an opinion about the performance of the project over time. A very simple procedure is to select a line of interest, for example the project cash flow, and then press F11 to draw a chart on a chart sheet. The objective here is to explain the shape of the line – can we (or the analyst) account for the various peaks and troughs? A further trick is that you can select another line in the model, copy it (Ctrl+C) and paste (Ctrl+V) directly onto the chart as a new data series; again, explain the shape. The chart is ephemeral; once the test has been carried out to your satisfaction it can be discarded (Figure 2.32).

CHANGE CHECKS

When working on a model over an extended period of time, with periods of perhaps days or even weeks between modelling activity, it can be difficult to develop a familiarity with the numbers being generated, or a sense of progress. The change check is not a proper audit check, but acts more as a continuity check. Noting the observations about the ratio and IRR tests above, we could identify a number of key results and record their values in the audit sheet – IRR, NPV, debt service cover ratio, whatever. Even though the results are not meaningful, because the model is not yet complete, they can remind us of our previous work and show the effects of recent and current work.

1. Put the appropriate headings on the audit sheet.
2. Write the appropriate key result calculations on the workings sheet, and put links to these formulas on the audit sheet.
3. At the end of the modelling session, copy these results and use Home, Paste, Paste(V) Values. Put the date above the pasted cells (use the time stamp shortcut Ctrl+; to insert the current date).
4. At the end of the next session, copy the updated results and paste values either on top of the previous or adjacent to them, and date accordingly.

The benefit of this technique is that at the end of each bout of modelling activity we can monitor the effect of the work on these key results and check that the changes tie in with our expectations or understanding of the effects we would expect to see. We will develop this idea further with the delta sheet technique in Chapter 8.

Model Comparison

Sometimes we have the situation where there are several copies of a model (e.g. it has been emailed to colleagues). With the tinkering that can then take place, it can be difficult to determine if each model is exactly the same. Why not add up the workings or an output sheet? A simple SUM can be tucked away tidily at the bottom of a sheet or on the audit sheet. The idea can be extended by putting in a

SUM at the bottom of each column, which might help identify where the discrepancies are creeping in. This technique is not completely reliable, for example, a balance has moved from one time period to another or from one account to another, but it is so simple and can be helpful.

MODEL MAP

It can be quite helpful to form an overall picture of the model and we can use a basic model mapping technique to create a graphical view of the model and its components.

1. Make a copy of the worksheet to be mapped – Ctrl+click and drag the sheet tab.
2. Select the entire sheet – Ctrl+A.
3. Adjust the standard column width to 2 units (Alt+H, O, W, 2). If the worksheet is particularly long or wide, try changing the Zoom to 50% or less.
4. Still with the whole worksheet selected, press F5 (Go To) and click the Special button.
5. Choose Constants, and clear the Text, Logicals and Errors check boxes. Choose OK. Excel has now selected all cells which contain numbers. Apply a fill colour. If Excel is not able to find any cells, make a note of this result.
6. Repeat Step 4, and then choose Constants, this time clearing the Numbers, Logicals and Errors check boxes. Choose OK. Apply a fill colour to all selected cells, which in this case contain text.
7. Repeat Step 4 for Constants, Logicals and Constants, Errors, using a different colour each time.
8. Then repeat Step 4 for Formulas, and each of Numbers, Text, Logicals and Errors.
9. Now select just the columns in the forecast period (if the model has one). Use F5 (Go To) Special and Row differences. Apply a fill colour to any cells found.
10. Finally, select the columns of the forecast period and run F5 (Go To) Special and select Precedents. Directly on completion of this command, use F5 (Go To) Special and choose Blanks. Apply a fill colour.

In the few moments it has taken to carry out these steps, we now have a full map of the worksheet, in which we can visually identify key exceptions to the modelling rules set out in this chapter and elsewhere, in particular the location of inputs and hard-coded values in formulas; breaches of the left-to-right consistency rule and references to empty cells. By clicking on any of the coloured cells, regardless of its size, we can still read its contents on the formula bar (Figure 2.20).

An alternative approach is to use conditional formatting, using the Excel ISERROR, ISLOGICAL, ISFORMULA, ISTEXT and ISNUMBER functions (see Chapter 6) (Figure 2.21).

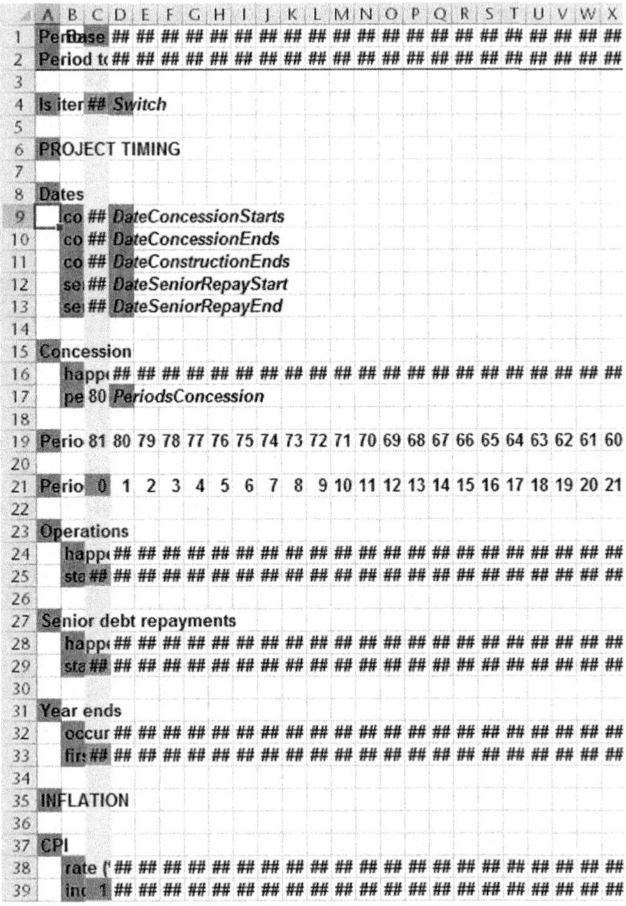

	A	B	C	D	E	F	G	H	I	J	K	L	M	N	O	P	Q	R	S	T	U	V	W	X
1	Per	Base	##	##	##	##	##	##	##	##	##	##	##	##	##	##	##	##	##	##	##	##	##	##
2	Period t		##	##	##	##	##	##	##	##	##	##	##	##	##	##	##	##	##	##	##	##	##	##
3																								
4	Is iter	##	*Switch*																					
5																								
6	PROJECT TIMING																							
7																								
8	Dates																							
9		co	##	*DateConcessionStarts*																				
10		co	##	*DateConcessionEnds*																				
11		co	##	*DateConstructionEnds*																				
12		se	##	*DateSeniorRepayStart*																				
13		se	##	*DateSeniorRepayEnd*																				
14																								
15	Concession																							
16		happ	##	##	##	##	##	##	##	##	##	##	##	##	##	##	##	##	##	##	##	##	##	##
17		pe	80	*PeriodsConcession*																				
18																								
19	Perio	81	80	79	78	77	76	75	74	73	72	71	70	69	68	67	66	65	64	63	62	61	60	
20																								
21	Perio	0	1	2	3	4	5	6	7	8	9	10	11	12	13	14	15	16	17	18	19	20	21	
22																								
23	Operations																							
24		happ	##	##	##	##	##	##	##	##	##	##	##	##	##	##	##	##	##	##	##	##	##	##
25		sta	##	##	##	##	##	##	##	##	##	##	##	##	##	##	##	##	##	##	##	##	##	##
26																								
27	Senior debt repayments																							
28		happ	##	##	##	##	##	##	##	##	##	##	##	##	##	##	##	##	##	##	##	##	##	##
29		sta	##	##	##	##	##	##	##	##	##	##	##	##	##	##	##	##	##	##	##	##	##	##
30																								
31	Year ends																							
32		occur	##	##	##	##	##	##	##	##	##	##	##	##	##	##	##	##	##	##	##	##	##	##
33		firs	##	##	##	##	##	##	##	##	##	##	##	##	##	##	##	##	##	##	##	##	##	##
34																								
35	INFLATION																							
36																								
37	CPI																							
38		rate (	##	##	##	##	##	##	##	##	##	##	##	##	##	##	##	##	##	##	##	##	##	##
39		in	1	##	##	##	##	##	##	##	##	##	##	##	##	##	##	##	##	##	##	##	##	##

FIGURE 2.20   The model map – blue (dark grey in print versions) for text, green (light grey in print versions) for hard-coded values, purple (very light grey in print versions) for logic values.

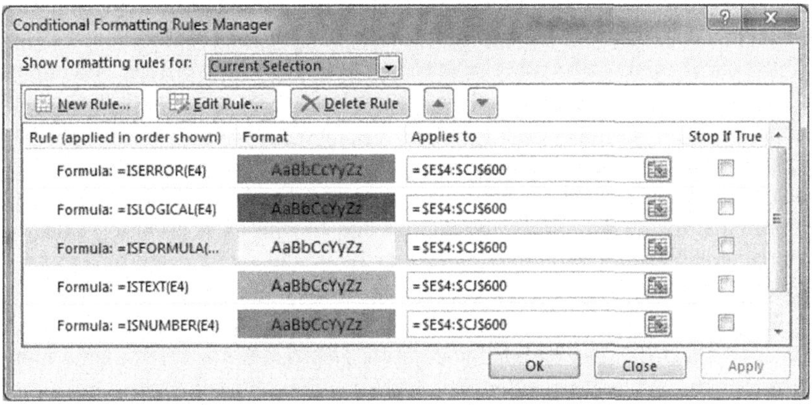

FIGURE 2.21   Model mapping with conditional formatting.

If you have reduced the zoom level to below 40%, you will notice an interesting feature in that Excel will display range names in the worksheet area itself. With our practice of naming single rows (see Chapter 4), this is not that useful because the display is so small, but if names have been used to describe blocks of cells then it can be quite helpful.

USING THE AUDIT SHEET

The audit sheet is a good introduction into the aims and objectives of model review and is particularly suited to the lower end of the audit spectrum, at the level of peer review, whether formal or informal. It can be developed within the organisation and reflect the risk controls that the management feels appropriate to the models in day-to-day use, or for special projects. As previously mentioned, the audit sheet can be introduced at the very outset of model development, so that the modeller can work on the audit checks as they write the code – the balance sheet tests being particularly relevant. Alternatively the introduction of the audit sheet can mark the formal shift from development to review, prior to implementation. A standardised, in-house, audit sheet can be used to set modelling standards – the modelling team will be aware that their models will be inspected and use the audit sheet as part of the error reduction and feedback mechanisms, and likewise management will have a defined set of controls to apply to the model.

Although we have used the expression 'financial model' throughout, there is no reason why the audit sheet, or audit workbook, methodology cannot be applied to nonfinancial models. For example, the public sector is often interested in concepts such as value for money, and affordability, or may be forecasting traffic volumes or local demographics; no financial statements but lots of calculations to control.

THE AUDIT WORKBOOK

The audit workbook extends the audit sheet idea and is a much more formal concept. It is used by model audit firms and forms part of the audit working papers which form the basis of the audit opinion letter. In addition to the routine audit checks, we have already considered that there are a number of more intensive checks to run. Using the language of the accounting auditor we differentiate substantive checks and controls checks, introduced in the previous chapter. It is important to understand that at this level we are not merely concerned with the content and structure of the model but also with the model's environment, which will include project or other documentation, legal agreements, banking agreements, contracts and subcontracts, bid documentation and the objective of the audit is to confirm that the model reflects these terms and conditions. A point in passing is that the model auditor will not comment on the business case itself, only that the model is an accurate representation of the cash flows for that business case.

The starting point will be the controls checks, which will include the model's audit sheet if it has one. If the controls give rise to concerns then a more rigorous approach will be called for, which may involve substantive checks of line items. Some audit firms will undertake a model reconstruction in which the financial statements are reorganised to a standard layout. For example, at Operis we follow the project finance approach of using the direct cash flow (revenue, operating costs, working capital, tax, capex); whereas many models follow the accounting convention of the indirect cash flow (net income, add back depreciation, etc.). This is a useful exercise when dealing with financial models from a variety of sources, but within an organisation, where there are set ways of layout out financial statements, this is of less value (Figure 2.22).

In the example above, the client model is using the direct cash flow approach but in a rather untidy way. The reconstruction sets it out more clearly and in a standard way which is used for *all* reconstructions.

Note that much of what follows can be applied to any spreadsheet model, not just financial models.

Layout

The audit workbook is of course a separate workbook to the MUT and therefore conforms to our rule about never changing the MUT. A sample audit workbook is shown in Appendix X, but as a minimum it should include:

1. Model summary: model title, description, version and location; contact details for the developer, auditor/reviewer, compliance officer and senior responsible officer/owner.
2. Issues reports: a log of matters found, an explanation of the issue and its consequences; links to the issue in the model and to documentation; the modeller's response and the resolution agreed.
3. Audit sheet: a standard audit sheet as described in the previous section, with environmental, structural, arithmetical, financial and change checks.
4. Documentation sheet: the locations or links to the model data book, accounting regulations, agreements and contracts and ancillary documents.
5. Specialist topics: descriptions of any specialist input or advice used by the reviewer, including tax and accounting, legal, operational and technical.
6. Key results: a worksheet containing links to the key results identified in the MUT (see below).
7. Reconstruction sheets: links to the MUT showing the precedents for the calculations of the key results (see below).
8. Sensitivity and delta sheets: sheets recording the effects of changes to the inputs and demonstrating the variance to the base case (see below).

The use of a standard audit workbook template ensures a consistency in the approach to model audit and can – and should – be developed to reflect organisation modelling risk controls.

Alignment of Timelines

Following the principle that we never change the MUT, we instead amend the audit workbook to the MUT and follow the primary timeline as it has been set

(a)

	A	B	C	D	E	F	G	H	I
1	Original			Total		01-Apr-16	01-Oct-16	01-Apr-17	01-Oct-17
2				£'000		30-Sep-16	31-Mar-17	30-Sep-17	31-Mar-18
3									
4	CASHFLOW								
5									
6	Unitary Charge			55,234		841	841	855	855
7	Service Payment			-		-	-	-	-
8	Third Party Revenue			420		-	-	6	6
9									
10									
11	Total Revenues			55,654		841	841	862	862
12									
13	Operating costs:								
14	RPI Related Operating Costs			(19,410)		-	(30)	(308)	(284)
15	Labour Related Operating Costs			-		-	-	-	-
16	Payments to RPI Swap Provider			-		-	-	-	-
17	Maintenance Costs			(2,622)		-	-	-	-
18	Technical Services Fee			-		-	-	-	-
19									
20	Net Operating Cashflow			33,622		841	811	554	577
21									
22	Construction costs			(12,893)		(7,048)	(4,995)	(850)	-
23	Development costs			(2,208)		(1,233)	(975)	-	-
24	Working capital costs			-		-	-	-	-
25	Capital receipt during construction (i.e grant)			3,091		-	535	2,556	-
26									
27	Pre-finance pre-tax cashflow			21,612		(7,440)	(4,624)	2,259	577
28									
29	Corporate Tax			(2,140)		-	(185)	(185)	-
30									
31	Pre-finance post-tax cashflow			19,472		(7,440)	(4,809)	2,075	577
32									

(b)

	A	B	C	D	E	F	G	H	I
1	Period from					1-Apr-16	1-Oct-16	1-Apr-17	1-Oct-17
2	Period to					30-Sep-16	31-Mar-17	30-Sep-17	31-Mar-18
3									
4	Revenue								
5	Unitary Charge					841	841	855	855
6	Service Payment					-	-	-	-
7	Third Party Revenue					-	-	6	6
8									
9	Costs								
10	RPI Related Operating Costs					-	(30)	(308)	(284)
11	Labour Related Operating Costs					-	-	-	-
12	Payments to RPI Swap Provider					-	-	-	-
13	Technical Services Fee					-	-	-	-
14									
15	Maintenance Costs					-	-	-	-
16									
17	Capex								
18	Construction costs					(7,048)	(4,995)	(850)	-
19	Development costs					(1,233)	(975)	-	-
20	Capital receipt during construction (i.e. grant + land sale etc)					-	535	2,556	-
21									
22	Working capital costs					-	-	-	-
23									
24	Corporate Tax					-	(185)	(185)	-
25									
26	PROJECT CASH FLOW					(7,440)	(4,809)	2,075	577

FIGURE 2.22   (a) The client's original cash flow and (b) the Operis reconstruction.

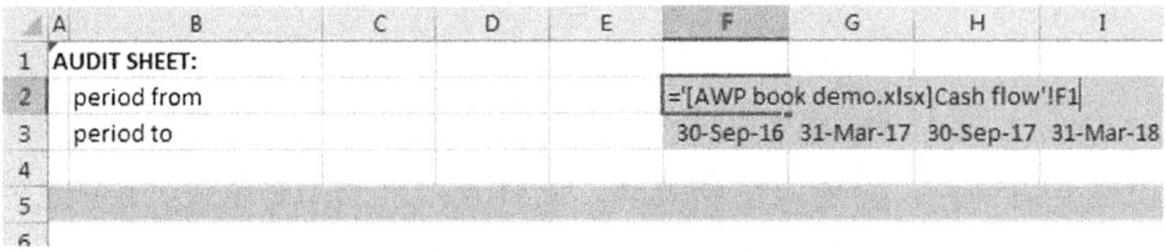

FIGURE 2.23   Linking to the timeline of the MUT.

up. If the forecast period starts in column F and ends in BY, then we amend the audit workbook to match, using Group mode to change all relevant sheets; and finally we link through the model dates. Note that when writing a file link formula by typing the = followed by clicking on the target cell in the MUT, Excel will automatically make the reference absolute, so press F4 three times to make it relative, and copy across the row. If using Copy and Paste Links the reference is relative anyway (Figure 2.23).

Key Results

The purpose of the key results sheet is to demonstrate the understanding and agreement of the overarching purpose of the model, following the top-down approach. Remember that we are not necessarily dealing with a model that has been developed in accordance with the principles set out in this book, and so the key results might be beautifully tabulated or, more commonly, scattered across several sheets. Our first step is to collate these results into the audit workbook. This can be done by writing the narrative description into the key results sheet and then linking to the MUT. We can use the Ctrl+[(open square bracket) and F5 Enter shortcuts to navigate to from the MUT to the audit workbook (Figure 2.24).

Reconstruction

Now that we have identified the key results we can attempt to check how they were derived. In the example here, we will examine the Internal Rate of Return calculation. From first principles this would use the Excel IRR function on a cash flow. The model results also mention real and nominal, suggesting that the cash flow is being discounted.

On the reconstruction sheet we link to the specific result we are testing. Using Ctrl+[we can locate the immediate precedents of this IRR to see that it uses the adjacent figures in the row. We now link these to the audit workbook. Now we write the IRR to prove that the model IRR is based on the same information. In this case we find a discrepancy because the IRR function does not take model periodicity into account; this particular model has a semiannual timeline. Rewriting the formula as =(1+IRR(F7:BY7))^2-1 gives us the same result as the model (Figure 2.25).

We now go back a further step. The cash flow used for the IRR should be the project cash flow, so we now locate it on the original MUT cash flow report and

	A	B	C	D	E	F	G	H	I
1	KEY RESULTS:		FALSE			30-Sep-16	31-Mar-17	30-Sep-17	31-Mar-18
2									
3									
4									
5	Project IRR, real			6.41%		-8,281	-5,360	2,205	581
6									
7	Project IRR, nominal			9.06%		-8,281	-5,360	2,260	595
8									
9	Blended IRR, real			11.03%		-10	-221	-1,057	83
10									
11	Blended IRR, nominal			13.75%		-10	-221	-1,083	86
12									
13	Loan life cover ratio (minimum)			1.15		n/a	n/a	1.15	1.15
14									
15	Loan life cover ratio (average)			1.15					
16									
17	Result 7			link to model					
18									
19	Result 8			link to model					
20									
21									
22									

FIGURE 2.24 The key results sheet.

D9			▼	:	✕	✓	*fx*	=(1+IRR(F7:BY7))^2-1	

	A	B	C	D	E	F	G
1	Reconstruction 1		FALSE			30-Sep-16	31-Mar-17
2							
3							
4							
5	IRR, nominal, from MUT			9.06%			
6							
7	Project cash flow, nominal					-8,281	-5,360
8							
9	Reconstruction IRR nominal			9.06%			
10							

FIGURE 2.25 The IRR formula.

link it through. This time there is a further discrepancy: although we are now using the correct formulation of the IRR, the result is significantly lower (Figure 2.26).

If we use the trace dependents tools (Ctrl+[) to track back through the formulas in the MUT, we discover that it includes the interest on cash balances for the IRR calculation. Again, we link this line to the audit workbook and repeat the calculation. This time we find agreement with the original. From this simple piece of analysis we have discovered a slightly different method of calculating the IRR and we should raise this in the issues report. We can now repeat the exercise for the real terms project IRR, and so on (Figure 2.27).

	A	B	C	D	E	F	G
1	Reconstruction 1		FALSE			30-Sep-16	31-Mar-17
2							
3							
4							
5	IRR, nominal, from MUT			9.06%			
6							
7	Project cash flow, nominal					-8,281	-5,360
8							
9	Reconstruction IRR nominal			9.06%			
10							
11	Prefinance, pretax cash flow			8.74%		-8,281	-5,360
12							

FIGURE 2.26 The IRR discrepancy.

	A	B	C	D	E	F	G	H
1	Reconstruction 1		FALSE			30-Sep-16	31-Mar-17	30-Sep-17
2								
3								
4								
5	IRR, nominal, from MUT			9.06%				
6								
7	Project cash flow, nominal					-8,281	-5,360	2,260
8								
9	Reconstruction IRR nominal			9.06%				
10								
11	Prefinance, pretax cash flow			8.74%		-8,281	-5,360	2,259
12								
13	Interest received on cash balances			9.06%		0	0	1
14								
15	Precedent 4			*link to model*				
16								
17	Precedent 5			*link to model*				
18								
19	Precedent 6			*link to model*				
20								
21	Precedent 7			*link to model*				
22								
23	Precedent 8			*link to model*				
24								
25	check		TRUE	*result 1 - reconstruction 1*				
26								
27								

FIGURE 2.27 The complete IRR reconstruction, with audit test at the bottom.

The benefit of the reconstruction technique is that it allows us to examine model components that could be scattered across several sheets, such that a manual inspection of formulas could prove difficult and time-consuming. For this example, we have looked at a key result, but the same methodology can be used for more basic elements, such as revenues or operating costs. By extracting the information we can see what has been included and potentially what has been excluded from any calculation.

Sensitivities and Deltas

The usual objective of any modelling activity is to carry out some form of 'what-if' analysis, by changing model inputs to test the impact on the outputs. We can use sensitivity testing as part of the model review process, as it will provide insight into the behaviour of the model, not just the formulas. There are two levels of this form of analysis: simple testing, in which we can vary the inputs by x amount and note the results; and stress testing, where we vary the inputs in such a way as to introduce serious problems, to see how they are managed – for example, a 50% fall in revenues to see if the reserve accounts react correctly, or that the cash shortfall is correctly recognised.

The delta sheet concept allows us to capture the before/after results so that we can clearly identify changes. Although we will look at deltas again in Chapter 8, we will set out the methodology here for its implementation in the audit workbook.

The first step is to make a copy of the key results sheet in the audit workbook.

1. Ctrl+click and drag the sheet tab. This will have the link formulas to the MUT. Double-click the sheet tab to rename it as 'Sensitivities - Links'.
2. Now copy the sheet twice more, naming them 'Sensitivities - Values', and 'Sensitivities - Deltas'.
3. On the 'Sensitivities - Values' sheet go to cell A1 and press Ctrl+A to select everything.
4. Now copy (Ctrl+C) and Paste Special, Values (Alt+H, V, V). This sheet is now a snapshot of the base case.
5. On the 'Sensitivities - Deltas' sheet, select the rows containing the formulas. Press F5 (Go To) and choose Special, and then select Formulas, and OK. This will select only those cells on the Deltas sheet which contain formulas (Figure 2.28).
6. Making sure that the cells are still highlighted, type an = (equals sign) into the active cell, and then click on the corresponding cell on the Links sheet.
7. Then type a – (minus sign) and then click on the corresponding cell on the Values sheet.
8. Finally press Ctrl+Enter to fill the Delta sheet with the new formula. While the cells are still selected, check the AutoSum on the status bar to confirm that the total is 0; if it isn't, undo (Ctrl+Z) and repeat from Step 6 (Figure 2.29).

The formula should be =Links! cell ref - Values! cell ref.

FIGURE 2.28 F5 Go To, Special.

▲	A	B	C	D	E	F	G	H
1	KEY RESULTS:		FALSE			30-Sep-16	31-Mar-17	30-Sep-17
2								
3								
4								
5	Project IRR, real			='Sensitivities - Links'!D5-'Sensitivities -Values'!D5				
6								
7	Project IRR, nominal			0.00%		0	0	0
8								
9	Blended IRR, real			0.00%		0	0	0
10								
11	Blended IRR, nominal			0.00%		0	0	0
12								
13	Loan life cover ratio (minimum)			0.00				0.00
14								
15	Loan life cover ratio (average)			0.00				
16								
17	Result 7			link to model				
18								
19	Result 8			link to model				
20								
21								

FIGURE 2.29 The Delta sheet.

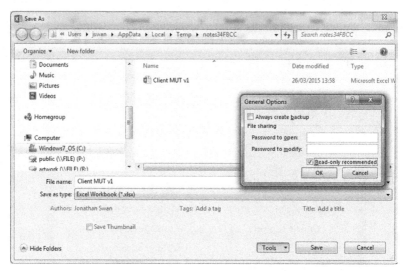

FIGURE 2.30 Setting the read-only attribute to the model under test (MUT).

	A	B	C	D	E	F	G	H	I	J
1	KEY RESULTS:		FALSE			30-Sep-16	31-Mar-17	30-Sep-17	31-Mar-18	30-Sep-18
2										
3										
4										
5	Project IRR, real			-0.05%		0	0	-1	-3	-3
6										
7	Project IRR, nominal			-0.05%		0	0	-1	-3	-3
8										
9	Blended IRR, real			-0.07%		0	0	0	3	-1
10										
11	Blended IRR, nominal			-0.07%		0	0	0	3	-1
12										
13	Loan life cover ratio (minimum)			-1.15				0.04	0.04	0.04
14										
15	Loan life cover ratio (average)			0.80						
16										

FIGURE 2.31 The delta sheet showing the effect of the sensitivity analysis.

Although the rule is never to change the MUT, if we run a sensitivity we need to change the inputs. Assuming the MUT is read-only, we can safely make these changes without harming the model itself, by discarding without saving when done. If we now change the inputs of interest, we can observe the effect on the delta sheet. In this case, I have increased operations and maintenance service costs by 10%, with a consequent negative impact on the IRRs (Figure 2.31).

THIRD PARTY MODEL AUDIT TOOLS

In addition to Excel's own auditing functionality, there are a number third-party add-in tools with extensive auditing features. Amongst the most well known are

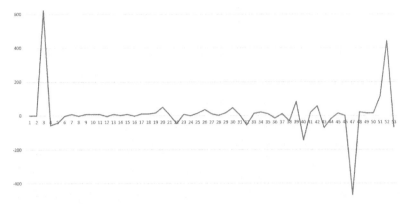

FIGURE 2.32   'Post-tax post-financing cash flow'? What's going on here?

Spreadsheet Professional, Spreadsheet Detective and the Operis Analysis Kit (OAK). Free trial versions of these can be downloaded from the Internet (see below). They provide a level of automation to the process of model review and in particular can prepare standard reports, which are of great benefit if a number of models of different origin or complexity are to be analysed. They can also generate model maps, which assist in the visualisation of the model and its components.

As with any of the audit checks described in this chapter, however, the assumption must be that you understand what the audit tools are telling you, and the significance or otherwise of the findings.

Operis Analysis Kit: www.operisanalysiskit.com.
Spreadsheet Professional: www.spreadsheetinnovations.com.
Spreadsheet Detective: www.spreadsheetdetective.com.

Chapter 3

Model Structure

INTRODUCTION

A good model is easily recognisable – it has clearly identifiable results based on clearly defined inputs. The relationship between them can be tracked through a logical audit trail. There is little empirical research into the needs and expectations of model users, but our experience suggests that most users want to know the location of the key results. The ability to perform sensitivity and/or scenario analysis is also very important, so the location of the key inputs should be explicit.

In this chapter, we will consider some of the general conventions concerning model structure. It is tempting to refer to them as rules, but in almost every case the suggestion that 'we must always do this …' can be immediately countered by the observation 'except when we don't'. It is important to recognise that when setting out a rule-based methodology we should have techniques for proving conformance with such rules and for locating and identifying exceptions, many of which we considered in the previous chapter.

As already mentioned, however, model development is not an ad hoc process and there should be an overall quality assurance framework controlling the modelling process, whether or not external compliance is required. Risk controls should also apply to the environment in which the model is used, in terms of those who can access and modify the model, and the use to which the results are put.

CHOOSING THE RIGHT TOOL

In a book about financial modelling it may seem obvious that we are talking about spreadsheets, but remember that this isn't always the case. Time and again delegates on my courses have described problems they are experiencing in their work where very clearly the spreadsheet was not suited to the task. Recently I met with a client who was trying to design a model that would be manipulated in several ways to generate management information relating to the operational costs of a number of business units. The calculations were arithmetically simple, and I soon realised that the analyst wanted to perform *data* modelling rather than *financial* modelling. It would be far more efficient to use a database application than a spreadsheet. Another client had to deal with a weekly data capture exercise that dumped an enormous amount of data into the spreadsheet, from which he was obliged to extract a small subset of content; most of the 20-Mb workbook was completely redundant. I would suggest that if your model uses pivot tables you should give some serious thought to switching to a database.

The focus of this book is on spreadsheet modelling.

THE THREE PRINCIPLES

In the introduction I outlined three principles:

Error reduction: This is the overarching philosophy of spreadsheet modelling. This principle accepts that errors are inevitable. Some techniques are more prone to errors than others. We reduce the risk of error by using alternative techniques and a consistent methodology that serves to enhance the detection of errors when they occur. This is the basis for the quality assurance process (Chapter 1).

Feedback: In the absence of apparent error, how do we ensure that we are right? The feedback principle is the first element of quality control – we *actively* seek to test and validate our work continuously throughout the model development process. This is the basis for the quality control process (Chapter 2).

Top-down: This principle helps us make sense of the complexities of the modelling environment. Rather than becoming immersed in immense amounts of detail (bottom-up), we retain a view of the model's overall purpose and results (this chapter and the rest of the book).

We should keep these principles in mind as we now start considering the modelling activity in more detail.

TWO APPROACHES

Although the structure of a model will depend for a large part on its purpose, there are a number of ground rules which should be recognised. Using the top-down principle I always recommend a **top-down approach**: we identify the purpose or objective of the model first, followed by a consideration of the usage of the model. Consider the following simple examples:

1. Model A will be used to calculate the net present value and internal rate of return of a manufacturing project, to be used by the company's management.
2. Model B is a loan calculator, which will be used and reused by a number of colleagues.
3. Model C is to produce consolidated monthly accounts using information from several business units, to be reported to the management.
4. Model D is a timesheeting system.
5. Model E is a budgeting model which will be used over a period of time, and will require the actual figures to be compared with the budgeted figures as they become available.

In the first model it is likely that we will be required to carry out sensitivity and scenario analysis, possibly using risk techniques. It is likely to be a one-off development, where we would build it, use it and probably discard it once the project goes ahead. The loan calculator, however, is specifically designed for multiple use, and for multiple users of unknown modelling experience. In this case, we would need to think about providing documentation and perhaps writing macros to automate the use of the model (and restricting the ability of the users to break anything!). The third model will generate standard management reports but the complexity will lie in obtaining and organising the input information. It might be that we would have to think about linking to the spreadsheets developed by each individual business unit. The timesheeting system would probably be developed as a template, and a single sheet should be sufficient. The budgeting model is a work-in-progress, in that it will be used over a period of time, during which the actuals will be entered into the model for comparison with the forecast or budget values, and reference will be made to last year's results for comparison.

Already, in each case, we are thinking about the overall structure and function of the model, before concerning ourselves with the detail, and ideally we are engaging our users or sponsors in the process; which is how computer programmers would go about it. Unfortunately, we find that the majority of modellers adopt a **bottom-up approach**, in which the collection and input of the raw data along with basic calculations take priority. This results in a rapid and unstructured early development phase, followed by a problematic and time-consuming late development phase in which the analyst attempts to structure and restructure the earlier work. Quite often the model grows by a process of accretion, in which different model elements are bolted on to the existing code, with some being definite enhancements whilst others do not really seem to do much. I also refer to the bottom-up concept as the 'stream of consciousness approach': a sequence of ideas thought up one after another, but without necessarily taking into account the relationships within the model itself. This type of modelling also tends to be idiosyncratic, by which I mean that each model, regardless of purpose, is as distinct and individual as the analyst who created it. In the absence of a clear plan or set of objectives it is often quite difficult for colleagues to understand the model. In the absence of the model builder it can be almost impossible to have full confidence that the model is actually doing what it is supposed to do, and because the users or sponsors have not been involved in the development process the results themselves may be unsatisfactory. Quite often discussions about such models become confrontational rather than cooperative.

Purpose

Returning to the top-down approach, we might summarise the key issues as being 'what is this model for?', and to an equal extent, 'who is this model for?' This means that we give careful consideration to model purpose and use before even thinking about firing up Excel. Another way of putting it is to *design the output first*. I often take a piece of paper and sketch out the model layout and structure. The first task in the spreadsheet is to design the model outputs, and by outputs we mean the physical reports that will be generated from the model. In doing this, we can then show others the outcomes we intend to achieve – without the numbers, of course, but in terms of the deliverable we hope to produce. I was once on a training assignment with a German investment bank during which I was asked if it was possible to develop a standard company valuation model. I was able to liaise with colleagues in London who prepared various drafts of the outputs, and by using an iterative process with local staff we were able to produce an agreed model structure by the end of the week. My colleagues were then able to set about the task of writing the model and the whole project was turned around in a very short time.

The top-down approach means that the outputs are agreed at the outset. From the modelling perspective, this then offers a work plan: the modelling assignment is simply to complete all the appropriate rows on the outputs sheet. And in doing so, the outputs then act as a work record, so that we can print the model at a moment's notice to show colleagues, management or the client. A further point is that many organizations have archives of models used for previous projects or transactions, and that these can serve as a template for subsequent, similar assignments.

Although we are considering model development, we can use the same approach when reviewing models: the key question is still 'what is this model for?' I like to set myself what I call the '2 Minute Rule' – can I identify the key results of someone's model within the first 2 minutes of examining it?

Structure

As mentioned above, model structure will depend on model purpose. As with many issues in financial modelling, different modellers will have different opinions concerning model structure, and it would be naive to suggest that there is a standard practice that could work for all models at all times. But there is some agreement about what might constitute good practice, and so we will review the key ideas and then look at some variations on the theme. Some of the ideas which follow may seem a little counterintuitive, but generally the principle of error reduction applies, and the time taken on developing a robust model structure will be repaid by reduced audit time and a flattening of the learning curve for users. I will not present these ideas as rules to be followed rigidly, because in almost every case there are valid exceptions. And always remember the cost/benefit analysis – if your model is for your own purposes and is likely to be discarded in the near future, then there is probably little need to spend a large amount of time and effort on the task. The assumption of this book is that you are involved with larger and more complex modelling assignments that merit a robust structure and a reliable development methodology.

Version Control

At this point we should expect to have a fairly clear idea of the proposed model and its reports, and we may be forming an opinion of the amount of work required. We also recognise that this is real life and despite the top-down approach things may well change. It is vital to impose a version control system so that any amendments are recorded and that the workbook that your colleague is commenting on is the same as the one in front of you. Excel has the ability to allow multiple users to access the same spreadsheet simultaneously and we should decide if this is acceptable during the model development. Excel has some fairly sophisticated version control features including the ability to track changes within a workbook, but ultimately the responsibility lies with the modeller, and quite often we find we need to know why a particular change was made, not just that it has happened. It is very important that we are absolutely clear about which is the latest version of a model – as Microsoft describe it, 'one version of the truth'.

At the most basic level we can use the grandparent/parent/child system: the first draft of the model is the grandparent; following the next set of modelling activities the workbook is saved with a new name or number as the parent and after the next development saved again with a new name or number as the child. As work progresses, the grandparent is deleted, the parent promoted to grandparent and the child to parent, with the current work as the child. In this way you will have a rolling series of files showing work-in-progress but with at least two backups. Alternatively, if disk space is not a problem, we can use an incremental file saving system, with each version of the model carrying a specific version number (which I would like to see documented in the workbook, for audit purposes, as described in the previous chapter). In this process we give the workbook a name and the version number, along with an incremental number and a description of the current activity. For example:

```
XYZ Wind Farm 02 15 subordinated debt
```

This reads as the '15th increment of version 2'. There are two ways of using the activity description, either to indicate what has just been completed (we have finished sub-debt), or what we intend to do next. The argument for the latter approach is that if I carry with workbook 15 and start writing the debt service reserve calculations and then press Ctrl+S, version 15 now has elements of what should be in version 16. Or we could make each version read-only.

Periodicity

As will be discussed in a later chapter, one of the trickiest of the common modelling problems is the handling of different time periods. Changing from quarterly to semiannual or annual is not merely a question of columns, but often the accounting treatment may change as well. We also find that we might be required to model the development or construction phase of a project or investment on a quarterly basis, switching to annual in the operational phase. And we need to recognise that start dates can be brought forward, or slip. These transition points often produce 'edge effects' with dependent formulas not quite working as they should. One option is to work at the level of the smallest time period across the whole of the forecast period, such that if there is a requirement for monthly calculations during the construction phase but quarterly during the operational phase, the whole timeline should be monthly.

An alternative is to set up a primary timeline that covers the majority of the forecast period, and a secondary timeline for the shorter period of higher detail. In Chapters 5 and 6 we will look at formula techniques to handle differing periodicities.

Extending the duration of the forecast period is much less of an issue but may still cause problems, which we will consider later in the book. Both periodicity and duration must be clearly specified before setting up the spreadsheet.

Accuracy

When setting up the inputs sheet it is appropriate to determine the level of accuracy and the level of detail that is required (known in the trade as 'granularity'). In some types of model we might start out with ballpark figures and then gradually refine the detail. With others we may be able to accept some imprecision or approximation, but some may require a high level of detail and accuracy from the outset. It may be tempting to include information simply because it is available. I often point out that it is the discrimination and common sense applied in selecting the correct inputs and excluding those that are trivial or irrelevant that can make or break a model. The problem is that this ability only comes with experience.

Colour

The use of colour in spreadsheets is worth thinking about. Some people dislike colour, feeling that it distracts them from the numbers, but I think that if used sensibly colour can add value. An old habit for some is to colour the inputs wherever they are located in the workbook. I am not too keen on this approach, because using the principle of error reduction these analysts have to remember to colour the cells every time they enter a value. Forgetting this even once means that the numbers are lost in the mass of calculations (although we do have techniques for locating them again in Chapter 2).

Generally a consistent approach to the use of colour throughout the model can be very helpful – if you have ever played around with Visual Basic you will have seen how colour is used to indicate different elements of the macro code. Sensible use of colour psychology can help others grasp the layout of your work. I prefer to use fill (background) colours – font colours don't always stand out, especially if the cell is currently blank or has a number format which returns a '–' for zero values. My colleagues and I use yellow for the base column, blue for unfinished formulas, green for input cells used for sensitivity testing and orange for cells picked up by audit checks.

Don't use too many colours, do make them different, and always remember that around 10% of your male colleagues are affected by some form of colour blindness.

WORKBOOK STRUCTURE

A very old modelling principle, from the first days of multiple sheets, is that each sheet should have the same layout and that each column should have the same function on each sheet. For example, column E is quarter 1 of the first year of the forecast period, on every sheet in the workbook. The operational researchers have shown that if sheets have different layouts the risk of error increases as the developers or users have to orientate themselves to the layout of each sheet, and that levels of confidence are generally lower (Figure 3.1).

We have considered the FAST, SMART and BPM standards in Chapter 1. The structural similarities of these methodologies can be seen in Figure 3.2.

The inputs/workings/outputs structure reflects the scientific training and education that I and most of my colleagues have received. Using a very simple

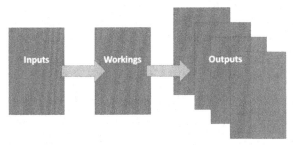

FIGURE 3.1   Model structure: inputs/workings/outputs.

⊿	A	B	C	D	E
1	Financial year ending			2016	2016
2					
3	Inflation				
4		rate		3%	=InflationRateIn
5		index	1	1.03	=D5*(1+InflationRate)
6					
7	Oil price				
8		real terms ($/barrel)		75	=OilPriceIn
9		money terms		77.25	=OilPriceReal*InflationIndex
10					
11	Oil production				
12		production (barrels per day)		0	=ProductionBarrelsPerDayIn
13		production days		365	=ProductionDaysIn
14		barrels/year		0	=ProductionBarrelsPerDay*ProductionDays
15					
16	Revenue			0	=ProductionAnnual*OilPriceMoney
17					

FIGURE 3.2   Input sheet with cell links.

interpretation of the scientific method, we might describe a major infrastructure project bid as a hypothesis. The data provided in support of the hypothesis form my inputs. I next formulate an experiment, which is the workings sheet. And then we evaluate our findings, on the outputs sheets.

THE INPUTS OR ASSUMPTIONS SHEET

This is where you should store all the numbers that are used in your model. It is generally agreed that it is very sensible to isolate the inputs or assumptions of the model. The premise is that you or your users should be able to change the numbers used in the model, but not the formulas. When you look at your Excel screen, how do you know if you are looking at numbers or calculations? The simple answer is that you click on the cell and inspect the contents on the formula bar, but this is not particularly efficient. I suggest that you keep all your inputs on a separate sheet. If needed, we can protect all other sheets in the file, so that users can flex the model and run sensitivity analysis without breaking anything.

You should always be able to track an assumption right back to its source, be it a data book or project document, and it should be expressed in the same units in the inputs, in the outputs and in the documentation.

It is perfectly permissible to use multiple inputs sheets, and indeed this might be recommended for multiple business units, project portfolios, time-dependent and time-independents inputs, and for file links.

Absence of Calculations

The inputs sheet should contain no calculations whatsoever, because that is the function of the workings sheet. The immediate exception to this sweeping general-isation is that data tables (Chapter 8) must be located on the same sheet as the input being tested. Also, I would not consider a link formula as a calculation. If we want to use the same production figure for each year in the forecast period, it is a simple exercise to write the figure in the first cell and put link formulas in the rest of the row. Other than this, the inputs sheet is made up of raw numbers (Figure 3.3).

THE WORKINGS OR CALCULATIONS SHEET

This is perhaps the more controversial issue when considering model structure. The suggestion here is that *all* the calculations used in the model are located on a single sheet, which by implication can then be rather large. However, the

54	Fixed assets: expansion				
55	depreciation rate		25%	25%	25%
56	capex, real		0	25,000,000	20,000,000
57	NBV bf		0	0	19,891,875
58	capex, money		0	26,522,500	21,854,540	→ goes to Cash Flow
59	depreciation		0	6,630,625	10,436,604	→ goes to Income Statement
60	NBV cf	0	0	19,891,875	31,309,811	→ goes to Financial Position
61					

FIGURE 3.3 Workings sheet with links to the inputs sheet (names ending with –In).

operational researchers have shown that the use of multiple sheets increases the risk of error, especially in large models where it can be difficult to form a mental map of the overall model layout and the relationships between different elements on different sheets. The principle of error reduction therefore applies, and we enter all the calculations on a single sheet.

Logic Cascade

Quite often we find that in the process of building the workings, a cascade effect is introduced, in which logic flows from left to right and from top to bottom (but not always). The flow is in general linear, which can be of great benefit in tracking logic and debugging errors. The audit techniques and tools in Chapter 2 work very effectively with this methodology.

The Size of the Sheet

Some people express concern about the potential size of the workings sheet. Variations might allow for the workings to be spread over several sheets to make them manageable, but the concern is that the overall linear flow of information from inputs to workings to outputs is compromised by workings logic flowing in the reverse direction. The judicious use of grouping and outlining techniques (Chapter 7) and the use of colour can make a large workings sheet less intimidating.

Some people complain that a lengthy workings sheet would be impossible to work with. I tend to point out that the conceptual model is already established if we have ever looked at a large document in a word processor. Imagine if Microsoft Word used the same sheet layout as Excel.

No Numbers

As with the earlier observation about the absence of calculations on the inputs sheet, we should also note that there should be no values on the workings sheet (but we will consider an exception – the base column – later on). This means both the input values proper, and also hard-coded values which have been typed directly into a calculation, for example, =E117*1.2 (remember that in Chapter 2 we have seen a technique for detecting such slips). Values from the inputs sheet are brought through to the workings by the use of link or import formulas:

```
=Inputs!E5
```

I would strongly recommend that we avoid writing calculations that combine input links with workings formulas, for example

```
=D10*(1+Inputs!E5)
```

I am quite happy to accept that this formula works, but from an audit/review perspective it requires us to check references on two sheets rather than one. I describe this type of formula as a three-dimensional calculation and I will

⊿	A	B	C	D	E
1	Financial year ending			2016	2017
2					
3	Revenue			-	=Revenue
4					
5	Operating costs			-	=0-CostsTotal
6					
7	Working capital change			-	=0-WorkingCapitalChange
8					
9	Capital expenditure			(82.4)	=0-CapexTotalMoney
10					
11	Tax paid			-	=0-TaxPaid
12					
13	Project cash flow			(82.4)	=E3+E5+E7+E9+E11
14					

FIGURE 3.4 Workings results feed through to the outputs sheets.

consider it further in Chapter 5. At this stage it is worth noting that by using links to pick up values from the inputs sheet, and then to write calculations based on the links, we end up with a full audit trail on one sheet (Figure 3.4).

We will explore the functionality of the workings sheet in more detail in the following chapters.

OUTPUTS

Rationale

If the concept of the single workings sheet is controversial, the design principles of the output sheets are the most counterintuitive. The two key suggestions are that the output sheets are populated with links to the workings sheets, and that none of the output sheets are linked to each other. To explain this, let us consider the calculation of depreciation. If my outputs include the pro forma financial statements such as the Cash Flow, the Income Statement (Profit and Loss) and the Balance Sheet, we would expect depreciation to be reported on the income statement and the effect of it would be to reduce the book value of the fixed assets on the balance sheet. However, rather than feeding the P&L depreciation through to the balance sheet, the calculations are set out on the workings sheet, as shown below (Figure 3.5).

We should find that each line of output contains a single formula which links back to the workings. The benefit is that revenue on the cash flow is the same as revenue on the income statement because they both link to the original revenue as calculated on the workings.

I would recommend that each output sheet should contain summary calculations, that is, wherever the output heading is Total, Subtotal or Net, there

	A	B	C	D	E	F	G	H	I	J
1										
2										
3										
4		Model name			NewCo FCA Regulatory Financials Forecast					
5		Version number			0.5					
6		Filename			C:\FCA\NewCo FCA Regulatory Financials Forecast.xlsx					
7		Date			11-Oct-16					
8		Deadline			01-Jan-17					
9		Author		JS						
10		Sponsor		NewCo Board						
11		Compliance officer		PM						
12		SRO		DC						
13		Work completed		Model structure						
14				Agreement with FCA financial requirements template						
15										
16		Work to follow		Confirmation of applicable FCA ratios						
17										
18		Amendments		Nil						
19										
20		Iteration cycle			1					
21										
22		Audit status		FALSE						
23										
24		Instructions		Nil						
25										
26		Navigation		Key inputs			Audit sheet			
27										
28				FCA Report			Workings			
29										

FIGURE 3.5   Outputs sheets contain links to workings and summary calculations.

should be a simple sum or addition (or whatever) of the relevant output rows. This serves to make each output sheet internally consistent; the numbers always add up (Figure 3.6). The imbalance check on the balance sheet, for example, should be based on the balance sheet itself and not on a suspense account tucked away on the workings sheet!

AUDIT OR CONTROL SHEET

This has been explored in some depth in the previous chapter.

VARIATIONS

As I teach this set of ideas concerning model structure on my courses, I normally find that at this stage I will have one or two individuals simmering with indignation at this ivory tower exposition of how models should be built, in contrast to the realities of model building in real organisations. But this is the real world, and there are many equally valid approaches to model structure. The key point

FIGURE 3.6   Basic workbook documentation, with navigation buttons.

is that we have a standard sequence of inputs–workings–outputs. If we change input I, we should see a change in output O. There is a linear path between the two, most of which is on the workings sheet. This basic methodology, once understood, becomes a very flexible basis for different modelling situations.

Earlier in this chapter we considered five different models:

1. Model A is used to calculate the net present value and internal rate of return of a manufacturing project, to be used by the company's management.
2. Model B is a loan calculator, which will be used and reused by a number of colleagues.
3. Model C produces consolidated monthly accounts using information from several business units, to be reported to management.
4. Model D is a timesheeting system.
5. Model E is a budgeting model which will be used over a period of time, and will require the actual figures to be compared with the budgeted figures as they become available.

I would suggest that Model A best illustrates the straightforward inputs–workings–outputs structure described above. The management would want to flex the inputs sheet for the sensitivity analysis, and the results are set out on the outputs. Model B, the loan calculator, introduces the first variation – we would probably want to show the inputs and outputs on the same sheet. We would need to ensure that the outputs could not be overwritten, and I would still recommend that we have a separate workings sheet.

Model C is also a variation, this time perhaps with multiple inputs sheets, one for each business unit. These could be copied and pasted from the source spreadsheets, or we could link the files. In general terms it is best to avoid file links in models (explained below), but in this case it might be the only realistic solution. The workings sheet is then used to consolidate this information before feeding it into the calculations; indeed it might be possible to have individual workings sheets for each business unit input sheet, with a consolidation workings sheet to pull it all together. The output sheets, in our methodology, are based on the workings and as such need little attention.

The fourth model, the timesheeting system, is perhaps so simple it can be set out on one sheet. The constants would be the employee name and number, the dates, the hourly rate and the overtime rate, and the only real variable is the number of hours worked. Once the information has been input, the model (if we can call it that) is printed and submitted to management. As long as we can differentiate inputs from workings and outputs, the structure holds.

Model E, the budgeting model, is an interesting mixture of historic data and forecast assumptions or estimates, with the added factor of the actuals which will be entered during the year. The number crunching is probably quite simple, with some year-to-date summary formulas and perhaps some extrapolations of budget under/overspend. Reporting should be straightforward, but the model will need to be set up so that the user is clear about what can and cannot be changed. A single, well laid out sheet might be an option, but it may be more appropriate to have a historic (previous years' figures) inputs sheet, a forecast assumptions inputs sheet, an actuals inputs sheet and then the workings and the outputs. The historic sheet is not going to change, the forecast sheet might be manipulated in response to the information made available during the year, and the actuals sheet itself is for the ongoing data entry. The outputs sheets would need to display all three input elements for comparison, along with any variance and extrapolation results.

Other variations are permissible. Model A, the net present value calculation, may contain a substantial amount of operating data relating to the manufacturing project, but in terms of sensitivity analysis the management might be interested in flexing just one or two key variables. In this context we might consider two inputs sheets – one for the key drivers and the other for the bulk of the unchanging assumptions. Or in the example of company valuation modelling, we would have historic data about the company and assumptions that relate to the forecast period. The historic data are not going to change but the forecast assumptions will be tested, so put them on separate sheets (one tip relating to historic data is to make sure that totals and subtotals are calculated and not simply typed in – this will flag up any errors due to rounding when the historic data were compiled).

Returning to Model C, the consolidation model, I mentioned that I am not particularly keen on linking to other files. The premise here is that each model should be self-contained, and file links are a notorious cause of error – particularly if the linked file is no longer in the location specified by the path in the link formulas – the classic example being when the model and its files are sent as email attachments. These are usually stored in the recipient's Temp directory and the links fail. Remember, if Excel is unable to refresh the links to the precedent files, your model is essentially broken. If file links are to be used, make sure they are isolated from the rest of the model. To manage file links, such as in model C, I suggest that we set up workbook-specific link sheets containing the relevant links, such that each link sheet contains links to only one external workbook. In other models it may just be appropriate to have a single links sheet, which contains all the file link formulas. These values are then fed into the model as required.

DOCUMENTATION

Inputs

I would recommend that inputs should be documented – there are three types of data you can put into a model: publicly available information, commercially sensitive information and the 'plug' number (i.e. an imaginary or temporary number). The latter should be very clearly identified. I once wrote an example of an interest calculation in response to an enquiry from someone who had attended a course of mine. A couple of months later I was dismayed to see that the analyst had simply copied and pasted this routine from my email into his model. The interest rate I had used was purely hypothetical and we both learnt an important lesson – I now clearly identify my plug numbers with colour and document them with cell comments.

Comments and Text Boxes

Excel is not particularly good at handling large amounts of text. Cell comments (Shift+F2) are very useful but of limited functionality. Do not be tempted to use merged cells as these break down the underlying structure of the spreadsheet. Although a cell can contain a substantial amount of text and can be formatted as required (use Alt+Enter to wrap text within the cell), the cell will not expand automatically, and we can end up with an irritatingly large entry in the formula bar. Cells can contain up to 32,767 characters, of which only the first 1024 will appear in the cell (formulas are restricted to a limit of 8192 characters). Large amounts of text should be placed in text boxes. These can be created from the Drawing toolbar or Insert tab, and have the benefit that they can be easily edited, formatted, resized and moved.

As the text box is an object we have the option that the box is neither shown nor printed. The print option can also be set using the text box shortcut menu (right-click on the box border) and choosing Properties in the Format Text Box dialog. Then File, Options, Display options, For objects, show: Nothing (hide objects). The print option can also be set using the text box shortcut menu (right-click on the box border) and choosing the Size and Properties command in dialog box.

KEY INFORMATION

Whether we are top-down or bottom-up modellers, once we get started on building a model the temptation is to crack on and get the job done. It is important to make sure that you document your work from the outset. I would recommend a separate documentation sheet, although you could include this information on the audit sheet as described in the previous chapter. Information we should include would be:

1. Model name.
2. Version number.
3. Filename – use the `CELL` function to return the full path of the workbook:`=CELL("filename")`.
4. Date – do not be tempted to use `=NOW()` functionality as this will only tell you the current date, not the date when the model was last used. The date must be hard-coded (try Ctrl+; as a date shortcut). Put the current date and time in the page footer.
5. Model author – your details, including telephone number and email address, in case anyone needs to get hold of you concerning the model.
6. Model sponsor – on whose behalf are you building the model? Contact details.
7. Model owner – if questions arise, who is empowered to make decisions concerning accounting policies? Who has ultimate responsibility for the verification of the inputs? Contact details.
8. Work completed – a record of main features/elements completed. With dates.
9. Work to follow – a list of priorities for future tasks. With deadlines.
10. Amendments – work previously completed but then revised. With dates.
11. Iteration cycle – how many times has the model been subjected to review/audit by the model sponsor/owner?
12. Audit – what is the overall audit status of the model (see Chapter 2).
13. Instructions to users – description of model purpose, locations of key inputs, key outputs. Description of macros. Instructions for printing.
14. Navigation – Go To macro buttons or hyperlinks (Figure 3.7).

MICROSOFT BACKSTAGE

The new Microsoft Backstage offers a number of tools and functions which should contribute to the model documentation and model audit (Figure 3.8). File, Info offers a Backstage screen with options to:

- Protect Workbook
- Inspect Workbook (check for issues)
- Versions
- Browser View Options
- Properties

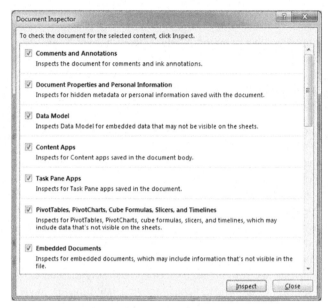

FIGURE 3.7   The file, Info Backstage view.

FIGURE 3.8   Document Inspector.

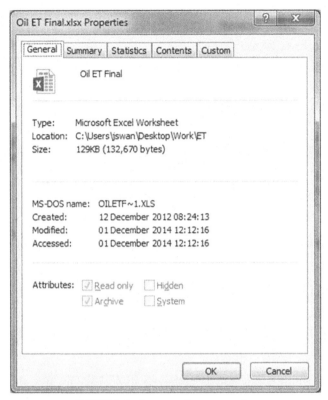

FIGURE 3.9 Document Inspector results.

- Related Dates
- Related People
- Related Documents

The Inspect Workbook option is interesting, and offers the Document Inspector dialog box which will check for document properties, hidden rows, columns and sheets and headers and footers (Figure 3.9).

The Document Inspector generates a report in a dialog box, which cannot be printed. The 'More Info' button is simply a link to a Microsoft support page which explains the nature of the issue. The Inspector also offers the 'Remove All' option, which is rather drastic; and it does not provide any navigational information to locate the problems. We were rather struck by Microsoft's use of 'issues', in the same sense we have been using it in this chapter (Figure 3.10).

FILE PROPERTIES

In my experience the workbook Properties is little used. It is a generic Microsoft Office feature and the five tabs in the dialog box store information ('metadata')

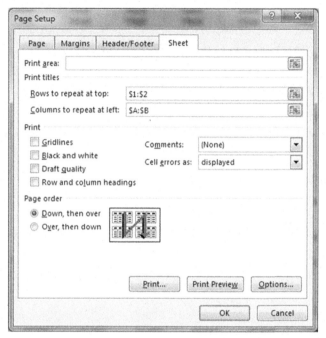

FIGURE 3.10   The Advanced Properties dialog box.

which may not be apparent in the workbook itself. Use File, Info and click on the Properties (QS) dropdown list. This offers the choice of Show Document Panel, which will appear below the ribbon; and Advanced Properties, which displays a tabbed dialog box.

General

This tab provides information about the file name, path and size, and about when the file was created, modified and accessed.

Summary

This contains information relating to ownership. As far as I can tell, the default Author and Company are derived from the details provided when Excel/Office was installed, but these fields can be edited (Figure 3.11).

Statistics

This duplicates the General tab but also stores information about the use of the workbook. The non-editable field for 'Last saved by' is linked to the name shown under Tools, Options, General, User name.

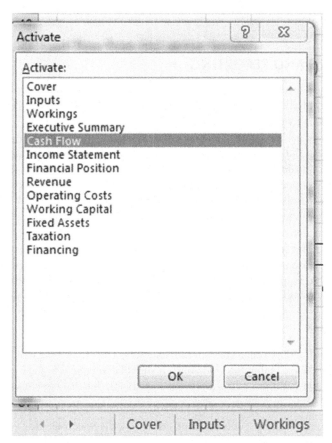

FIGURE 3.11 Setting print titles.

Contents

This lists all sheets, charts and range names used in the file. These are all derived from the workbook and cannot be edited.

Custom

Additional headings are provided in which further information can be stored. There is a list of predefined properties or you can define your own.

Although I recommend that it is good practice to complete the workbook Properties for each model, it should also be remembered that it may contain information that you may not wish others to see – I have lost count of the number of models I have been invited to comment upon in which I have discovered that I am apparently the author. People have attended my courses and taken away the course models and developed them for their own purposes; eventually ending up back on my desk!

PRINTING AND REPORTING

I have suggested that by using the top-down approach to modelling we focus on the outputs first – the tangible product of the largely intangible process. The outputs, or reports, are designed in consultation with the users so that the reports are of genuine value. And we ensure that the outputs are designed from the outset, so that at any stage of the model development we can demonstrate the progress made. We should therefore make sure that we can print our work at a moment's notice. When it comes to reporting some modellers rely on macros, which in some cases is the only way to handle complex reports. But it is helpful to understand basic printing techniques.

Do not underestimate the importance of printing. One of the first actions we take when we receive a model is to press Ctrl+P (print) and see what comes out of the printer. For reasons explained in the previous chapter, a model lacking print settings (headers, footers, print titles) is unlikely to have ever been printed, which suggests that nobody outside the modelling team has ever examined the model's results.

Print Area

Before printing, go to each sheet in turn and press Ctrl+End. This will select the bottom right-hand cell in the worksheet. It should correspond to the intersection of the last non-blank column with the last non-blank row that contains anything. To fix this:

1. Select the empty columns or rows (Ctrl+Spacebar for columns, Shift+Spacebar for rows)
2. Delete them using Home, Delete, Delete Sheet Rows or Ctrl+−
3. Save the file, close it and reopen it.
4. Run the Ctrl+End shortcut again to confirm that the end cell is where it should be.

It is worth noting that Ctrl+End relates only to cells in the worksheet. If you have objects such as macro buttons, combo boxes or embedded graphs, Excel does tend to recognise them and increases the print area accordingly, which you may or may not want, in which case you will have to define the print area manually.

The print area is usually defined automatically by Excel. To specify your own print area you can select the range manually and use Page Layout, Print Area, Set Print Area. Range names can speed up this selection process if you have set them up in advance. It would seem that we are restricted to one print area at a time, but we can work around this using noncontiguous selection: Ctrl+click and drag over nonadjacent ranges. Using print preview to see what this does, we find that Excel puts each range on a separate sheet. I would welcome a workaround for this but I have never found a non-macro solution.

In the page break preview model (View, Page Break Preview) we can redefine the boundaries of the areas by clicking and dragging, and ranges can be added or removed by right-clicking and making the appropriate choices from the shortcut menu (Add to Print Area). Page breaks can be inserted using Page Layout, Breaks, Insert Page Breaks.

Whichever technique we use, we are confronted by Excel's inability to assemble print areas from different sheets unless we are content that each print area should be printed on a different page. We could record a simple macro in which the source print areas are copied and pasted (as values perhaps) to a separate sheet and assembled for printing, this sheet then being discarded or retained on completion of the subsequent print command.

Group Mode

If you have used the inputs–workings–outputs structure described previously, it is likely that we only need to print the outputs. These should all have the same page layout to give a consistent look-and-feel to the reports. You will know that you can group all your output sheets by Ctrl+ or Shift+ clicking on the sheet tabs, which then sets up group mode. An alternative is to right-click a sheet tab and choose Select All Sheets.

Page Setup

Page setup can catch out the unwary, because there are two ways of using it. If you have grouped the sheets together and you use the Page Layout, Page Setup command, the settings you specify will apply to all sheets in the group.

Fit to Page

If a standard layout has been adopted for the report sheets, we will find that we have the same number of columns on each sheet so the width is constant. However, each sheet is likely to differ in its length. Page setup offers the scaling options to increase or decrease by a percentage value, or to fit to a specified number of pages. With the latter, it is worth noting that we need only specify one value; for example, I have adjusted the column widths and layout with the intention of printing on a landscape page, but we do not know the length. Rather than specifying one page wide by one tall, we simply enter the width requirement and leave the height blank. The effect of Fit to Page on font size must be appreciated if you are working with a house style.

Headers and Footers

Headers and footers should be classed as part of the model's documentation and treated accordingly. Each page of the printout should show the sheet name and page number, and at least one page should have the filename. It should be compulsory to include both the date and the time on the printout – we have seen models approaching financial close that are being adjusted and updated and subsequently printed on an hour-by-hour basis. You must be able to confirm that the printouts on your desk are the most up-to-date available. The footer should also contain such caveats as 'Numbers may not agree due to rounding', 'Numbers in £000s' or 'Numbers in millions unless stated otherwise' if applicable.

It is not widely known, but headers and footers can be used as a form of security stamp. For some reason Excel 'remembers' all custom headers and footers created in a workbook. If you make sure that your details are entered in this way, even if you don't then use the header or footer for printing, they will be recorded for posterity when the file is saved.

You may be aware that if we attempt to write an & character into a header or footer, for example, XYZ & Partners, Excel will omit the &. To solve this, use XYZ && Partners.

To change page numbers we can either set the First page number on the Page tab of the Page Setup dialog box, or we can change the page number code in the header or footer. To increase the page number by 1, for example, the code should read: &[Page]+1 (note that there is a space after the 1)

I would not recommend putting the version number of the model into the header or footer because it often gets overlooked when updating a file. The version number should appear on the model's documentation sheet as part of the normal printout.

Excel still doesn't have the ability to put a link to a cell in the header or footer, although there are times when we need to include more information than can be entered using the header/footer codes. Excel now has a button in the Header/Footer dialog box to insert the path as well as the filename.

Print Titles

Use Print Titles on the Sheet tab to include information from the worksheet, making sure that Group mode has been switched off. Rather than selecting rows or columns to include, we can use row or column referencing – for example, to print the period dates across the top of the worksheet use $1:$2; and $A:$B to print the first two columns. We cannot include nonadjacent rows or columns. A limitation to print titles is that they are worksheet-specific and cannot be applied to multiple worksheets using Group mode, so we set them up on each worksheet individually (Figure 3.12).

Reports and Custom Views

We should be able to generate reports at short notice. Once the page setup routines have been followed, printing reports can be as simple as Ctrl or Shift clicking the sheet tabs to group them, and then running the print command (Ctrl+P). When using this method remember to switch off group mode afterwards – click on a sheet tab outside the group, or right-click a sheet tab and choose Ungroup Sheets from the shortcut menu.

FIGURE 3.12   The scroll tabs and the sheet navigation dialog box.

Another way to set up reports is to use custom views. The time spent setting these up is recouped from the ease of use in generating reports later on. It is similar to the process of setting up range names (see Chapter 4) but it includes the print settings. This technique is particularly useful if individual elements of the reports need to be printed, rather than a job lot which may have standard print settings.

1. Clear any existing print area using Page Layout, Print Area, Clear Print Area.
2. Select the first range for printing: Page Layout, Print Area, Set Print Area.
3. Use Page Layout, Page Setup launcher to specify the settings required, headers and footers, etc.
4. Use Views, Custom Views, Add and give the view a name.
5. Click OK.

Repeat this for each additional range to include, making sure that the existing print area is cleared each time. This technique is particularly useful if individual elements of the reports need to be printed, rather than a job lot which may have standard print settings. When you need to print, use Views, Custom Views, Show and print the selection.

MODEL DEVELOPMENT

Drawing on the ideas set out above, and anticipating further suggestions in the following chapters, it is helpful to consider the first step in setting up a model.

Above all else, make sure that the location of the inputs is specified, and that the key results are set out clearly. The amount of effort you put in at this stage should be commensurate with the ultimate purpose of the exercise – the quick and dirty monthly figures spreadsheet does not really require us to labour over the finer points of detail and methodology, whereas the model supporting the business case for opening a new office will benefit from the extra effort spent setting up a clear and robust structure from the outset.

New File

Create a new workbook in Excel, add new sheets as required by right-clicking a sheet tab, choosing Insert, and Worksheet or pressing Shift+F11. Name the sheets. You will know that you can click and drag the sheet tabs to rearrange them, and you can copy a sheet by Ctrl+click and drag its tab. Decide if an audit sheet is necessary (Chapter 2).

Saving

At this stage, save your work. Version control was introduced above, and it must be followed rigorously.

Learn the shortcuts Ctrl+S for File, Save, and F12 for File, Save As.

Grouping

The general modelling rule is that each sheet should have the same lay-out ('look-and-feel'). To apply the same settings to each sheet, group them together by right-clicking on any sheet tab and choosing Select All Sheets. To select groups of sheets, select the first sheet tab, hold down the Shift key and click on the last sheet tab. To select nonadjacent sheets, hold down Ctrl whilst clicking on the required sheet tabs. Caution: any editing or formatting carried out with group mode on will affect all grouped sheets. You can check the grouping status by looking at the sheet tabs or by reading the Excel title bar – it will have the warning [Group] after the file name. To disable group mode, click on a sheet tab outside the group, or right-click a sheet tab and choose Ungroup Sheets. Note that you will find that some commands appear to be disabled while Group mode is active.

Layout

With group mode enabled, adjust the column widths and enter the column headings that are common to all sheets. Apply any standard borders. You may want to consider providing a 'hard edge' to the model, by hiding all the columns beyond the end of the forecast period or equivalent. Put the active cell in the column which you would like to be at the right-hand edge of the spreadsheet. Press Ctrl+Shift+right arrow, followed by Ctrl+Spacebar. These two actions select the surplus columns. Press Ctrl+0 or run the Home, Format, Column, Hide & Unhide, Hide Columns command, to hide these columns.

To restore the hidden columns, press Ctrl+A and use Home, Format, Hide & Unhide, Unhide Columns.

Although we have a rule that we do not hide rows or columns, this relates to content. The columns beyond the end of the forecast period do not contain any data, so we are not in breach of the rule.

Units and Base Columns

Identify and label any units columns, and set up a base column if required (see Chapter 5). Apply a fill colour to both.

Number Formatting

You may wish to apply number formatting at this stage. I would agree that comma (thousands) format is useful, but I would not recommend any of the custom millions-type formats at this stage (see Chapter 7). Note that if you apply the thousands format, values such as percentages will appear as zeros until formatted appropriately. If we have numbers in the millions we can enter them more efficiently using the exponential format. For example, we can write 10,000,000 as 10E6. Excel displays this as 1.00E+07, and the thousands format makes this more readable (people simply do not like the exponential format). Learn the shortcuts for the common number formats:

Ctrl+Shift+% for percentage, two decimals.
Ctrl+Shift+! for thousands, two decimals.
Ctrl+Shift+$ for your default currency format.
Ctrl+Shift+~ applies the default general number format (i.e. it clears any existing number formatting).

Use Home, Increase Decimal (Alt+H, 0) or Home, Decrease Decimal (Alt+H, 9) as required.

AutoComplete

Disable the AutoComplete feature. This analyses your text entry whilst you type and if it corresponds to a previous entry in the same column, Excel will suggest how to complete your typing for you. I find this immensely irritating and I switch it off using File, Options, Advanced and clearing the Enable AutoComplete for cell values check box.

There are occasions when it would be helpful to copy from the cell directly above and in this case I use the little-known shortcut Ctrl+Shift+" to copy the value, or more rarely Ctrl+' to copy the formula.

Printing

Now prepare the model for printing, as mentioned in the previous section. We should be able to print our work at a moment's notice. At the very least we should get the page layout setup, with appropriate headers and footers. Run a test print, and show the results to colleagues or the project sponsor to ensure that your layout matches expectations.

Data Entry

For quick data entry, select the range to contain the information (row or column) and type in the figures or text. Press Enter to move the active cell down after each entry, or Tab to move the active cell to the right. Hold down Shift with either Enter or Tab to move in the reverse direction. While the range remains selected Excel will cycle you through each cell within that range in turn.

- To fill a range with the same information, select the range first, type the entry and press Ctrl+Enter.
- To select a range of cells which already contain data or formulas, press Ctrl+Shift+*.
- To select cells in a particular direction, press Ctrl+Shift+ arrow key.
- To select a row, press Shift+Spacebar. To copy across the row, press Ctrl+R.
- To select a column, press Ctrl+Spacebar. To copy down the column, press Ctrl+D.
- To select the whole sheet, press Ctrl+A twice.

Cell Comments

As you start work on the model, you may find it helpful to document your work as you go using cell comments. You can easily set these up by using Review, New Comment; or press Shift+F2. To remove cell comments, use Review, Delete. You can change the user name which appears by default in the comment by using File, Options, General, User Name.

Fill Right

As you start writing formulas, you will almost invariably need to copy them across the row. Using the mouse to copy across can be frustrating, particularly when the mouse pointer reaches the right-hand edge of the screen and the spreadsheet starts scrolling rapidly. A more effective technique is to write the formula, select the cells in the row using (Ctrl+) Shift+right arrow, and then press Ctrl+R, which is the shortcut for Home, Fill, Right.

Sign Conventions

At this stage we should also give thought to our sign conventions – do we show liabilities as negatives or positives? As far as the outputs sheets are concerned, this is determined by reporting conventions which seem to differ from one organisation to the next. However, for workings or calculations purposes, there is a good reason to calculate all liabilities as positives (liabilities here being used in a broad sense, covering all charges, costs and expenses). The reason for showing them as positive numbers is that in our accounting and finance training we tend to learn textbook formulas which express, for example, profits (or earnings) before tax as being revenue *less* costs, *less* depreciation, *less* interest. If costs, depreciation or interest were calculated as negatives, we would have to add them back, which just would not look right. And worse, an inconsistent approach might result, for example, in positive costs and interest, but negative depreciation. This formula would be messy, and it would take additional time to check the precedent values to ensure the signs were correct.

Do not confuse the observations here about sign convention on liabilities with the sign seen in cash flows: we may well expect to see a cash account or a company's reserves increasing or decreasing over time, using the appropriate sign to show the direction of the movement.

If we had a reporting convention of showing liabilities as negatives, we can change the sign using =0-, as in

```
= 0-InterestPaid
```

This might look a little fussy, but on UK/US keyboards the – and the = keys are adjacent to each other and we see this as a fairly common typing mistake, so I would not recommend simply typing =-InterestPaid, because we could not be sure if this was an error or not. This =0- method of changing sign is also easier to spot.

NAVIGATION

As we start the model build it is important that we can navigate our way around. A sensible layout with appropriate documentation will greatly help, but when checking formulas and references we need to be able to move quickly and efficiently around the workbook. I would expect any competent modeller to be familiar with the following techniques.

Ctrl+PgUp/Ctrl+PgDn

These basic shortcuts are used to move from one sheet to the next.

Alt+PgUp/Alt+PgDn

Not so widely used as shortcuts, but serve to move a screen to the left or screen right.

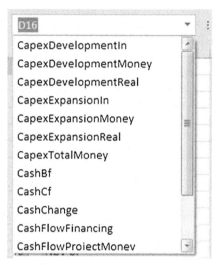

FIGURE 3.13 Go To and Go back.

Right-Click Scroll Tab Buttons

Right-clicking anywhere on the scroll tab buttons at the bottom left of the workbook will bring up a dialog box which lists all the worksheets and can be used to navigate rapidly across multiple sheets (Figure 3.13).

Home/Ctrl+Home

The Home key will move the active cell to column A, or to the left-hand edge of the worksheet if Window, Freeze Panes has been used. Ctrl+Home takes the active cell to A+, or to the top left cell if the panes have been frozen.

Ctrl+End

This keystroke combination will move the active cell to the bottom right-hand cell of the active sheet. This should correspond to the intersection of the last column and last row of the active area. Sometimes we find that this cell is way beyond the expected end of the sheet, which normally indicates that at some stage we copied something too far across a row (or down a column), and subsequently deleted the material.

The solution to this is to:

1. Select the appropriate rows and/or columns.
2. Delete them.
3. Save the file.
4. Close the file.
5. Reopen the file.

On pressing Ctrl+End again, the active cell should now be in a meaningful position.

Ctrl+arrow

Press Ctrl+an arrow key to move to the edge of the spreadsheet in that direction. Alternatively press End and the word End appears in the status bar; press any of the arrow keys to be moved to the last cell in that direction. If the row or column is empty, or the active cell is already beyond the last cell, you will find yourself at the outer edges of the spreadsheet. This can be irritating if you frequently need to read across a row, so one workaround is to give the worksheet a 'hard edge'. If, for example, column T marks the right-hand edge of your workings area, fill the column with a number or a character. Now when you use Ctrl (or End) + arrow, you should find that the active cell will always stop in column T. A sneaky variation on this is to use the ' apostrophe character – when this is entered in a cell, it appears blank, with the (non-printing)' only visible in the formula bar.

F6

If the window has been split (View, Split), use F6 to move the active cell from one pane to the next (although it now cycles through the Status bar and the Ribbon as well). Use Shift+F6 to reverse.

Go To

You can use either F5 or Ctr+G to call up the Home, Find & Select, Goto dialog box. Enter either the cell reference or range name and choose OK (or press Enter). One interesting feature of Go To is that if you then press F5 again, Excel enters your previous location as the default, as a Go Back function. If I used F5 to move the active cell from E36 to E73, when I press F5 again the destination cell is assumed to be E36. Excel in fact stores up to the last four locations of the active cell, which allows for some useful auditing. Although the dialog box lists all your range names (if you have any), Excel will list the cell references of the ranges in the dialog box (Figure 3.14).

Name Box

The box on the left-hand edge of the formula bar is the Name Box. It normally shows the cell reference of the active cell, but you can click in the box and type a cell reference for a Go To functionality. You can also select a range name from the list with the same result (Figure 3.15).

The Name Box can be widened as required. We will look at names in more detail in the next chapter. A little-known trick is to copy cell references from formulas and paste them into the Name Box.

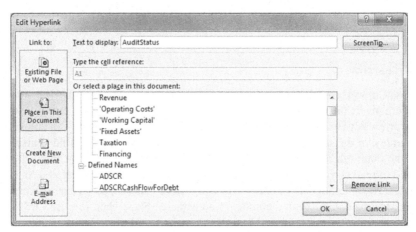

FIGURE 3.14   The Name Box.

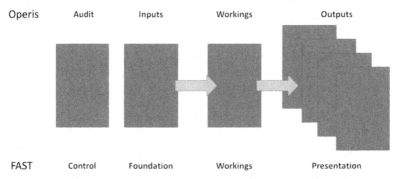

FIGURE 3.15   Inserting hyperlinks.

Ctrl+[

You will of course be familiar with F2 Edit Cell, and that when used on a formula Excel highlights all precedent cells with different colours (assuming File, Options, Advanced, Allow editing directly in cells is enabled). With many formulas, however, the references are off-screen and you will need to browse to find them, and in so doing run the risk of losing the active cell. One powerful shortcut is Ctrl+[(open square bracket), which is Select Precedents. This in itself is a shortcut for F5 Go To, Special, Precedents (Home, Find & Select, Go To Special, Precedents). The trick with Select Precedents is that the precedent cells are highlighted, and you do not need to scroll around to find the selected cells but instead press Enter repeatedly. You will know that when you have several cells selected the active cell will scroll around within the selection when you press Enter (or Tab). I will often take this a

	A	B	C	D	E	F	G	H
1	Financial year ending			2016	=D1	=E1	=F1	=G1
2								
3	Inflation rate			3%	3%	3%	3%	3%
4								
5	Oil							
6	real terms price ($/barrel)			75	=D6	=E6	=F6	=G6
7	production (barrels per day)			0	4,000	4,000	6,000	6,000
8	production (days)			365	=D8	=E8	=F8	=G8
9								
10	Costs, in real terms							
11	unit variable ($/barrel)			20	=D11	=E11	=F11	=G11
12	fixed ($)			0	40,000,000	40,000,000	40,000,000	40,000,000
13	abandonment ($)			0	0	0	0	0
14								

FIGURE 3.16 Operis versus FAST model layout.

step further and while the precedent cells are still selected, apply a Fill Color. In this way, for example, all the precedent cells for my EBITDA[1] calculation can be coloured light blue, and I can examine the audit trail at leisure, or even leave it as a marker for other users to follow. Use F5 Go To to return to the cell under inspection.

The benefit of Ctrl+[is that you can inspect both the values and the formulas in the precedent cells. Pressing Ctrl+[repeatedly will push you further up the precedent pathway.

It is no surprise that Ctrl+] (close square bracket) will select dependents. One thing to note with these two techniques is that they are formula driven, by which I mean that there must be a formula on the same sheet to push or pull the selection. If you have an inputs sheet, for example, which contains only values, Ctrl+] does not work. Also, if a formula feeds into one formula on the same sheet and another on another sheet, the shortcut will only pick up the dependent on the same sheet. However, with the workings sheet methodology introduced earlier in this chapter, this is not such a problem.

Hyperlinks

Hyperlinks do not seem to be used much in modelling. Used carefully they are a very efficient way of navigating to very specific locations in the workbook (Figure 3.16).

1. Select the cell to contain the hyperlink and use Insert, Hyperlink (or Ctrl+K).
2. Click on the Place in this Document tab.
3. Type the text to display in the cell (and if you want to, a ScreenTip).
4. You can then either enter a cell reference or a range name for the destination cell(s).
5. Click OK to return to the workbook.

---

1. Earnings Before Interest, Tax, Depreciation and Amortisation.

Test the hyperlink by clicking on it. Use F5 Go To to return to the hyperlink formula cell. Hyperlinks can be edited by selecting the cell using the keyboard and pressing Ctrl+K – do not try to click on the cell otherwise you will activate the link.

Excel also has a **HYPERLINK** function which has the following syntax:

```
=HYPERLINK("[model.xls]'Balance Sheet'!A1,"Balance Sheet")
```

When the user clicks on this example the active cell will move to the home cell position on the balance sheet. Note that the filename must be included, and the entire filename+sheetname+cell reference string is enclosed in quotes. The second part of the formula is the prompt or text which appears in the cell as a hyperlink.

Warning: neither method will update the link references if the sheet or file names change, and as such are very prone to error.

Part II

The Modelling Process

Chapter 4

Referencing and Range Names

RELATIVE AND ABSOLUTE REFERENCES

The vast majority of Excel formulas are written using cell references. In your very first Excel lesson back at school you were taught that instead of writing =1+2+3 you should instead use cell references: =A1+A2+A3. In other words, you were taught to write code – that A1 is used to represent the first value, and so on. Your first spreadsheets were probably no more than one screen in size, so it was easy to relate the references to their corresponding values (and their adjacent text labels). But in this book we are concerned about the development and use of very large spreadsheets, where references describe cells hundreds of rows away, perhaps on other sheets. In this context, a reference such as ='Fixed Assets!'=!$D$116 conveys little, if any meaning. Perhaps this is a reference to the depreciation life, so is it too much of an insult to the intelligence to consider writing =DepreciationLife?

Cell reference formulas can become difficult to read when sheet references are included, especially if the sheet names are ambiguous. Here is a real formula which illustrates the point; with references to three sheets:

```
=-(SUM(Funding!F27,Funding!F186,Funding!F37,Funding!F38,Funding
!F196,Funding!F189)-SUM('Depr. & Tax'!F39,'Depr. & Tax'!F40))+R
evs!F51+Revs!F52
```

Most people will continue to use cell references. The basics of relative referencing will be well known: if we write a formula into cell D10 such as =D4+D6 and copy it across the row, we assume it will change to E4+E6, F4+F6 and so on. But what happens if we copy the same formula from D10 to D20? It will now read =D14+D16, the relative referencing here meaning add the value from six cells above to the value from four cells above. To make the new formula refer to the original references we should make them absolute, using the $ sign to fix the cell address. Edit the first formula and click on each reference and press the function key F4: =$D$4+$D$6. However there is a problem if this formula is copied across the row – it stays the same, pointing at D4 and D6 only. If we think about it, we actually want the row referencing to remain fixed, but the column reference to change across the row. We can edit the original formula again to create a mixed reference. Selecting each absolute reference in turn, press F4 again so the formula now reads =D$4+D$6. This can be copied across the row. It can also be copied to row 20, as it will still point to rows 4 and 6.

The F4 function key, if pressed repeatedly, will cycle through full absolute ($D$4), row absolute (D$4), column absolute ($D4) and back to relative (D4). It is a good practice to make the reference as only as absolute as it needs to be, so, for example, a formula that should lock on to row 3 should be a mixed reference such as =D$3. This can be copied across the row so that the column referencing changes. If this formula is copied and pasted elsewhere it will still refer to row 3.

R1C1 REFERENCING

We describe the normal cell address methodology as A1 referencing, as in the previous example of writing =D4+D6 into cell D10. The calculation instruction is to 'add the content of the cell six cells above to the contents of the cell four cells up'. When this formula is copied to the adjacent cells in the row, the instruction remains the same but the formula is visibly different: =E4+E6 and so on. R1C1 (Row 1, Column 1) referencing is a technique that develops our understanding of formulas, in which we remove the usual row and column addresses and instead our formulas display the underlying 'instruction' (Figure 4.1).

Use the File, Options, Formulas, R1C1 reference style command. Note that the column headers are now replaced by numbers.

The original formula in cell D10 was: =D4+D6. With the R1C1 style, it appears as: =R[-6]C+R[-4]C. The [-x] indicates that the reference is above or to the left, and with the sign omitted it is below or to the right. We can read this as -6 rows (up, or above) plus -4 rows (above). There is no column number so the precedent cells are in the same column. When this formula is copied across the row you will notice that each formula is identical – this links into the formula consistency approach we will see with the range names shortly.

We can use R1C1 with functions, so that the sum of the four values in row 10 is written as =SUM(RC[-5]:RC[-1])

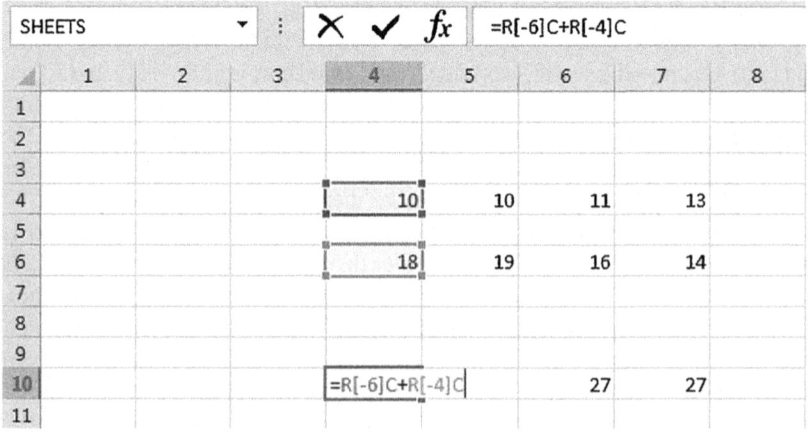

FIGURE 4.1 The R1C1 workbook.

Absolute references are written without the square brackets [ ] so to multiply the formulas in row 10 by a value of 10 in D2 (or row 2 column 4, as it now appears), we could write =(R[-6]C+R[-4]C)*R2C4. The F4 absolute key can still be used to create absolute and mixed absolute references.

In routine work, it is unlikely that we would ever find a need to use R1C1 referencing, other than as means to protect our code; users simply won't touch formulas written or displayed this way (Figure 4.2).

There is one aspect of R1C1 functionality that gives it an immediate use for the modeller. If we have written a formula in row 80 that refers, for example, to row 10, and we wish instead to point to row 20 we would normally have to locate the formula, edit it and then copy across the row. We can't use Find & Replace because the cell references are different in every cell; and it would be misguided to attempt to find the 10 and replace it with 20 as these values could occur anywhere. Instead, we can simply switch on R1C1. The formula is of course identical across the whole row, and the row referencing is enclosed by the square brackets, which makes it sufficiently distinct to now use Find & Replace, changing R[-70]C to R[-60]C.

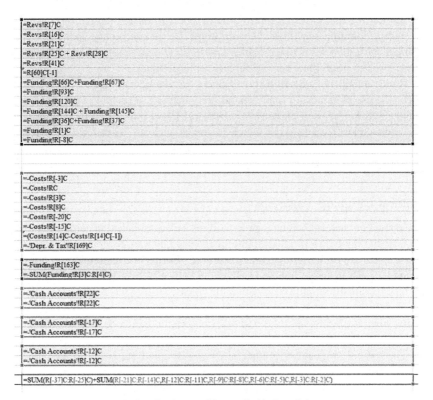

FIGURE 4.2   Would you edit this formula?

Although range name formulas are unaffected by this, the Name Manager (and indeed any other feature that displays or uses cell references) will use the R1C1 notation, and remember that the R1C1 setting is global, so any other open workbook will display this way.

RANGE NAMES

The use of range names is probably one of the most contentious issues in financial modelling. For some they are just plain common sense, but for the majority they seem to represent the dark side of modelling practice. In this chapter, we will look at range names in some detail, and in doing so explore the arguments for and against. As will be seen, I am a strong advocate of the use of names, but in the context of model complexity and the mitigation of the risk of error. A simple one sheet workbook is unlikely to require the use of names and indeed it will take more time to set them up; the cost outweighs the benefit.

In recent years, there has been some research into the use of range names in spreadsheets. Generally, the findings are negative, that users find them difficult to work with and either introduce errors through their use or fail to find existing errors. I am somewhat critical of this research: the experiments are rather contrived and in many cases require the participants to have a degree of familiarity with accounting and finance terminology. The research participants are not familiar with the use of range names and in almost all cases the experimental models are so small that even I would use cell references.

Range names have been in spreadsheets for many years. Lotus 1-2-3 introduced the use of names for range operations, such as SUM or COUNT, but the range name could not be used on its own. Microsoft Excel introduced the column or row intersection technique, in which formulas such as =Revenue-Costs refer not to the entire ranges but instead to individual cells – this will be explored further below.

Natural Language Formulas

The concept of natural language processing is well established in computing and in particular the fields of artificial intelligence and human–computer interaction. These fields are primarily concerned with the systems and techniques by which computers can interpret human language, whether as text or speech. We work in the opposite direction: computer (in this case spreadsheet) code expressed in a way that the end user can understand. Programmers have been doing this for years, when declaring variables and other objects in their code. So have spreadsheet users – imagine using a workbook without sensible sheet names?

The natural language formula (NLF) was adopted but badly implemented by Microsoft in Excel 97. The range labels feature, if enabled, automatically assigned row and column headings as labels which could be used in formulas. This was predicated on the fact that each row or column had a proper and meaningful text label. Clearly this didn't allow for any other organisation of the narrative or for the repetition of headings. The feature caused so many problems that it was quietly withdrawn in Excel 2007.

NLFs in fact predated the range label technique, through the use of range names. I consider range names and their implementation in NLFs as a fundamental part of the principle of error reduction.

Geographical Precision

Many modellers seem to prefer the geographic precision of the cell reference – there is no dispute over the location of Inputs!D4. Indeed there isn't – but what exactly is Inputs!D4? Most of the time we are more interested in *what* the cell contains, rather than *where* it is located. In Chapter 2 we covered a number of simple navigation techniques which would allow us to visit the cell if required; these techniques work equally efficiently for names and for cell references. I have encountered modellers who claim that they can read a formula and intuitively understand the elements referred to by cell reference. I might suggest that intuition is not the most reliable of modelling skills.

Speed

Some modellers argue that it is much faster to write formulas using cell references. This is undoubtedly true, for anyone reasonably proficient with the keyboard and mouse, *if* the distance from the formula cell to the precedent is not too far. But the most common error in financial models is that of the pointing error – the wrong cell reference. If using cell references we should avoid typing them, but instead should point to the cell using either the mouse or keyboard. It is all too easy to click on the wrong cell, and it can be quite tricky to spot this mistake as it happens, particularly if the user is inexperienced or under time pressure. But although not impossible, it is quite difficult to use the wrong range name, and often such a mistake is immediately apparent on inspection of the formula. As the model increases in size, so too does the time spent scrolling up and down or across sheets, in the attempt to write a cell reference formula.

Poor Teaching

I have found that the subject of range names is often poorly explained. Many people are shown how to set up range names using the text at the start of the row. For example, the text 'total sales' is used to name the adjacent row (Figure 4.3).

First, Excel does not care much for the space between the words and substitutes in the underscore character total_sales, which looks scruffy. But second, and more importantly from a modelling perspective, we might have several 'total sales' lines, for example, one for each business unit or region. There is no differentiation between each one, and Excel will only allow one definition, so range names do not appear to offer any value. At this point most analysts dismiss range names altogether.

3	London
4	total sales
5	
6	Paris
7	total sales
8	
9	New York
10	total sales
11	
12	Total sales
13	

FIGURE 4.3   Row headings do not make sensible range names.

A Rule of Thumb

There is a trade-off between development time and model usage, and I would agree that certainly in a small model (e.g. the monthly management accounts) the use of range names is superfluous. My simple rule of thumb is that if you cannot see the item being referred to on screen, then it should be named, and the name must exist in the worksheet. I can think of examples of calculation blocks in which only the final line has an impact elsewhere in the model, so in this case it is only this line which requires a name.

The FAST Viewpoint

The subject of range names is the key distinction between the methodology described in this book and that promoted by the FAST Standard.[1] The authors of the FAST methodology are fundamentally opposed to the use of names, such that FAST 3.03-08 states, simply, 'Do not use Excel Names'. They do appear to accept that names may be used for external links (3.03-08.1), references for macros (3.03-08.2) or 'where non-local precedent references are warranted' (3.03-08.3); this latter principle is actually how we will be formulating our use of names in this chapter. The explanation given (in 4.03 Excel Names) is that:

> The FAST Modelling Standard advocates very limited use of Names, that is adherents to the Standard are generally against Names. Adherents of the FAST Modelling Standard believe that Names positively harm flexibility and transparency; benefits they may provide are often achievable through simpler techniques and design. In fact, Names are better (or only) suited to simple spreadsheets with limited complexity, where reading a simple natural language formula such as =Price*Quantity is a real possibility.

---

1. FAST Modelling Standard 01b 16.11.12 (http://www.fast-standard.org/document/FastStandard_01b.pdf).

The Principle

The underlying principle of using range names is that formulas are readable, as NLFs. Consider the following example:

```
Earnings before tax =Revenue-CostsOperating-InterestNet
```

If you are familiar with the concept of the earnings (or profits) before tax and you are familiar with the language it should not take too long to spot that I have left out depreciation.

Now consider this formula:

```
Earnings before tax =E16-E87-E114.
```

What's missing from this? In order to discover the missing reference, we need to inspect the other references first. Using the F2, Ctrl+[and auditing tools from Chapter X this shouldn't be too time-consuming, but this would only establish what has been included in the formula.

Name Conventions

Before going too much further with this exposition of range names, it is worth recognising that even in a relatively simple model you could end up with a couple of 100 range names. We should give some thought to how we will orga-nise the names in order to make them manageable, and to ensure that they have real meaning and conform to the 'natural language' approach. It may seem a daunting task to document each row of calculations with a distinct and mean-ingful name but the names support the row headings – they aren't some infernal creation, designed to confuse and obscure. If the row heading says expenditure, in the section for life cycle costs, then the range name will reflect this. We even find confirmation from the FAST modellers on this point: FAST 3.05-3 states that each line item must have a unique label.

I normally suggest the following naming convention:

```
CategoryDescriptionSubDescription...
```

For example

```
CostsFixedReal
CostsLabourHour
CostsVariableMoney
CostsOperating
```

Each of these names should match, as closely as possible, the headings at the start of the row. All of the above names are in the overall category of costs. Within this I have provided appropriate descriptions to differentiate one element from the other, and the name should be as long as it needs to be to allow for this. I have also written the names as compound words, with no spaces, with each component identified with an upper case letter. As noted above, Excel will sub-stitute the underscore _ character into any spaces, which works but looks untidy.

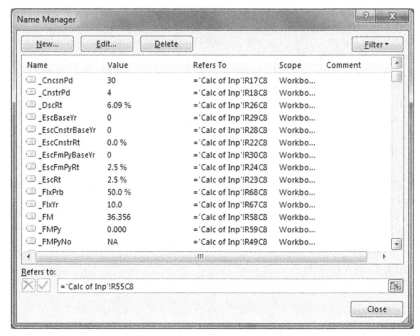

FIGURE 4.4 Some very poor range names.

Some people suggest that a full stop can be used in this context, for example, Costs.Variable.Unit (similar to the command syntax in Visual Basic for Applications, in Chapter 9). Excel does not allow the use of arithmetical operators in range names. Numbers cannot be used for names unless you prefix them with an underscore, but this is not recommended.

Avoid using names that could confuse or mislead, and use common sense if abbreviating or using acronyms. EBITDA is recognisably earnings before interest, tax, depreciation and amortisation, but would you recognise PCTCT as profits chargeable to corporation tax? What about TVA or MwSt[2]? Do not use range names that look like Excel functions, for example, SUM or NPV. This does not confuse Excel but may cause problems for your users. Avoid names such as Q1 and Q2 because these are also valid cell references. In fact, Excel will not allow you to do this, and will add a trailing underscore _ character to the name without telling you (Q1_ and Q2_), which can lead to trouble if you have not spotted it. An Excel workbook now has 16,384 columns and abbreviations such as PBT, PAT, GBP, TAX and USD potentially conflict with column headers. Excel will not allow certain characters to be used in names, for example the arithmetic operators +, −, *, /, and characters such as &, $, £. In each case, Excel will replace the invalid character with an underscore (Figure 4.4).

---

2. Taxe sur la Valeur Ajoutée and MehrwertSteuer respectively – French and German sales tax.

Range names must be unique. If you attempt to create a name that already exists on the same sheet, Excel will prompt you and offer the choice between going ahead with the new name and eliminating the earlier definition, or to stop and set up an alternative name for the current range. Think this one through if it should happen: any existing formulas containing the original name will automatically refer to the new definition. If you create a duplicate name on a different sheet, however, Excel will not provide any warning and will create something known as a local or sheet level name, which we will look at shortly.

The key point is to make sure your range names are meaningful, for use in NLFs. We use them so that we can write readable formulas in such a way that other users can understand our work. A logical and consistent approach will enhance this. And at any stage, if the existing name proves unsatisfactory, it is a simple operation to use Ctrl+H (Replace) and substitute in a new name.

Benefits

There are several further benefits of using range names. As a model is developed, it is likely that blocks of code are moved around, with rows being inserted or deleted as required. Cell reference formulas will still work, of course, but the references will be different, for example, you may have recognised that E45 is your Revenue line, so when it next appears as E63 you may have to spend a moment checking that this is correct. The range name Revenue, however, will remain unchanged regardless of where it is located.

I am often asked, fairly aggressively, 'How am I supposed to remember all the names'? There is a simple answer – you aren't, and why would you? I normally respond, 'Do you remember all your cell references'? As mentioned above, the range name is supported by the row heading. You can always use the F3 Name Manager dialog box to refresh your memory.

Reusable Code

Additionally, range names can be reused. The earnings before tax formula referred to above is the same in all of my models. The elements to which it refers, however, will be in different locations in each new model that I set up. But if I use range names I can simply copy and paste the formula from one workbook to the next. If the names in the formula do not exist in the new workbook, Excel will by default treat the names as absolute references and refer to the corresponding cells in the new workbook, until such time as the names are redefined. If the appropriate range names already exist in the new workbook, Excel will offer a choice between using the name as defined in the new workbook or using the name in the original file. The option exists to change the names in the source formula before pasting into the new workbook (Name Conflict). Given that over time, colleagues and users become familiar with your name conventions and the language used, new model development can become quite efficient as you reuse code from previous models.

The Certainty of Names

Range names offer considerable advantages in heavy duty modelling, large complex models perhaps with file links and with macros. Range names provide an element of certainty that cell references lack: if you need to prepare a monthly income statement derived from 14 business units you probably do not want to waste time hunting around the source files for the detail you require, when you know you need to pick up revenues, costs and so on. When running command sequences to pick up data from other files, the consistent use of names in the source files can allow for very effective data capture, where the use of cell referencing may be much less reliable – the insertion or deletion of a single row can wreck the process. Visual Basic for Applications (VBA) macros which are written using name ranges will be more robust, and of course the VBA code can be reused in new models (see Chapter 9).

One Dimension versus Two Dimension

Range names will be used consistently throughout this book. In the vast majority of examples you will see formulas written in the format =Revenue-CostsOperating. For this to work, the range Revenue must be a single row, or one dimensional (1-D) (or it could be a column). There are a few examples later of names referring to blocks of cells, described as two dimensional (2-D). The latter are not generally used for calculation purposes (except for look-up tables). This distinction between 1-D and 2-D leads us to the two methods for generating range names: Create and Define.

CREATING NAMES

It is a good practice to document your names in the workbook and this is easily achieved using the Create Names command. We have already considered the problem in using the row headings as potential names, in that the text down the left-hand side of the sheet is descriptive but also can be repetitive. Instead, put the names on the right-hand side of the range. In this way names are unique,

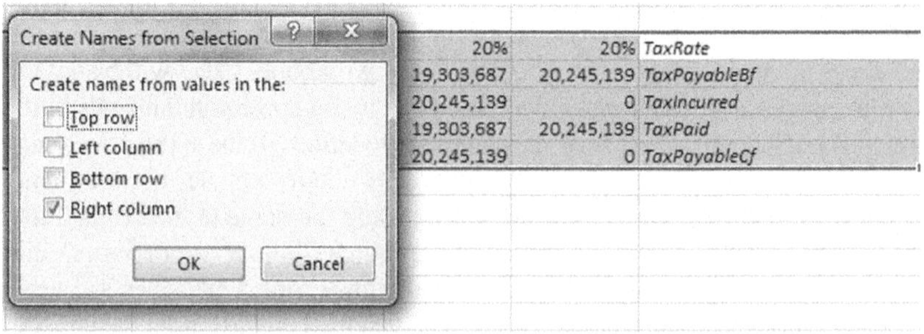

FIGURE 4.5 Names are created from text located at the edges of a range.

descriptive and immediately adjacent to the range to which they refer. Select the name and the cells and run the Formulas, Create from Selection command (or Ctrl+Shift+F3). This produces a simple dialog box (Figure 4.5):

Excel examines your selection and identifies that the names are in the right-hand column (using the simple assumption that this is the only text in the selection; values or formulas cannot be used as names). Click OK. In Chapter 2, we saw the Go to functionality of the Name Box and this can be used to confirm that the name has been created and to confirm the range. The Name Box can be widened as necessary. A further tip is to click and drag over a range of cells, and then inspect the Name Box. If Excel recognises the selected range, it will show the name in the box. Selecting an individual cell within a named range will result in the cell reference only appearing in the box.

It is possible to name individual cells as well as rows or columns. The name must be adjacent to the cell, and the usual Create Names command used. An individually named cell is effectively an absolute reference.

Create Names is not infallible: if you have selected multiple rows and names and there are several blank rows in the selection, Excel may fail to identify the position of the names and the dialog box is blank. You can help by selecting the appropriate check box. If you run the command and yet the name does not appear to have been created, check that you have selected both the row and the name. If you have a range which contains more rows than columns, Excel can get confused and it will offer to create names in both the top row and the right column. If you do not spot this, you will find that Excel creates a name from the text in the top right cell in the selection, and assigns it to the cells to the left and below. This is typically noticed when the name is used in a formula and returns the #VALUE! error, because one name is attempting to reference more than one cell (see below) (Figure 4.6).

An alternative to using names on the right-hand edge of the range is to set up an extra column on the left-hand side and put the names at the start of each row. This can be useful when your forecast period is very wide. Some users suggest hiding this column once it has been set up, but I prefer to keep it visible so that I can inspect names and ranges in the workbook.

I have referred to range names describing rows in both this and subsequent sections, but the same methods can be used in the context of columns.

FIGURE 4.6   Excel sometimes gets confused.

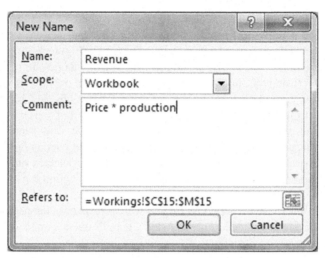

FIGURE 4.7   The Define Names dialog box.

Interestingly, the Undo command does not work for Create Names, but it does work for Define Name.

DEFINING NAMES

The Create Name method requires the range name to be written into a cell adjacent to the range to which it refers, which is an important element of documentation. The Define Name technique allows us to set up range names without writing them in the workbook, so for example you can use it to set up names for ranges such as, 'PrintArea' or 'BalanceSheet'. Define Names (Formulas, Define Names, Define Names) allows the definition of names for selected areas in the worksheet and also to define the scope of the name (workbook or sheet level, see below) (Figure 4.7). An interesting addition is the ability to provide a comment about a range name, for example, explaining what an abbreviation might mean, or what the underlying formula is doing. But because good practice recommends that names should be documented in the worksheet itself, range names should not be set up using this command, the point being that the defined name only exists in the Name Manager.

NAME MANAGER

This is a powerful feature which provides much useful information about the names in the workbook. Use the command sequence Formulas, Name Manager (or Ctrl+F3). Names are listed alphabetically and the values stored in the named cells are shown as an array. The source cell references are provided, along with the scope and any comments. Clicking on the category heading sorts the details in ascending or descending alphanumeric order. There is also

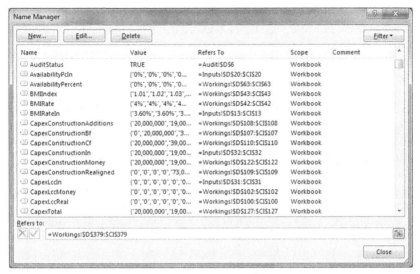

FIGURE 4.8   The Name Manager.

a filter tool which allows names to be ordered by scope or if they contain errors – a useful audit tool (Figure 4.8).

Names can be added to or deleted from the list (the only place where names can be deleted, in fact). Names can also be edited by double clicking, which launches a dialog box similar to the Define Names box, above. This editing technique should be used with caution: Excel will not only accept the revised name but will update all formulas which use the name. However if the name was set up using Create Names (i.e. written in the worksheet), the original name will remain in the cell.

USING NAMES

If we consider the Earnings before tax formula mentioned previously,

```
=Revenue-CostsOperating-DepreciationTotal-InterestNet
```

we need to understand what the names mean in this context. I have often encountered very strong criticism from the cell reference modellers who demand to know which Revenue is being referred to in the formula. There is a very simple answer: it is the cell at the intersection of the Revenue row with *this* column. If the model has been set up so that each column represents one year, then the revenue figure referred to is the revenue figure for that year. By virtue of the use of the range name, it cannot be the revenue for any other year.

In technical terms we might describe a range name as a vector (it has a magnitude and a direction). However Excel is able to interpret it as a scalar if the formula intercepts the direction. To understand this further, type the following formula into a cell: =3:3. This formula is a relative reference to row 3 – by omitting the column reference Excel assumes that this formula therefore refers to row 3 in *this* column, whatever this column actually is (and this is a very efficient way of writing code). A range name is a more meaningful way of setting up such references. An apparent vector formula such as =Revenue is read as the instruction to look up 'this column' to its intersection with the row called Revenue and to return the (scalar) value from that cell. This range/column intersection is as unique as its cell reference. If it is not on the current sheet Excel will then look in the same column on each sheet until it finds the correct, intersection, cell. This should emphasise the key modelling layout rule, that each column has the same function on each sheet. If you cannot guarantee the same layout and structure on each sheet in the workbook, you should avoid the use of range names from the outset.

If the formula is in a cell which does not have a corresponding name in the same column, the usual result is the #VALUE! error. Editing the cell will reveal that the formula is valid (the name is in upper case and in colour); but Ctrl+[(Go To Precedents) should reveal the problem.

All of this is fine, assuming that every formula you will write should refer to something in the same column. If, for any reason, you need to refer to something in a different column (e.g. a previous balance) you will need to use cell references, although we will consider the use of relative range names later on.

Having set up your range names, there are a number of ways of using them. First, you can type the names directly into your formulas. Tip: if you have created range names using the compound word with initial capitals convention (e.g. CostsOperating), try typing the formula in lower case:

```
=revenue-costsoperating-depreciationtotal-interestnet
```

If Excel recognises the names, you will find that it will capitalise and colour the names automatically:

```
=Revenue-CostsOperating-DepreciationTotal-InterestNet
```

If you get a #NAME! error, edit the cell and look for the name that has remained in lower case (or in black)

```
=Revenue-CostsOperating-deptotal-InterestNet
```

Individually Named Cells

A range name can be created, or defined, for an individual cell. Once this has been done, the cell reference will no longer appear in the Name Box when the cell is selected, only the name will be seen. The key feature of an individually named cell is that it is effectively used as an absolute reference. If we have a cell which contains the current GBP:Euro exchange rate and name it ExchangeRate, we can write =ExchangeRate anywhere in the workbook and it will return the single value.

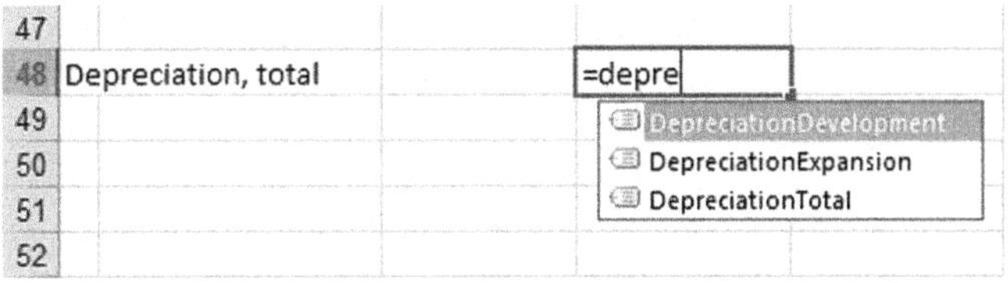

47		
48	Depreciation, total	=depre
49		
50		
51		
52		

FIGURE 4.9   Formula AutoComplete: use Tab to select the name from the list.

Paste Name

Another way to use names in formulas is to use the Formula, Use in Formula, Paste Names and selecting it from the list in the dialog box (the shortcut is F3). As the list of names can be quite long, you can type the first letter of the name you are looking for to scroll more rapidly through the list (if you are particularly fast on the keyboard, you can type several letters).

Formula AutoComplete

This a quick and effective way of using range names when writing formulas. If Formula AutoComplete is enabled, a drop-down list of functions and valid names appears whenever you write a formula. To select a name from the list, type part of the name and when the name appears in the list, use the arrow keys to select it and press the Tab key to paste it into the formula. For some users this feature can be quite irritating and it may have been disabled. The settings for Formula AutoComplete are in File, Options, Formulas, Formula AutoComplete (Figure 4.9).

Note that this is not Cell AutoComplete, the very irritating feature where Excel attempts to complete text entries.

Applying Names

As mentioned earlier, it is undoubtedly quicker to write some formulas using cell references, and it would be laborious indeed to then rewrite the formula using the appropriate names. To substitute names into cell reference formulas, use the Formula, Define Name, Apply Name command. Select the name to apply (Ctrl+click for multiple names) and Excel will scan through the worksheet and identify any cell references that correspond to named ranges, converting the references to names (Figure 4.10).

When using this command, we often find that Excel has automatically selected one or more names in the dialog box – this is not because Excel is intelligent enough to work out which names need to be applied, but simply because it remembers the last names that were created. Most of the time, we need to cherry-pick the relevant names from the list.

If, after running this command, the references have not been converted to names, check that the reference is to a cell in the same column (names work

FIGURE 4.10   Applying names to existing cell reference formulas.

on the principle that the reference is to the intersection of the current column with the named row), or that the reference is not to another sheet, for example, =Inputs!E5 will not be converted to Inflation In even if that is the correct name to substitute, because of the sheet name in the formula. In this case it will have to be updated manually. Also, the column/range name intersection idea was illustrated above using the =3:3 referencing technique; Apply Names will not work here either.

Editing Range Names

Sometimes a name needs to be changed, for example, Revenue should be Turnover. More commonly we recognise that typing mistakes happen at any time, regardless of the modelling methodology, and a misspelled range name is as likely as a misspelled row heading. There are a number of ways to manage this. Using the Create Names technique, the (misspelled) name is in the worksheet. Assuming the name has already been used in formulas, follow these steps:

1. Locate the name and range in the worksheet.
2. Use the Name Manager (Ctrl+F3) to delete the name from the list. This should produce #NAME? errors.

3. In the worksheet, type in the correct name for the range and rename the range (Ctrl+Shift+F3).
4. Use the Replace command (Home, Find & Select, Replace or Ctrl+H), entering the old name as the Find what string, and the new name as the Replace with string. Choose OK.
5. Repeat step 4 on other sheets as required. Check that the #NAME? errors have now disappeared.

The benefit of this approach is that the new name is correctly documented in the workbook. This is an example of the 'Break and Make' technique – an error has appeared in the workbook but we know the cause. Only by following the correct steps will the error disappear, however we can get a sense of the impact of the amendment and assurance about the resolution of the error.

The alternative is to use the Name Manager:

1. Open the Name Manager (Ctrl+F3).
2. Locate and select the target name in the name list.
3. Click on the Edit button.
4. Type in the new name and choose OK.

Excel will update all dependent formulas with the new name.

This method does not generate any #NAME? errors, nor does it change the original name next to the named range. The extent of the change to the name is not as apparent as with the first method.

Deleting Names

Good practice suggests that you should delete misspelled or redundant range names at the earliest opportunity, and is based on the technique for editing names. The Name Manager (Ctrl+F3) is the only way to delete range names.

If the deleted name has already been used in a formula, the #NAME? error value appears. Use F2 to examine the formula; invalid names will be shown in black. To debug this issue further use the audit tricks from Chapter 2 to locate and fix the problem, or use Ctrl+H (Replace) to substitute a new or corrected name for the deleted name.

Use the usual Ctrl- and Shift-clicking techniques to select multiple names for deletion.

Removing Names

It is reasonably common for me to work on a model development project with a client, only to have them reject the use of range names, usually at a late stage. Although it is a simple operation to convert references to names (Apply Names), Excel offers no functionality to revert names to references. A manual rewrite of the formulas is a time-consuming and difficult exercise.

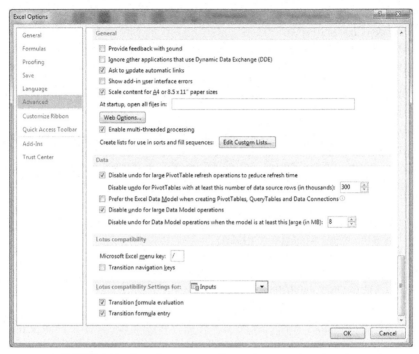

FIGURE 4.11   A cumbersome way of removing names from formulas.

There is one rather messy way in which we can solve this problem. Lotus 1-2-3 was a spreadsheet application that dominated the market in the early 1990s. Although Lotus 1-2-3 used range names, it did not have the same ability to identify the intersection of the column containing the range reference with the named row. Excel was deliberately designed to contain functionality that would help users make the transition from 1-2-3, and so we can take advantage of this to force Excel to behave like its former competitor. Assuming that we have a model containing formulas using range names, we can use File, Options, Advanced, scroll right to the bottom to locate the Lotus compatibility settings to switch on Transition formula entry, note the options for sheet or workbook level (Figure 4.11).

Identify a cell containing a range name formula and press F2. No difference. Press Enter, and then edit the cell again. The range names have now been converted to cell references for the whole of the named range, although you will notice that the formula bar reveals that the names are still there. Tidy up the formula so that the references are to the formula column, and copy across the row. Repeat as required for each formula. When complete, repeat the Transition sequence and deselect the Transition formula entry box. Both the formula bar and F2 show that the names have now been removed (Figure 4.12).

Assuming that we have followed the left-to-right consistency rule, we need only carry out this operation on the left-hand formulas and then copy across

7	Oil price				
8	real terms ($/barrel)	75	75	75	75
9	money terms	77.25	79.57	81.95	84.41
10					
11	Oil production				
12	production (barrels per day)	0	4000	4000	6000
13	production days	365	365	365	365
14	annual production	0	1,460,000	1,460,000	2,190,000
15					
16	Revenue	=D14:M14*D9:M9		119,653,607	184,864,822
17					

FIGURE 4.12   The formulas resulting from the 1-2-3 remove names trick.

					new columns			
0.0	8.4	14.5	21.0	30.7		=H9		OpeningBalance
16.6	13.2	13.7	17.3	15.5			14.7	Income
8.2	7.1	7.2	7.6	8.0			8.2	Expenditure
8.4	14.5	21.0	30.7	38.2	▼	▼	44.7	ClosingBalance

FIGURE 4.13   A formula problem from inserting new columns.

when complete. You will now need to use the Name Manager command to delete the unwanted or redundant names.

Extending Ranges

A mild criticism of named ranges is that if the range is extended (extra columns or rows are added), the name may or may not recognise this. It is relatively easy to work around this. If the new columns are inserted from the edge of the working area, then the named ranges do not change. If the new columns are inserted inside the working area, then the range names will expand accordingly. Tip: whether you are using range names or cell references, take care when inserting new columns. Any formula that referred to the previous column will now skip the new columns. Copy the formulas from the last working column to the new edge of the workbook (Figure 4.13).

Moving Named Ranges

During model development, it is not uncommon to restructure sections of the model. If named ranges are to be moved, we should make sure that the entire range is selected, including the name. If we then Ctrl+X Cut and Ctrl+V Paste, the cells and the name will move to the new location. If only part of the range is moved, the range name will refer to the original location. The same applies if we copy and paste ranges and appropriate caution should be exercised when writing dependent formulas, to ensure that they are not referencing the original ranges.

Names and Functions

Range names can cause problems if used with some Excel functions and it is appropriate to consider this now, in advance of Chapter 4, although you may wish to refer to that chapter in this context. There are several array functions (MAX, MIN, COUNT, SUM, AVERAGE, etc.) which, by definition, are designed to operate on a range of cells, so if a range name is used as an argument, the function will act on that range. For example, =MIN(CashAvailable) will, quite rightly, return the smallest value in the range called CashAvailable, regardless of which column contains the formula. But if I need to return, say, the smaller of this year's available cash compared to my annual debt repayment, the following formula would give me unexpected results:

=MIN(CashAvailable, DebtRepayment)

Instead of returning the smaller of this year's cash or repayment, the MIN returns the smallest value from both ranges. The principle is that CashAvailable and DebtRepayment are treated as arrays (or vectors). Instead of the individual cells in the formula column, they are evaluated in their entirety. For example, if they are both 10 cells wide, the MIN algorithm solves for the smallest of the 10 Cash Available values and the smallest of the 10 DebtRepayment values – 20 values in all, rather than the two we might have expected from our previous understanding of how names work in formulas.

In order for us to use these functions and benefit from range names, we need to provide some extra detail. If I wrote =CashAvailable, Excel would have no problem, because it would return the CashAvailable value from this column. If I rewrite the formula slightly, =0+CashAvailable, this calculation works as well. But if I now substitute the calculations into the original formula, I discover that it now works:

=MIN(0+CashAvailable,0+DebtRepayment)

F2 now reveals that Excel has gone back to the (scalar) column intersections as expected. The reason for this is that Excel does not read formulas and functions from left to right, it applies the rules of arithmetic priority and in this example, it evaluates the contents of the brackets first. So it carries out the two calculations as they are written, and it then passes the results to the MIN algorithm to process. However, adding 0 to a range name does not look too clever, so Excel shows a glimmer of intelligence in allowing us a final trick – omit the 0. The final formula is:

=MIN(+CashAvailable,+DebtRepayment)

Do not omit the comma (argument separator) – we are not adding the two values together. Use the +range name technique for any array type functions. The clue that this amendment is required is that usually (but not always) on writing the formula and copying across the row you get the same result in each cell.

This is not a bug fix, as several writers have suggested. Array functions read range names as arrays; we wish to use range names as individual references, and we now have an elegant solution.

ADDITIONAL NAME FUNCTIONALITY

The previous sections introduced the key name concepts and techniques, sufficient for most routine modelling purposes. The following sections describe additional techniques which are less commonly used.

Combination Names

You can assemble nonadjacent ranges using range names, which can be useful for printing and other purposes. This method will only work if all the named ranges are on the same sheet. For example, I could assemble the ranges `BalanceSheet`, `IncomeStatement` and `CashFlow`, into a single range called `FinancialStatements`. To do this, set up the individual names first using Define Names. Then return to the Define Name dialog box and type in the new name. In the Refers to section, type an equal sign followed by the names separated by commas. Click OK. Tip: if you type the names in lower case you should see them convert to upper case as appropriate.

Combination names can be a little difficult to use. If you press F5, you will not see them listed, but if you type the name, Excel will happily highlight the source ranges as required, which is a very handy way of selecting multiple ranges. You can perform calculations on combination names and this is very useful for summary calculations (`SUM`, `COUNT`, `AVERAGE`, etc.).

Combination names can be used for printing: use the Page Layout, Page Setup launcher, then select the Sheet tab in the Print area box, type in the combination name (or use F3 Paste Name). If you next select Print Preview, you will see that if the source names are not physically adjacent to each other in the workbook, Excel will put a page break between them.

Intersection Formulas

It goes without saying that cell `C1` is the intersection between column `C` and row `1` and provides a unique reference. If we have row and column names, we can repeat the trick with range names. If we had a column named `London` and a row called `Sales`, I could write a reference to the `London Sales` cell in the following way:

```
=London Sales
```

In case you have not spotted it, there is a space or 'intersection operator' between the two names. As this intersection is as unique as a cell reference, there is no requirement to write the formula in the same row or column as the named ranges. If it turns out that there is no intersection between the row and the column, Excel will return the #NULL! error. I include this short paragraph on intersection formulas out of completeness; I do not find them particularly useful.

Sheet Level or Local Names

If you set up a range name using Create or Define, the name is described as a global name; which is described as the scope of the name. Provided you are in the correct column, you can write a formula on any sheet referring to a name and Excel will return the appropriate value. As we also noted earlier, if on creating a name, Excel spots that the name already exists on the same sheet, it will warn you. If, however, the duplicate name is on a different sheet, you will receive no warning at all. When you come to use the name in a formula, you may be baffled to find that the name does not return the value you expect. For example, if the original name (e.g. Revenue) was on sheet 1, the duplicate on sheet 2, you will find that the formula =Revenue on sheet 3 refers to the sheet 1 version, always. Ctrl+[(Go To Precedents) will also select the sheet 1 reference. However, writing =Revenue on sheet 2 results in the sheet 2 value. To pick up the sheet 2 value on the third sheet you would need to type the sheet name prefix, as =Sheet1!Revenue. This is a local or sheet level name. Let us assume, in the first instance, that this was a genuine error.

If you have a look in the Name Manager (Ctrl+F3), you will find that the duplicate name has the sheet name showing in the scope list. If this is the case, you can simply use the Delete button in the Name Manager to remove the name.

However, you may wish to set up sheet level names deliberately. If we have a workbook in which each sheet represents a separate business unit, it may be appropriate to have the same layout and the same names on each sheet (e.g. Revenue and Costs). This can be done quite simply by setting up one sheet first with all the headings, formulas and names required. Then copy the sheet (Ctrl+click and drag the sheet tab) as many times as is required. Because the same names occur on each sheet, Excel sets up sheet level names for the duplicates. The formulas use the sheet level names, and if you wish to write further formula you can do so.

The original sheet contains the global names, and this sheet should be deleted if not required. The now-redundant global range names should be deleted using the Name Manager (note that if the original sheet has been deleted these should all have #REF! values). To then summarise the figures from each sheet onto a main report, write the appropriate formulas but this time using the sheet name prefix for each name, for example:

```
=South!Sales+North!Sales+East!Sales+West!Sales
```

Problems can arise if you mix and match global and local names. For example, if I fail to delete the source sheet in the exercise above, in addition to the local

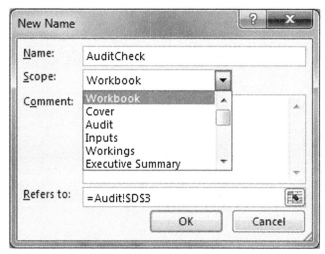

FIGURE 4.14 Defining a sheet level or local name.

names `South!Sales`, `North!Sales`, etc., I still have the original global `Sales`. If I attempt to include it in a formula using its own sheet name, for example:

`=Original!Sales+South!Sales+...`

Excel pulls an odd little trick by substituting the filename for the sheet name:

`=consolidatedsales.xls!Sales+South!Sales+...`

Not very helpful.

To create a sheet level name without copying names from other sheets, we use the Formulas, Define Name, Define Name command and set the scope to the relevant sheet. A name must be unique within its scope (Figure 4.14).

Three-Dimensional or Cross-Sheet Names

It is possible to set up range names which refer to elements on different sheets, which would be useful for consolidations, but in practice little else. In this example, we have three sheets which have exactly the same layout but represent the profit and loss statements for three business units.

1. If necessary, add a summary sheet at the start.
2. Use Define Names (Alt+M, M, D) and type in the range name.
3. In the Refers to box, delete the existing suggestion.
4. Click on the first sheet tab in the range, hold down Shift and click on the last sheet tab. Then click on the cell to be named.
5. Repeat steps 1–3 for each 3-D name.

Test that the 3-D names work by using the SUM function on the summary sheet.

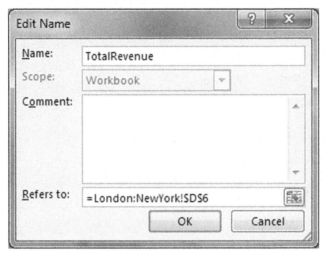

FIGURE 4.15   Defining a 3-D names.

I am not particularly enthusiastic about 3-D names because the standard audit/ go to functionality does not work: neither Ctrl+[or F5 will show the precedent cells. Also, if they are to be used at all they should be used for a single dimension – as with naming rows as one row high and several columns across, and columns as one column wide and several rows in length, the 3-D range should be one cell drilling down through each sheet. If multiple cells are named, Excel will make no attempt to use the column matching principle from earlier on; and a SUM function will return the value of the sum of all cells in the range, regardless of which column the SUM is copied to. Likewise, the reference must be to the same cell on each sheet – we cannot have a 3-D name which refers to E16 on one sheet and E20 on the next. Finally, 3-D names must be defined, they cannot be created, and therefore are unlikely to be documented in the spreadsheet (Figure 4.15).

Relative Names

I pointed out previously that we can be very comfortable using range names once we understand that they can only refer to the intersection of the named range with the current column: if your formula in column E reads Revenue, then we know with absolute certainty that the Revenue figure is also that for column E – it cannot be anything else. Hopefully, as far as your modelling goes, that will be the case.

But you may encounter relative names. An example of this might be where I set up a routine that begins with an opening balance, which is by my definition would be a link to the previous closing balance (this is the corkscrew technique, in the next chapter). Because the previous balance is in the previous column, a normal range name would not be allowed. However, we could set up a range called PreviousBalance using the Name Manager.

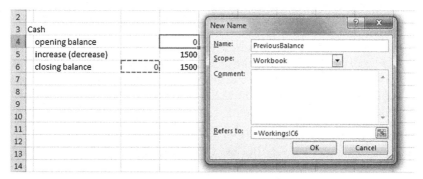

FIGURE 4.16   Setting up a relative name.

1. Select a cell in the opening balance row, and press Ctrl+F3.
2. Select New. Type in the name `PreviousBalance`, then click in the Refers to box and delete any reference.
3. In the worksheet, click on the actual previous balance cell and note the absolute reference that then appears in the dialog box. The trick here is to press F4 (Absolute) three times until the $ signs disappear. Then click OK.

Now rewrite the opening balance formula using the new name. It should work – if you press F2, Excel should highlight the previous balance. Now try using F5 Go To and choose `PreviousBalance` as the destination. What happens? You should find that it is always relative to the current cell, whether or not it is actually the previous balance at all. In this example, `PreviousBalance` is always two cells below and one the left of the active cell (Figure 4.16).

If your colleagues or users are new to range names they are unlikely to thank you for using relative names and in any case I suggest that relative names are best avoided.

Mixed Absolute and Relative Names

Accumulated depreciation is an example of a rolling total type of calculation, where in this case we need to add up all the depreciation previously charged up to and including the current period. You will probably know that the cell reference version of the formula is:

```
=SUM($E80:E80)
```

As the formula is copied across the row, the `$E80` reference is fixed, and the relative reference changes. To achieve the same effect with range names, try the following:

1. Name the row as required using Create Names (Ctrl+Shift+F3).
2. Write the formula required in the appropriate row. Copy across the row and ignore the result.
3. Move to the first formula in this row.

4. Use the Name Manager (Ctrl+F3) and select the name and click the Edit button.
5. In the Refers to box, amend the reference so that it only refers to the first cell in the range and make it column absolute, then delete the $ signs (F4) from the second reference to make a relative reference (e.g. $E80:E80). Tip: you may need to press F2 when editing the reference.
6. Choose OK.

Test that it works (Figure 4.17).

This technique is not very flexible and may result in unexpected circularities. If you copy the formula to another row, Excel will include the cells between the formula and the original named range. The use of F5 Go To will highlight the potential problems of this technique.

Naming Values and Formulas

Take, for example, this afternoon's exchange rate between sterling and the euro. I should write it into my model, appropriately named. Instead, I shall use Define Names. I shall use a plausible name, such as ExchangeRateGBPEuro, but instead of referring to a specific cell or range, in the Refers to section of the dialog box I type the value. I can now amend my currency calculations by multiplying by my new exchange rate, but nobody can see it in the workbook (Figure 4.18).

Even worse, using F5, ExchangeRateGBPEuro returns an invalid reference. Where is the exchange rate? The only way to check is to inspect the Name Manager dialog, or to use the F9 trick from Chapter 2. It may be that you can think of a moral reason for hiding key values such as this, but a good practice suggests that all values used in the model should be both easily visible in the worksheet and properly documented.

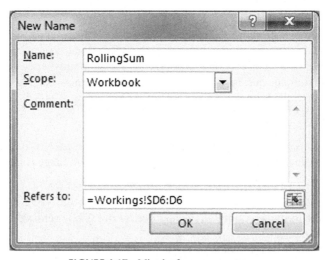

FIGURE 4.17   Mixed reference range name.

We can slide further into the ethical abyss by naming formulas. In this case, you can use the Name Manager, New name to set up names for formulas which are entered into the Refers to section of the dialog box. It is not quite as straight-forward as it could be – a formula such as GrossProfit which is made up of Sales-Costs will return the same value if copied across the row, because Excel only uses the left-hand cell from each of Sales and Costs. However, if you write the named formula using cell references it should work – make sure you use relative cell addresses.

Dynamic Range Names

Returning to the issue of having named ranges grow or shrink as data are added or deleted, it is possible to solve this using expanding or dynamic range names. This needs some careful thought, but is worth exploring. It may be helpful to refer to the section on the OFFSET and Lookup functions in Chapter 6.

Let us create a chart based on a series of sales figures. We would like to add the sales figures for each week as they become available, but we do not want to have to keep updating the chart. Because of the open-ended nature of the exercise, it would be sensible to put the range name in a column to the left of the figures, rather than on the right as usual.

What we would like to do is to automatically increase this range as the figures are updated.

1. We can use the COUNT function to return the number of values in the row (COUNTA would include the text in the headings).
2. We can use the OFFSET function to define a range that starts in the first cell in the row and ends *n* cells further on, where *n* is the value returned by COUNT. If COUNT increases, the OFFSET reads further across the row.

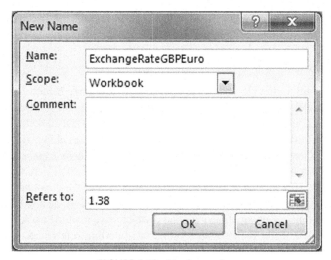

FIGURE 4.18   Naming a value.

3. We combine the two functions in the Name Manager, New name dialog box.
4. The syntax is: =OFFSET(SheetName!$D$34,,,,COUNT($34:$34)) (note the four commas, further explanation below).
5. Set up a chart, based on the existing range. Use the Chart Tools, Design (JC), Select Data commands to specify that both the Chart date range and the Series values are derived from the named range. Remember to include the sheet reference otherwise Excel will complain, because once you click OK it substitutes in the current cell references for the range.

Now add new data and test to see that the range has updated.

The COUNT function is used to count the number of values in row 34 (in this example). We do not know how many values this will eventually contain, and this referencing looks at the entire row. Make sure the referencing is absolute ($34:$34).

The OFFSET function uses $D$34 as its starting point and reads off the number of cells in the row identified by the COUNT. As further cells are added, the COUNT increases and the range expands. Note the four commas – these are placeholders for arguments that are not relevant here but are explained further in Chapter 6. In simple terms, the COUNT returns the argument for the width of the range.

The dynamic name functionality is useful in the context of the sales chart exercise used here, and in the topic such as lookup tables, where it is important that if new data are added to the table, its definition must be updated.

Dynamic names are useful when data are being added. If you start deleting data, specifically from the left-hand edge of the range, the COUNT value falls and the OFFSET does not read across the full range. You can solve this by changing the start point cell reference, for example, $D$34 could be changed to $H$34 to exclude the first four weeks. Make sure that the redundant values are then deleted.

Dynamic range names are of interest to the modeller but they bring in the ambiguity inherent in the use of OFFSET. Although F5 Goto is effective, F2, Ctrl+[and the auditing tools are a little vague in identifying the cells in use, because of the full row referencing used in the COUNT function.

Listing Names

It can be useful to provide your users with a list of the range names you have set up in the model. Select a cell on your inputs or documentation sheet, and use the Formulas, Use in Formula, Paste Names command (or F3) and click the Paste List button. Excel lists all your range names in alphabetical order, along with their cell references. There are a couple of useful tricks you can pull here: a quick scan down the list will show you any names that refer to deleted ranges, as they will refer to #REF!. You can use the Name Manager to then delete any of these redundant names. But we can also use the list to answer two important questions: do any names refer to blank references, and are there any ranges which have multiple names?

If you look at the list of names and corresponding references, you might ask yourself how Excel has actually provided the cell references. It displays what is apparently a formula (e.g.) =Workings!$E$4:$K$4. It is possible to do this manually, if you prefix the formula with an apostrophe. But if you look carefully you will see that Excel has not done this. If you now edit the cell and press Enter, you will either return a #VALUE! error or a value, depending on the column. If you then use the Ctrl+[Go To Precedents shortcut, you will highlight the source range. (Note that you must edit the cell first; this method does not work whilst Excel is displaying the cell references.)

Empty Ranges

To use this method to locate empty ranges, try the following sequence:

1. Paste the name list onto the workings or calculation sheet.
2. F2 Edit each of the cell references.
3. Select all the references.
4. Press Ctrl+[Go To Precedents.
5. Press F5 Go To Special, and select Blanks.
6. Using the Fill Color palette to apply a background colour.
7. Browse the sheet for any coloured cells.
8. Select any cells that you find, and check the name that appears in the Name Box (assuming the original name text has been deleted from the sheet already).
9. Use the Name Manager (Ctrl+F3) to delete the name from the list. You may wish to Ctrl+F Home, Find & Select, or Ctrl+] the name first, in case it has been used in a formula.
10. Repeat as required.

Record the results on the audit sheet, if necessary.

Multiple Names

We can use the name list to locate multiple names used for a range. This typically occurs when a name has been misspelled and then corrected, without having then deleted the misspelled name. However it can also occur during the early stages of a model's development, before a naming convention has been agreed, and the names already in use are then replaced with new names. This can lead to a lot of confusion.

1. F3 Paste List onto any sheet.
2. Do not edit the cell references.
3. The names are listed alphabetically, so we use the Home, Sort & Filter command to sort the references into ascending order.
4. In the column adjacent to the references, write a logical formula to test if the range reference is the same as the one in the cell below, for example: =E10=E11.
5. Copy the formula down the column. Unique references will return FALSE.

OilPriceForecast	=Workings!$D$20:$M$20	FALSE
TaxLossIncurred	=Workings!$D$200:$M$200	FALSE
TaxLossUsed	=Workings!$D$201:$M$201	FALSE
TaxLossCf	=Workings!$D$202:$M$202	FALSE
PCTCT	**=Workings!$D$204:$M$204**	**FALSE**
TaxAmountSubjectToTax	**=Workings!$D$204:$M$204**	**TRUE**
TaxRate	=Workings!$D$207:$M$207	FALSE
TaxPayableBf	=Workings!$D$208:$M$208	FALSE
TaxIncurred	=Workings!$D$209:$M$209	FALSE
OilPriceReal	=Workings!$D$21:$M$21	FALSE
TaxPaid	=Workings!$D$210:$M$210	FALSE

FIGURE 4.19   Using Paste List to locate multiple names for a range.

6. You can write a function to count the number of TRUE values: =COUNTIF(list of references, TRUE).
   Obviously, if this returns 0, then no further work is required.
7. Locate all TRUE values and identify the problem names; correct using the Name Manager.

Record the results on the audit sheet, if necessary (Figure 4.19).

External Name References

Paste List also allows you to identify names that refer to other files. We noted in Chapter 3 that this is not the best practice but in some cases is unavoidable. The name list will include the references to other files as file link formula. These can be easily located if you use Ctrl+F (Find) and search for the square brackets [or], back slash/or for the string '.xlsx'. Alternatively we can sort the list of names by the cell reference column and browse through the addresses.

It should be noted that Paste List will not list sheet level names that have been defined on other sheets. Nor does it differentiate between sheet level and global names.

Phantom File Links

It is not uncommon to find a model that generates the file link update dialog box when opened, but a search through the workbook fails to identify any file link formulas. One potential cause is that there are range names which are them-selves file link formulas, even if the name isn't being used in the spreadsheet. These names can be located using the Name Manager; once deleted the problem should go away.

Chapter 5

Mainly Formulas

INTRODUCTION

The purpose of this chapter is not to show you how to write formulas in the first place, but to consider ways in which you can set them out more clearly and which will conform to the principle of error reduction. One of the concerns we have about writing calculations is what I call the 'intellectual challenge' approach: the attempt to solve modelling problems in the least amount of space, usually a single cell. The results are formulas of bewildering length and complexity, which require considerable time and effort to understand, and are difficult to audit and review. We have all done it – we have spent some time trying to solve a problem and in so doing we have created a monster of a formula, which takes up four lines on the formula bar and has six closing brackets (along with a statistically increased risk of error). And then we look back at the formula a week or so later and amaze ourselves that we were so clever, because we are not quite sure how (or why) we did it.

There are a number of articles and websites whose authors recommend this approach. In almost every case I would urge caution, because long, complex calculations are challenging to read, and the operational research suggests that the longer the formula, the less chance of it being either read correctly or understood. If the reviewer or user is unable to understand a formula, we are failing to give them the confidence they need to rely on the results of the model. We can still tackle complex problems, but by breaking the task into manageable steps, using as much of the worksheet as required. It may appear more time consuming, but the logic is simply expressed and should be easy to follow. We have 1,048,576 rows per sheet in Excel – an awful lot of real estate into which to break down and spread out the calculations.

This chapter explores ways in which we can make formulas simpler to understand and the next chapter considers how functions can be used in this context, although I have included the use of a handful of functions in this chapter to help illustrate the use of particular techniques. A good modeller should be familiar with the use of corkscrews, logical masks, counters, switches and flags; all of which individually should be simple formulas, but in combination allow us to perform very complex tasks.

In many cases we will be using range names as introduced in the previous chapter. Conforming to the overall purpose of the book, the intention is to encourage you to reflect on alternative practice in the light of these suggestions.

I am confident that you would be able to generate additional solutions to the problems and issues that follow. Even if you reject my solutions, you will have greater confidence in your own modelling abilities.

BODMAS OR PEMDAS

Brackets, order (power), division, multiplication, addition and subtraction, or in the United States, parentheses, exponents, multiplication, division, addition and subtraction: the principle of arithmetic priority, or the order of operations. The key point is that Excel doesn't read formulas from left to right. One of the ideas promoted in this and the following chapters is to keep formulas short – the longer the formula, the more chance we have of running into a Bodmas error. A simple example: `=1+2*3` gives the result as 7, and `=(1+2)*3` is 9. In the formula `=1+(2*3)` the brackets are redundant. From long experience I find that some analysts will use the brackets in long formulas as we might use the comma in a long sentence, simply to make it more readable. However the use of brackets this way will change the order in which Excel will solve the calculation, which leads to errors (and which can be very difficult to spot). Generally the use of brackets around each 'clause' is helpful, but in more complex examples I often recommend breaking the formula into a number of smaller calculations. It may seem time consuming and an insult to the intelligence, but I've seen too many megaformulas in my time which contain simple Bodmas errors. This is a real formula from our archive:

```
=IF(SUMIF(Assumpt!$F$884:$BL$884,ConstrPADCo!DZ$2,Assumpt!
$F$1261:$ID$1261)=0,IF(DZ208,IF(AND(DZ208=1,EA208=0),
-DY217,PPMT((1+DZ212)^DZ$30-1,SUM($F208:DZ208),
$D208,$D210)),0),MIN(MAX(IF(DZ208,IF(AND(DZ208=1,EA208=0),
-DY217,PPMT((1+DZ212)^DZ$30-1,SUM($F208:DZ208),$D208,
$D210)),0),-SUMIF(Assumpt!$F$817:$BL$817,DZ$2,Assumpt!$F$1262:
$BL$1262)/CtnP-DZ214-DZ278-DZ323),0))
```

TIMING

The management of timing is one of the most important aspects of cash flow forecasting models. Apart from simple calculator-type models, which contain sequences of single calculations which are time independent, most models will have some period of time under analysis, either as historical data or forecast assumptions. As introduced in Chapter 1, the first rule that applies is that the time periods must be consistent across each sheet (the same column has the same function on each sheet), and we should use the same periodicity on each sheet in the workbook. This is simple in concept, but in practice it can be difficult to apply, particularly in relation to managing multiple periodicities, such as quarterly and annual reports. There are a whole series of time-related problems, including the timing of cash flows, the timing of discounting (or compounding).

The timing or duration of certain events is uncertain, with difficulties in writing dependent formulas. We have events such as capital expenditure that trigger time-limited formulas such as depreciation (with a fixed life), but the depreciation only begins once the asset is put into use. Working capital and sales tax, repayment periods, interest payments, reserve accounts, all have timing implications. In the following section, we will consider various techniques which help us work around some of the inherent difficulties in writing robust, time-dependent calculations.

The following techniques can be used to manage this type of problem, based on the key principle that the timing of any event or phase in the forecast period is driven by the input only.

Time Dependency and Time Independency

One of the issues to consider is whether a value will change over time. If it is a constant in the sense that it remains unchanged over time, for example, the depreciation life, then it is described as time independent. If it is likely to change then it is time dependent. I normally reserve column C or D to hold time-independent inputs, and time-dependent inputs are entered across the forecast period. In some models this distinction may be so important as to merit separate inputs sheets.

On the workings sheet we may assume that the forecast period calculations are based on time-dependent inputs. Some calculations may refer to time-independent constants (entered in the base column, below). There are also time-independent formulas, such as results like the net present value or internal rate of return, or the debt ratios. These are based on the forecast cash flows but return single results, and again I would put them in column C or D.

Left-to-Right Consistency

One of the fundamental rules of models that involve more than one period is that each row should have only one formula, and this was briefly introduced, along with its corresponding audit check, in Chapter 2. Consider a discounted cash flow scenario in which we are considering investing in a new production facility. The investment will probably take place in the third and fourth quarters of this financial year. The accounting rule is that the new asset will not be depreciated until it is put into use, in the first quarter of the next financial year. We need not consider the depreciation treatment in detail, but we need to recognise that for the first two quarters of the analysis there should be no depreciation, and that it should kick in after that. It might be tempting to leave the first two cells in the depreciation line blank; after all, there is no need for a calculation. But what happens if we decide to bring the project forward – on the inputs side the management will type the investment figures in the appropriate cells, but they are then required to locate and update the depreciation formula. The same problems arise if we defer the expenditure – the onset of depreciation should also be delayed. We should avoid users having to update formulas, however well-intentioned.

The modelling rule is that the formula for depreciation must be the same all the way across the forecast period. We need the same formula for the period before depreciation starts, for the duration of the life of the asset, and the same formula must handle the period after the asset has been fully depreciated, with no user intervention required. We will explore techniques to solve this problem in the sections which follow.

Base Column

To adhere to the rule of left-to-right consistency, we need to recognise that some formulas would almost by definition need to be different, in particular the first cell of a row. For example, consider a simple inflation compounding formula that takes the previous value and multiplies it by the current inflation rate:

```
=E5*(1+InflationRate)
```

This works fine when copied across the row, but only if there is a value of 1 in D5 to start off the logic. However, we cannot type this into E5 as this is in the forecast period and breaches the rule about the hardcoded values in the workings area. Furthermore, perhaps D5 itself should be an escalation value, for example, 1.03. This causes a further problem, because the value of 1.03 is dependent on inflation having a value of 3% in the time period represented by column E. If this value changes, the hardcoded 1.03 will not reflect this. It might be tempting to simply write =1*(1+InflationRate) in this first cell, but then again we breach the left-to-right consistency rule.

This problem is solved using a base column. The purpose of this additional column at the left-hand edge of the forecast area is that it handles such initialisation values and other numbers that may be required for formulas but without breaching the left-to-right consistency rule, nor that of having hardcoded values in the calculations area. The values in the base column are not inputs as such and are not variables, in that their value will not change. They are simply there to make the formulas work (Figure 5.1).

Another way of using the base column is to recognise that it falls outside the forecast area as such, and can be described as the 'now' or 'current' column. In

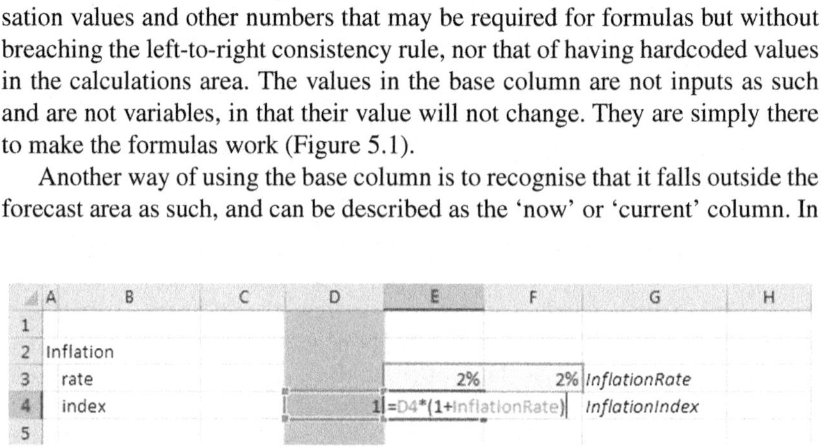

⊿	A	B	C	D	E	F	G	H
1								
2	Inflation							
3	rate				2%	2%	*InflationRate*	
4	index			1	=D4*(1+InflationRate)		*InflationIndex*	
5								

FIGURE 5.1 Column D acts as the base column.

this way it can handle time-independent information, such as the depreciation life of an asset, which will not vary over the forecast period. Also, it can be used to store genuine current information, such as the actual current value of an asset, which then feeds into the forecast calculations. In some types of modelling, for example, company valuation, we may need multiple base columns, which in this case would handle one or more years of historic data (Figure 5.2).

Corkscrew

This is a very simple technique which will be used in material in the following chapters. It allows us to pass information from one period to the next. It can be illustrated using the example of a simple bank account. At the start of the period we have an opening balance, we then deposit funds into the account, and we make withdrawals. At the end of the period we have a closing balance, which becomes the opening balance for the next period. We call it a corkscrew because if we run a Trace Dependents audit check on the code, we see a zigzag as the balances are carried/brought forward (Figure 5.3).

When we set up this routine we note that without exception, the opening balance formula is a simple cell reference to the previous balance – it is never a calculation, and it never contains a range name (why not? See Chapter 4). In the first period, this means that it is looking outside the forecast period proper, which is why we use the base column. However, it is a cardinal modelling rule that formulas must never refer blank cells, so we initialise with a value of 0 for the closing balance in the base column.

	A	B	C	D	E	F	G	H
1								
2	Forecast inflation			2014	2015	2016	2017	2018
3		rate					2%	2%
4		index				1	1.02	1.04
5								
6	Growth assumption							
7								
8	Forecast (real terms)				historic data			
9		revenue		20	21	23	23.92	25.36
10		costs		15	15	16	16.64	17.64
11		operating profit		5	6	7	7.28	7.72
12								
13	Forecast (nominal terms)							
14		revenue					24.40	26.38
15		costs					16.97	18.35
16		operating profit					7.43	8.03
17								

FIGURE 5.2 Extending the base column idea to handle 3 years of historic data. Column F now acts as the calculation base column.

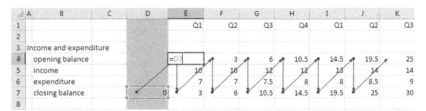

	A	B	C	D	E	F	G	H	I	J	K
1					Q1	Q2	Q3	Q4	Q1	Q2	Q3
2											
3	Income and expenditure										
4		opening balance			=D7	3	6	10.5	14.5	19.5	25
5		income			10	10	12	12	13	14	14
6		expenditure			7	7	7.5	8	8	8.5	9
7		closing balance		0	3	6	10.5	14.5	19.5	25	30
8											

FIGURE 5.3   Using the Trace Dependents tool to illustrate the corkscrew.

3	Fixed assets							
4		opening balance			0	10	8	
5		capex			10	0	0	goes to the Cash Flow
6		depreciation			0	2	2	goes to the Income Statement
7		closing balance		0	10	8	6	goes to the Financial Position
8								

FIGURE 5.4   The corkscrew can handle information that is reported on different output sheets.

In the context of the depreciation problem mentioned above, the corkscrew offers a mechanism where we can identify the cash flows as they occur and roll them up until such time as the depreciation formula should kick in.

You may see different ways of describing the opening and closing balances. The closing balance is sometimes referred to as the ending balance. In English accounting, we often use the expressions 'brought forward' (b/f or bf) and 'carried forward' (c/f or cf). You may also see beginning of year/end of year (boy/eoy), or beginning of period/end of period (bop/eop). As always, be consistent with your own terminology, to avoid confusion later on.

An interesting feature of the corkscrew is that the closing balance is a balance sheet item. Depending on how the corkscrew is set up, it may also include the profit and loss and cash flow items (Figure 5.4).

I have often found that corkscrews can offer a simple solution to apparently complex problems, in which analysts have found themselves bogged down in technical problems trying to identify items that have occurred previously instead of thinking about bringing the item forward. Some countries report accumulated depreciation on their balance sheets, which can be solved as a continuous sum of all previous depreciation, or more simply as a basic three-line corkscrew (Figure 5.5).

In the three-line corkscrew we can perform the following calculations:

```
=closing balance-opening balance=increase, or
=opening balance+increase=closing balance
```

In the four-line corkscrew we can calculate:

```
=opening balance
=additions to the corkscrew
=deductions from the corkscrew
=opening balance+additions-deductions=closing balance
```

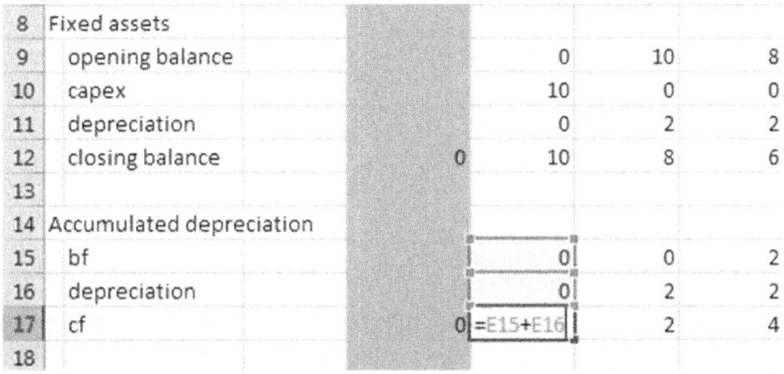

8	Fixed assets				
9	opening balance		0	10	8
10	capex		10	0	0
11	depreciation		0	2	2
12	closing balance	0	10	8	6
13					
14	Accumulated depreciation				
15	bf		0	0	2
16	depreciation		0	2	2
17	cf	0	=E15+E16	2	4
18					

FIGURE 5.5 Accumulated depreciation corkscrew. The annual depreciation from row 11 is linked to row 16.

TECHNICAL FORMULAS

The next set of techniques help simplify potentially complex calculations. Using the depreciation example again, the problem is basically in two parts: divide the asset by the life (simple arithmetic), but only after the asset has been put into use and for a fixed period only (timing dependent). Rather than solve this with a single formula, break it into steps.

Masks

The technique of masking is simply that of enabling or disabling a particular calculation or routine based on a zero or unit value. If the formula is multiplied by 0, it evaluates to 0, if it is multiplied by 1, we get the expected result. This is another method for tackling the issue of left-to-right consistency. The mask can be either input, in which case the string of 0s and 1s is entered manually on the inputs sheet, or calculated using logical functionality. This is explored in much more detail in Chapter 6, but it is worth looking at the basics here. A simple example should help – I would like to pay a dividend to my shareholders, but under the terms of a loan covenant I am not permitted to do so until the loan has been paid off. We will assume that the bank are willing to vary the duration of the loan subject to our financial circumstances, so we cannot simply type in the dividend formula from the point at which the loan is repaid (and this would breach the left-to-right consistency principle). I have a loan corkscrew in my model which shows the loan being drawdown and then there are a series of repayments until the loan is finally paid off. Whilst the repayments are underway, therefore, I cannot pay a dividend. All we need here is an extra line for the mask.

Rather than writing an IF routine, we simply write the test condition:

```
=LoanRepayment=0
```

When you enter this (described as a Boolean formula), Excel returns FALSE or TRUE. FALSE has a value of 0 and TRUE a value of 1. If we now multiply the

8	Loan									
9	opening balance		10	8	6	4	2	0	0	0 *LoanBf*
10	drawdown		0	0	0	0	0	0	0	0 *LoanDrawdown*
11	repayment		2	2	2	2	2	0	0	0 *LoanRepayment*
12	closing balance	0	8	6	4	2	0	0	0	0 *LoanCf*
13										
14	Dividend mask		=LoanRepayment=0	FALSE	FALSE	FALSE	TRUE	TRUE	TRUE	*DividendMask*
15										
16	Dividend		=DividendCalculation*DividendMask			0	3	4	4.5 *Dividend*
17										

FIGURE 5.6   Loan repayment corkscrew and dividend mask.

dividend calculation by the loan repayment mask, dividends are only shown for those years in which there is no loan repayment. Do not worry if you can see problems with this, for example, an interest-only loan, or the possibility of paying a dividend provided we exceed a particular interest or repayment cover ratio, because this is fully explored in Chapter 6 (Figure 5.6).

Generally one logic test per mask should be sufficient. This may mean setting up additional lines for each test. We can then combine the mask results by multiplying them together (the equivalent of the AND function in the next chapter). If we extend the dividend payment example by adding a further requirement that profits need to be in excess of 1.2 and that the loan must have been repaid, we can add a further test:

```
=Profit>=ProfitMinimum
```

We then multiply the DividendMask by the ProfitMask, and the dividend calculation by this combined mask. Note that the result is shown as a 1 or a 0 (see Coercion, below). To pay a dividend if either the loan is repaid or the profit target is reached (equivalent to the OR function), we can simply add the two masks together:

```
=DividendMask+ProfitMask
```

In this way we can create complex tests overall, but each line is as simple as possible. Again, the masking technique will be developed further in the next chapter.

Flags

Flags are a type of mask but tend to indicate single events, such as the start of operations or the expected date of the completion of a transaction. They use the same TRUE/FALSE functionality, and may be calculated or input. These can be used in the counter technique, below (Figure 5.7).

Switches

Switches and masks are similar, but we tend to think of masks and flags as time-dependent, extending across the forecast period with the results being generated for each period. Switches, on the other hand, tend to be single cells and are

	A	B	C	D	E	F	G	H	I	J	K	L	M
1					2015	2016	2017	2018	2019	2020	2021	*Year*	
2													
3	Start of operations			2017	*StartYear*								
4		flag			=Year=StartYear		TRUE	FALSE	FALSE	FALSE	FALSE	*StartYearFlag*	
5													

FIGURE 5.7   The StartYear flag – is the year in row 1 the same as the year shown in C3?

therefore time independent. They may also have more functionality than simple TRUE/FALSE outcomes, and a common example of a switch would be a cell used to drive the scenario to be used by the model (see Chapter 6 for a more detailed explanation).

Coercion

The examples above are based on displaying TRUE and FALSE as the results of formulas. We know that they have numeric values of 1 and 0 respectively and we can easily multiply against these values when using masks and other techniques. However, if we attempt to SUM a row containing TRUE and FALSE values, the result is 0, because Excel does not accept the logical operators as values (ignoring the SUMIF function for the moment). In order for this to work, we need to convert (or coerce) the operators by the simple operation of adding 0 or multiplying by 1. For example,

```
=DebtRepayment>0
```

reads TRUE for periods in which repayments take place, and FALSE if they do not. If we need to return the number of loan repayments, a sum of this mask will not work. If we coerce the formula:

```
=(DebtRepayment>0)+0 or =(DebtRepayment>0)*1
```

we now see a line of 1 and 0 values. The sum of this row will now be valid.

Additionally the N function can be used to the same effect:

```
=N(DebtRepayment>0)
```

The use of SUMIF and COUNTIF in this context will be considered in the next chapter.

Counters

If we have a loan which we are due to start repaying in period 5 of our forecast period, clearly we need to know when this happens. At its simplest we number each column, but to be consistent with our 'no inputs on the workings' rule, we write a 0 in the base column and a formula: =previous+1, where 'previous' is a cell reference to the cell to the left. This gives an incremental number series (Figure 5.8).

20	Debt repayment									
21	counter		0	=D21+1	2	3	4	5	6	7	8 *DebtRepaymentCounter*
22										
23	Debt repayments									
24	start in period		5 *DebtRepaymentStartPeriod*							
25	mask			FALSE	FALSE	FALSE	FALSE	TRUE	TRUE	TRUE	TRUE
26										

FIGURE 5.8   A simple counter and mask combination.

28	Forecast period				
29	number of periods	48 *PeriodNumber*			
30	periods left	49	48	47	46	45
31					

FIGURE 5.9   Counting down.

We could try the reverse – how many periods are left? This time we could write a COUNTA(forecast period)+1 function in the base column, and write =previous-1 as the counter formula (Figure 5.9).

We can develop more sophisticated counters using the mask and coercion techniques. If we have a depreciation life of 5 years but the asset is not acquired until year 2, we don't stop the depreciation in period 5 but in acquisition year+5. We could set up a mask (flag) to identify when the acquisition takes place and a second line to coerce this to a value. A third line begins with a 0 in the base column and then =previous+above. This will give a string of 1s once the flag reads TRUE. Repeat this formula once more to get a number series; and write a logical mask formula that returns TRUE or 1 during the depreciation period only (i.e. while the counter is between 1 and 10). This can be done using the AND function or using =(counter>0)*(counter<=depreciation life). This will only return 1 when both arguments are TRUE. Check that the sum of this row does not exceed the depreciation life (Figure 5.10).

We will be using counters again in the next chapter.

CHANGING PERIODICITY

If we agree with the rule of left-to-right consistency, we are faced with a number of problems where it would seem that this is going to be a very difficult rule to comply with. In this section, we will consider a number of techniques to solve this problem.

Quarterly to Annual

This is a common issue that modellers struggle with: how do we set up a model so that we can report either quarterly or annual results (or monthly to quarterly, etc.)? A basic modelling rule is that the model is set up using the smallest time units required – if there is a requirement to report monthly then the whole model is set up at this level. This in itself is problematic, although with 16,384 columns this should no longer be a problem. The usual solutions

35	Capital expenditure										
36	additions		0	0	10	0	0	0	0	0	*CapexAdditions*
37											
38	Capex investment										
39	flag		=CapexAdditions>0	TRUE	FALSE	FALSE	FALSE	FALSE	FALSE	*CapexFlag*	
40	flag to value		=CapexFlag+0	1	0	0	0	0	0	*CapexValue*	
41	number	0	=D41+E40	0	1	1	1	1	1	*CapexNumber*	
42	counter	0	=D42+E41	0	1	2	3	4	5	6	*CapexCounter*
43	mask		=(CapexCounter>0)*(CapexCounter<=DepreciationLife)						1	0	*CapexMask*
44											
45	Depreciation life		5	*DepreciationLife*							

FIGURE 5.10   Depreciation counter using masks.

	A	B	C	D	E	F	G	H	I	J	K	L	M	N	O
27							Year 1						Year 2		
28					Q1	Q2	Q3	Q4	Totals	Q1	Q2	Q3	Q4	Totals	Q1
29															
30	Earnings														
31	operating				17.95	17.20	12.49	11.30	**58.94**	10.60	16.30	15.10	11.42	**53.42**	12.11
32	before tax				5.21	7.33	7.33	5.94	**25.81**	8.58	7.84	9.16	6.89	**32.47**	5.35
33	after tax				1.88	4.26	2.99	1.97	**11.10**	3.05	2.12	1.97	1.12	**8.26**	2.93
34															

FIGURE 5.11   Wrong solution: profits calculated quarterly, with annual totals in columns
I and N.

tend to be a bit messy: the annual total formulas are interposed amongst the quarterly figures, and by judicial use of hidden columns we can laboriously convert from one time period to the other (Figure 5.11).

The immediate problem with this type of solution is first it requires a lot of effort (which usually ends up being macro-driven) and second, that it completely breaches the principle of left-to-right consistency. If any formula needs to be amended or updated, it is no longer a question of simply copying across the row, because this will then overwrite the annual totals. Let us look at a couple of solutions – the principle is the same whether we need to convert from quarterly to annual or from monthly to quarterly, or any other permutation.

Some models are structured with quarterly or monthly columns for the first few years, then becoming semiannual or annual over the extended forecast period. Again the left-to-right consistency rule is breached, and we often encounter 'edge effects' where the accounting treatments over the transition period are incorrectly modelled, and this includes the concept of the 'stub period' or partial periods, where an activity begins (or more rarely ends) during a period, rather than at the start. This would need more attention and will be seen in the next chapter.

Rolling Total

One solution is to separate the quarterly and annual calculations into two rows. The quarterly row works as before, and we set up a corkscrew and mask for the annuals.

1. Set up a four-line corkscrew with the headings brought forward, additions, retirements and carried forward.
2. The brought forward (or opening balance) is a link to the previous closing balance.

					Year 1				Year 2			
27												
28				Q1	Q2	Q3	Q4	Q1	Q2	Q3	Q4	Q1
29												
30	Earnings											
31	operating			17.95	17.20	12.49	11.30	10.60	16.30	15.10	11.42	12.11
32	before tax			5.21	7.33	7.33	5.94	8.58	7.84	9.16	6.89	5.35
33	after tax			1.88	4.26	2.99	1.97	3.05	2.12	1.97	1.12	2.93
34												
35	Quarter mask											
36												
37	Operating profit											
38	opening balance			0.00	17.95	35.15	47.64	58.94	69.54	85.84	100.94	112.36
39	additions			17.95	17.20	12.49	11.30	10.60	16.30	15.10	11.42	12.11
40	retirements											
41	closing balance		0	17.95	35.15	47.64	58.94	69.54	85.84	100.94	112.36	124.47
42												

FIGURE 5.12 Rolling total #1: basic cumulative corkscrew but with no retirements.

	A	B	C	D	E	F	G	H	I	J	K	L	M
						Year 1				Year 2			
27													
28					Q1	Q2	Q3	Q4	Q1	Q2	Q3	Q4	Q1
29													
30	Earnings												
31	operating				17.95	17.20	12.49	11.30	10.60	16.30	15.10	11.42	12.11
32	before tax				5.21	7.33	7.33	5.94	8.58	7.84	9.16	6.89	5.35
33	after tax				1.88	4.26	2.99	1.97	3.05	2.12	1.97	1.12	2.93
34													
35	Quarter mask				FALSE	FALSE	FALSE	TRUE	FALSE	FALSE	FALSE	TRUE	FALSE
36													
37	Operating profit												
38	opening balance				0.00	17.95	35.15	47.64	0.00	10.60	26.90	42.00	0.00
39	additions				17.95	17.20	12.49	11.30	10.60	16.30	15.10	11.42	12.11
40	retirements				0	0	0	58.94	0	0	0	53.42	0
41	closing balance			0	17.95	35.15	47.64	0.00	10.60	26.90	42.00	0.00	12.11
42													

FIGURE 5.13 Rolling total #2: insertion of the quarter mask and the retirements formula.

3. The additions is a link to the quarterly figure.
4. We will skip the retirements for a moment, and set up the carried forward (closing or ending balance) as the brought forward plus the additions, less the retirements (Figure 5.12).
5. At this stage, the corkscrew accumulates the quarterly figures over time. We want to drop out the total in the fourth quarter of each year, so we need to set up a mask that identifies the fourth quarter (remember that Q4 is also a valid cell reference, so we enclose it in quotes in the following example): =Quarter="Q4"
6. The retirements formula adds the opening balance to the additions and multiplies by the mask: =(Bf+Additions)*QuarterMask
7. The retirements line now shows the annual figures (Figure 5.13).

If we use range names for this, we might end up with the following: OperatingProfitQuarterly and OperatingProfitAnnual. For reporting purposes, we could either have a single version of each report which then contains a reference to, for example, the quarterly value. We can then use Ctrl+H Replace and change all … Quarterly references to … Annual, and then hide the unwanted columns. Or we could set up two copies of each report, one of which is the

	A	B	C	D	H	L
27					Year 1	Year 2
28					Q4	Q4
29						
30	Earnings					
31		operating			11.30	11.42
32		before tax			5.94	6.89
33		after tax			1.97	1.12
34						
35	Quarter mask				TRUE	TRUE
36						
37	Operating profit					
38		opening balance			47.64	42.00
39		additions			11.30	11.42
40		retirements			58.94	53.42
41		closing balance		0	0.00	0.00
42						
43					Year 1	Year 2
44	Income statement					
45		operating profit			58.94	53.42

FIGURE 5.14   Hiding the columns to produce an annual report.

quarterly report, the second of which is the annual, with the columns hidden in advance (Figure 5.14).

The benefit of this solution is that we have preserved full left-to-right consistency. The downside is that we will probably have to build an awful lot of corkscrews. With some models we are required to produce quarterly reports for the development phase and annual reports thereafter. This technique easily lends itself to this requirement – and is flexible if the requirement changes.

Relative Totals

This is a simpler variation of the rolling total method and can be set up using cell references or relative range names. The concept is similar, in that we add up the values from the current and previous three quarters. Every fourth total then represents the total for that year. To do this, your first quarter of the first year must be in column D or further to the right, to avoid it referring to cells beyond the left-hand edge of the worksheet.

1. Write a SUM function that adds up the four cells above and to the left.
2. Copy the formula across the row. Test to confirm that the Q4 totals represent the total for the year (Figure 5.15).

Use the same column hiding and reporting techniques described previously. Use the relative naming procedure described in Chapter 4 if you wish to use range names. This method is simpler than the corkscrew and far less time

	A	B	C	D	E	F	G	H	I	J	K	L
27								Year 1				Year 2
28					Q1	Q2	Q3	Q4	Q1	Q2	Q3	Q4
29												
30	Earnings											
31		operating			17.95	17.20	12.49	11.30	10.60	16.30	15.10	11.42
32		before tax			5.21	7.33	7.33	5.94	8.58	7.84	9.16	6.89
33		after tax			1.88	4.26	2.99	1.97	3.05	2.12	1.97	1.12
34												
35	Operating profit				17.95	35.15	47.64	=SUM(E31:H31)		50.69	53.3	53.42
36												

FIGURE 5.15   The relative sum technique is used in row 35.

consuming, and if you are confident about your model layout, it is very robust. However, the corkscrew retirements produced zero results in quarters 1, 2 and 3, so an accidental link to one of these would be rather obvious. The relative total method has values for all quarters and it would be more difficult to spot a mistake. Of course, there is no reason why you couldn't use the mask in this technique as well.

We should give some thought to the ways in which we convert quarterly figures into their annual equivalents. For some figures a total is sufficient, but for others we may need to return an average, for example, with interest or inflation rates. Again the corkscrew offers a simple solution for this. I leave it to you to extend these techniques to consider converting monthly to quarterly to semiannual to annual.

CIRCULARITIES AND ITERATION

A circular formula is one which directly or indirectly refers to itself. Most of the time they are produced in error, and Excel wastes no time in filling your screen with dialog boxes and blue audit lines. Quite often it is a simple matter to locate and rectify a circularity, but in some cases it can be rather difficult, especially if the predecessor trail extends over multiple sheets. However, sometimes we are faced with calculations that are inherently circular. In this section, we will review some techniques for locating the accidental circularity, and then consider how to solve the deliberate or intentional circularity.

You should recognise that a circular model is fundamentally broken. Somewhere you have a calculation that is no longer recalculating, and dependent formulas similarly fail to recalculate. At this point, your model has the functionality of a table in Microsoft Word.

The screen shots in this section are based on an interest calculation, where we calculate the amount of interest we earn on a cash balance. This interest is then paid into the account by the bank, thereby increasing the amount of cash, which will then increase the amount of interest earned. This is clearly circular (although there are workarounds). However, earned interest is included in the pre-tax profit calculation. This profit is then used in the tax calculation. Neither the profit nor the tax is in the circular path, but they are linked to it, and become

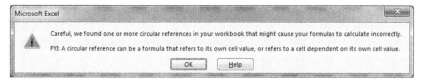

FIGURE 5.16   The circular warning. Do NOT ignore.

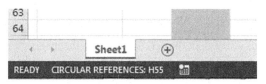

FIGURE 5.17   The circular warning on the status bar.

noncalculating-dependent cells. This can lead to major problems if the relationship between different items in a model is not clearly understood. We can end up with noncalculating output sheets, which are completely insensitive to changing the inputs.

Debugging Circularities

We have all had occasions when we have written a trivial formula and suddenly Excel fires up the circular warning. If you are lucky, the blue audit lines which then fill your workbook are meaningful and you can locate the source of the problem. Use the Formulas, Error Checking, Circular References, and Excel will provide a list of cells in the circular path. But sometimes the problem is rather more intractable – it is hard to believe but some users continue working on the model despite the warning. Unfortunately, Excel has never had something as useful as a #CIRC! error, which would make life so much simpler. Instead we have to examine the model carefully (Figure 5.16).

It is worth noting that we now have four types of formulas in the workbook:

1. The circular formulas themselves;
2. Calculations within in the circular path but which aren't circular themselves;
3. Dependent formulas that refers to cells in the circular path (noncalculating-dependent cells) – the model's outputs are good examples;
4. Noncircular calculations. Note that these can occur before, after, and inside the circularity, and alongside the noncalculating-dependent cells.

We need to find the cells in the circular path, and not get distracted by the noncalculating-dependent cells (Figure 5.17).

Having dismissed the circular warning dialog box, note the circular warning on the status bar. If there is a cell reference next to it, one or more formulas on the active sheet are not recalculating due to the circularity. They may or may not be in the circular path. The cell reference next to the warning will refer to a noncalculating cell. If there is no cell reference then the active sheet is clear. Note that the circular warning remains even if you are working in another workbook – never ignore this warning, because something, somewhere, is broken. Once you have identified which sheets are involved in the circularity, you can then examine the formulas. There are two things to note here: because Excel is unable to calculate, the formula which gave rise to the circularity will evaluate to 0. Also, formulas in the circular path are not recalculated, so changes to predecessors or to inputs will have no effect on these cells. One neat little trick is to select a cell, press F2 and then press Enter. If the cell is in the circular path, the value originally shown in the cell is lost and a 0 appears. Continue with this and eventually you will be able to differentiate between noncircular calculated cells and the circular noncalculated cells. Do not use this technique for a large circularity.

There are two basic approaches to tracking down circularities, both of which are somewhat risky, so the first step is always to back up the file first (Figure 5.18).

Trial and Error

The first method is an unsophisticated trial-and-error approach. If you are dealing with a forecast-type model, you will have many rows of calculations, and hopefully you will be observing the left-to-right consistency rule established earlier in this chapter, whereby the formula in the first cell of each row is simply copied across the row. This means that you do not need to examine the formulas other than in the first column, so delete all the additional columns. Once you have done this, start deleting individual sections, pressing Ctrl+Z (Undo) after each deletion. At some point the circularity will disappear, returning on Undo. Once this happens, delete individual elements within each routine, looking for the same effect. If you are lucky you may be able to locate the circularity quite quickly. Once you have found it, make a note of the problem and its solution, close down the workbook. You should then be able to make your correction in the original file.

This technique is not wholly reliable, in that some circularities are caused by problems in the now-deleted forecast period, for example, MAX/MIN, and some of the look-up type functions. If the circularity disappears when you

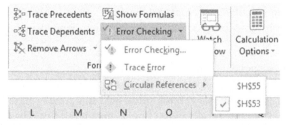

FIGURE 5.18 The Circular References tracking tool on the Formulas tab.

delete the columns other than the first one, you may have a problem involving calculations across columns, so Ctrl+Z Undo and delete all columns after the first two.

Error Tracking

A more reliable solution is to introduce an error value into the model. As noted above, there is no #CIRC! error, so we will have to do this manually. Again, back up the workbook first. Locate an input that is at the head of the longest dependency trail which you think runs through the circularity, for example, inflation or price. It is up to you which error you introduce, but I would normally divide the input by 0, which gives the #DIV/0! error value (and I am assuming that there are no such errors already in the model). Alternatively, if you have a strong suspicion concerning the location of the circularity, introduce the error closer to the suspected code (Figure 5.19).

Inspection of the dependent formulas should now reveal that the error has cascaded through the model – press F9 (Recalc) a couple of times to force the issue. You will see that the error does not penetrate into the circular code, which should still contain numbers. This is a problem, in that the error message is in the clean parts of the model, and the numbers are in the broken part. It would be more helpful if the position was reversed (Figure 5.20).

1. Use File, Options, Formulas, Enable iterative calculation (this is explored in more detail shortly).
2. Press F9 (Recalc) a couple of times to force the error message into the circular path.

	A	B	C	D	E	F
1	Financial year ending			2016	2017	2018
2						
3	Inflation rate			=3%/0	#DIV/0!	#DIV/0!
4						

FIGURE 5.19   The original input value has been divided by 0.

			C	D	E	F
124						
125	Project cash flow					
126	money terms			#DIV/0!	#DIV/0!	#DIV/0!	#DIV/0!
127	real terms			#DIV/0!	#DIV/0!	#DIV/0!	#DIV/0!
128						
129	Financing cash flow			105,000,000	-64,710,586	-55,790,905	-126,310,784
130						
131	Net cash balances, made up of...					
132	bf			0	22,600,000	5,247,525	0
133	change			22,600,000	-17,352,475	-5,247,525	8,128,212
134	cf		0	22,600,000	5,247,525	0	8,128,212
135						

FIGURE 5.20   The error has cascaded through the workings but has not appeared in row 129.

3. Next, repeat the command sequence and switch Iteration off. You should see the circular warning reappear, and at this stage the error message should permeate the whole model.

4. Locate the original input cell and remove the division formula. The error message disappears throughout the clean sections of the model and remains trapped within the circularity.

You could use conditional formatting to assign a colour to the error cells (see Chapter 7), or a background colour – use F5 (Go To), Special, Formulas, Errors to select the cells (Figure 5.21).

Now that the circular path has been isolated, you can work your way through the code in an attempt to locate the source of the problem. Note that F2 (Edit) will cause the cells to revert to 0. If you switch to manual recalculation (Formulas, Calculation Options(X), Manual) the numbers will remain. Initially you should concentrate on excluding those routines which you firmly believe are not actually causing the circularity. You could also try variations of the error routine – once you have narrowed down your investigation, try replacing the '=' in a precedent formula with a text character such as '^'. The formula is now a text string, and dependent formula now have the #VALUE! error, which can be helpful to differentiate from the surrounding #DIV/0 errors. As text, it cannot be in the circular path, and at some point you will find that the circularity disappears. Restore the formulas as required, make a note of the cause of the circularity, and update the original workbook. Iteration is explained in more detail in the next section.

FIGURE 5.21 Selecting cells with error values.

You should always bear in mind that there could be more than one circularity in a model, and the use of different error values can be useful in this context. It can also be helpful to sketch out the components of a model in order to determine the relationships between them and the audit path.

Handling Circular Code

We are occasionally faced with a problem that involves an inherent circularity which cannot be avoided. We will explore this issue by using an interest calculation as the example but please note that this is simply for the purposes of illustration, and I am making no suggestion that this is necessarily the correct way to do it.

Let us consider the interest-earning cash account mentioned above (Figure 5.22).

We have the opening and closing balance, and we earn interest at 5%. Using the average balance method, this gives us 7.5 of interest. The effect of this would be to increase the total cash balance carried forward, so we add the 7.5 of interest to the existing end balance. But we are using the average balance method to calculate interest, in which case we must repeat the calculation, which increases the amount of interest, which then increases closing balance, so we calculate the interest again, and so on. There is a circularity involving the carried forward balance and the interest amount.

If we put this into the model, Excel complains about the circularity and the model locks up. So we go to File, Options, Formulas, Enable iterative calculation. We then find that the interest and the closing balance have been calculated to some detail: 7.692308. We also discover that Excel will happily recalculate the formulas if the inputs change and all dependent formulas now work, so the model is apparently in good working order.

Take a look at the status bar. The original circular warning has been replaced by the Calculate prompt. This normally appears when you have set recalculation to manual, and Excel prompts you to press F9 to recalculate. But we aren't using manual recalculation, and pressing F9 has no effect and indeed the Calculate prompt remains. This is normally the only clue that you will have that someone is using iteration. But what's the problem? The model is working.

Now try the following. Enter a value of 1 in one cell and 2 in the cell below. In the third cell write a sum to add all three cells together (Figure 5.23).

8	Cash	
9	interest rate	5%
10	interest	=AVERAGE(D11,D12)*D9
11	opening balance	100
12	closing balance	200
13		

FIGURE 5.22   A simple interest calculation.

D16			▼	⋮	✕	✓	f_x	=SUM(D14:D16)	

	A	B	C	D	E	F	G
8	Cash						
9		interest rate		5%			
10		interest		7.692308			
11		opening balance		100			
12		closing balance		207.6923			
13							
14				1			
15				2			
16				300			
17							

FIGURE 5.23 Iteration is on. Where does the 300 come from?

You will have spotted that this formula is circular, but Excel did not complain when it was entered. You may want to consider why the sum of 1 and 2 should equal 300. Before we look at that, just press F9 a couple of times.

If we go back to the File, Options, Formulas dialog box, we note that iteration is part of the Excel recalculation engine. The first point is that we cannot simply iterate part of the workbook, it has to be all or nothing. The second point is that iteration is controlled by two constraints. Excel will either iterate the formula 100 times, or until there is a maximum change of 0.001 (both of these are defaults: the maximum number of iterations is 32,767, and the maximum change is up to 15 decimals). The interest on the cash account was constrained by the maximum change setting, whereas the simple sum was governed by the maximum iterations (1 + 2, repeated 100 times). The interest value will not change until its precedents are changed, but the simple sum will reiterate 100 times every single time the model recalculates (Figure 5.24).

The interest routine is described as a converging circularity (i.e. the results are governed by the maximum change constraint), the simple sum is a diverging circularity (the results are governed by the maximum iterations). It is this latter type that is the most dangerous.

The key issue is that after switching iteration on, Excel will iterate all subsequent circular formulas without comment or warning. As we know, the majority of circularities are errors, so we must be very cautious about the use of iteration. Note that we can't simply turn it off because Excel will only complain about 'a circularity'. If we have other or multiple inadvertent circularities there is nothing to warn us: my simple sum is a deliberately obvious example of what might go wrong; we have seen real-life errors ticking over at much lower levels, but with the result that the model gave a different answer each time it was run.

Most investment banks and financial institutions prohibit their analysts from using iteration because of this inherent problem of differentiating deliberate from accidental circularities. These poor souls are left wrestling with the

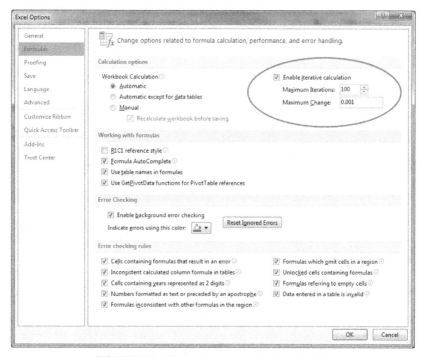

FIGURE 5.24   The iteration command and constraints.

algebra in an effort to work around the problem. With a little planning, however, it is possible to use iteration and to preserve career prospects.

Let us look again at the interest routine: it is a good calculation if the iteration is on, but I would prefer it to make itself noncircular if iteration is off. We could consider the use of an IF test here: in Excel-speak,

```
=IF(Iteration=ON,AVERAGE(+Opening Balance, +Closing Balance)*
IntRate,0)
```

If iteration is on, therefore, run the circular interest calculation, if iteration is off, return 0 (noncircular).

The problem here is the test condition because we cannot write Iteration=ON. There is no direct way of testing the iteration status from a formula. But we can do it indirectly, if the user provides the information about iteration. In a cell at the top of the worksheet, enter the prompt 'Is iteration on?' In the adjacent cell, enter the appropriate response (you may find it helpful to name the cell, Switch) (Figure 5.25). Now update the interest calculation to read:

```
=IF(Switch, AVERAGE(+Bf, +Cf)*IntRate,0)
```

(note the plus signs prefixing the range names – refer to Chapter 4 for explanation).

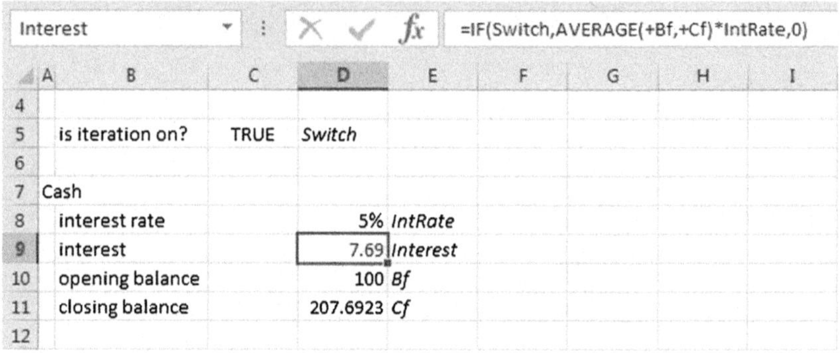

| Interest | | | ▾ | ⋮ | ✕ | ✓ | *fx* | =IF(Switch,AVERAGE(+Bf,+Cf)*IntRate,0) |

◢ A	B	C	D	E	F	G	H	I
4								
5	is iteration on?	TRUE	*Switch*					
6								
7	Cash							
8	interest rate		5%	*IntRate*				
9	interest		7.69	*Interest*				
10	opening balance		100	*Bf*				
11	closing balance		207.6923	*Cf*				
12								

FIGURE 5.25   Implementing the switch mechanism.

Note that you do not need to specify the condition that Switch=TRUE, because the content of the Switch cell is either true or false and the IF condition must evaluate to either true or false.

We can now test the mechanism. Switch on the iteration and do not forget to update the Switch cell to TRUE. The interest should be calculated. Set the Switch to FALSE and switch off the iteration. The interest reads 0 and the circularity has disappeared.

One observation is that when the switch is false, the interest (or whatever is being calculated) reads 0. The following formulas will produce values when the iteration is off:

```
=IF(Switch,AVERAGE(+Bf, +Cf)*Rate,Bf*IntRate) or
=IF(Switch,AVERAGE(+Bf, +Cf),Bf)*IntRate
```

In both cases, the false outcome is to multiply the opening balance by the rate, which generates a result. This is useful if you are developing code in which you need to see the effect of interest (or whatever); the zero value previously used is not very helpful. My own preference is for the original formula: if a user notes that there is no interest being shown on the profit and loss statement, for example, it is a significant omission and would be caught. The Bf*IntRate version of the formula results in incorrect numbers and may not be picked up by the users. This does not quite fit in with the Principle of Error Reduction, in that users may believe that the temporary interest value is the correct value.

Some people have suggested that the false outcome could be a text flag, for example, 'Iteration is Off'. This is an option, but any dependent formulas will generate the #VALUE! error, which is probably not worth the trouble.

We can now write circular code that is controlled by the switch. At any stage, we can switch iteration off to test for unintentional circularities. Any and all code that involves iteration should have the switch control built in. As it is most likely that accidental circularities are introduced during the development of the model, it would make sense to leave iteration off until such time as the circular components are under test. Once the model is complete and is being used for sensitivity analysis (see Chapter 8), you can leave the iteration on.

A question that may arise, in using the inputs/workings/outputs methodology described previously, is where should the iteration prompt and switch cell be located? The TRUE/FALSE response is indeed an input, and a variable as such, but I would keep them on the workings sheet because the switch drives the circular code. Once the model is ready for the users, iteration is switched on, and the users should not really have any reason to switch it off. Given the importance and risks of the iteration technique, another suggestion is to put the iteration switch on the audit sheet. With the Switch set to FALSE, the audit check fails and the model results would not be accepted. Setting the Switch to TRUE would be one of the final model development actions and the final audit test.

It is very good practice to document the use of iteration so that other users can be confident that other circularities are not being masked. You should note that it is also possible to lie – the Switch could read FALSE and yet iteration is still on. For this reason I always recommend that on seeing any sort of switch mechanism you should immediately check the iteration status in the File, Options dialog box. This should form part of the audit routine and the outcome should be recorded on the audit sheet. In this context it is worth noting that the iteration state is persistent. The default setting is always off, but if a workbook has been saved with iteration on, when it is next reopened Excel will switch on iteration without any warning to the user. This is dangerous because the user may well consider themselves to be working in a safe environment and will not be aware of any accidental circularities that may arise.

The iteration off/on routine lends itself to macro automation (see Chapter 9). I prefer not to make it too easy to set up iteration, because users may not understand the full implications of using it and may end up in trouble. If a user does not understand the prompt 'Is iteration on?' it is unlikely that they would go much further with it. You could use the data validation tricks in Chapter 7 to ensure that the user does not input 'Yes' or 'No' in response to the prompt.

A fringe benefit of using the switch mechanism is that if error values appear in iterated circular code they are almost impossible to resolve, as the error is trapped in the circular loop regardless of any correction. Setting the Switch to FALSE and immediately back to TRUE has the effect of purging the error.

A final point is that some users have been shown how to use iteration as part of their general Excel training and fail to understand the dangers of the technique. Their reaction to any circularity is to switch on iteration, almost as a reflex action. They then continue working as if nothing has happened. As a consequence I always make sure that I inspect the status bar for the 'Calculate' warning whenever attempting to review someone's model, and indeed we included this check in our initial audit tests in Chapter 2.

ADVANCED FORMULAS

We conclude this chapter with an overview of two approaches to formula writing that a good modeller should know about but not necessarily use. Array formulas, and formulas written using R1C1 notation, can be difficult to work with and generally I've only seen them used as security measures, as users find them impossible to edit successfully.

Array Formulas

We have already seen an example of an array formula being used as the audit check in Chapter 2. This is probably the only time I would use this technique – array formulas can perform some spectacularly complex calculations, but in routine use they are of little value and generally fall foul of the principle of error reduction. They are difficult to edit, difficult to understand, and because of this in my experience the most common use of array formulas is for security purposes – end users find themselves unable to edit formulas. In this context we should also recognise that few analysts, in practice, would claim to be familiar with array formulas, so you may find colleagues unwilling or unable to help you if you get stuck.

According to Excel Help, an array formula 'can perform multiple calculations and then return either a single result or multiple results'. In practice this means that we can, for example, multiply one block of cells by another

F3			× ✓ f_x	{=B3:B17*D3:D17}			
	A	B	C	D	E	F	G
1							
2		this column	multiplied by this column			makes	
3		13		13		169	
4		18		10		180	
5		19		20		380	
6		14		17		238	
7		19		14		266	
8		16		20		320	
9		20		12		240	
10		20		16		320	
11		18		19		342	
12		15		11		165	
13		17		11		187	
14		20		10		200	
15		17		20		340	
16		19		10		190	
17		13		10		130	
18							

FIGURE 5.26 A trivial example of an array formula.

block of cells. Firstly select the destination cells F4:F17, then in F4 write: =B4:B17*D4:D17 (Figure 5.26).

The trick is to press Ctrl+Shift+Enter to enter the formula. The commonest errors are failing to select the full range of cells to contain the array formula, and having either too few or too many cells in the selection. The next commonest error is then editing the formula and forgetting the Ctrl+Shift+Enter trick, so that Excel complains that it cannot change part of an array – press Esc to continue (Figure 5.27).

Another example is to perform an array calculation with the results in one cell. We can use the audit sheet created in Chapter 2 as an example of this. We used the ABS function to remove the sign from the balance sheet check formulas. We discovered that ABS works on cells, not ranges, and wrote an array formula that converted the values in the range into their absolute values, which we combined with the MAX and the logic test to prove that none of the values were about the rounding threshold:

```
=MAX(ABS(range))<Tolerance
```

In a similar way you may recall that we set up an AuditCheck cell, which returned TRUE if all audit tests had been passed, and FALSE if even one had failed. However, if one of the tests returned an error message, the audit check displays the error. We can easily amend the formula to include an ISERROR check as in the following:

```
=NOT(ISERROR(AND(C:C)))
```

The ISERROR returns TRUE if there is an error value in column C. The NOT converts the result to FALSE to give us the audit failure.

We already have a code that identifies how many tests have failed overall, and so it would be helpful if we could return the total number of audit tests that were giving an error message. SUMIF and, more correctly, COUNTIF immediately come to mind, with ISERROR as the logical test. However ISERROR does not differentiate existing FALSE values from errors. The array method will do this as a single calculation:

```
=SUM(IF(ISERROR(C:C),1,0))
```

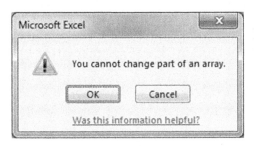

FIGURE 5.27 Excel complains if you try to edit array formulas.

Remember to press Ctrl+Shift+Enter, and test to prove that it works.

It is worth noting that range names themselves are a type of array formula, and I have seen examples of calculations in which this point seems to have been missed:

```
{=Revenue-Costs}
```

When writing this type of calculation the formula row must be selected first, then write the formula, then press Ctrl+Shift+Enter. The array formula structure of this calculation is redundant, unless used for security purposes. If security really is an issue, perhaps combine the array formula technique with the R1C1 notation system described in the previous chapter. For security purposes it is not ideal because the user can simply switch back to normal cell referencing, but it serves as a robust barrier to inspection and can be combined with array formulas and other techniques to prevent any modification of calculations.

Chapter 6

Mainly Functions

INTRODUCTION

There seems to be a distinct learning curve associated with Excel functions. Most people begin gently with the likes of SUM and COUNT and AVERAGE, and soon graduate to IF and VLOOKUP, and perhaps SUMIF and COUNTIF. And that, for many, is as far as they get, so once they start developing financial models they are overly reliant on this limited group of functions. The purpose of this chapter is to provide you with the dozen or so most useful functions for the general financial modeller. As with Chapter 5, we will look at some examples in the context of techniques combining formulas with functions, and again we will be using range names from Chapter 4.

There are a couple of shortcuts we can use to get help with functions. Type the = into the cell and press Shift+F3 to get to the Insert Function dialog box; or type the function name (e.g. =XNPV) and press Ctrl+A to go straight to the Function Arguments dialog box. Remember that when writing a formula or function we can use F2 to change from Edit to Point mode and back again, and we can use this trick to specify ranges in dialog boxes. Formula AutoComplete allows functions to be selected and entered into the worksheet very efficiently. If this feature has been disabled, use File, Options, Formulas, Formula Auto-Complete to restore it; this can also be enabled/disabled whilst editing formulas using Alt+↓ (down arrow) (Figure 6.1).

Excel function Help can be rather technical, particularly with its explanations of function arguments and syntax. I take the liberty here of rephrasing some of these elements using expressions that my students have found more understandable.

LATE BINDING FUNCTIONS

We begin with a topic that will help us understand something about how formulas and functions work. If we write a calculation to the effect of =a+b−c and copy it to 20 cells in the same row, we can be reasonably confident that we know what the formula is doing in each cell. If we write =IF(a>b,a+b−c,a−c) and copy it to the same cells, we no longer know what to expect, if we don't know the value of a. Using an expression from computer programming we describe this type of operation as 'late binding', in the sense that the result in any one cell using this formula can only be known at the moment of recalculation. There are several examples of late binding functions, including the LOOKUPs, INDEX,

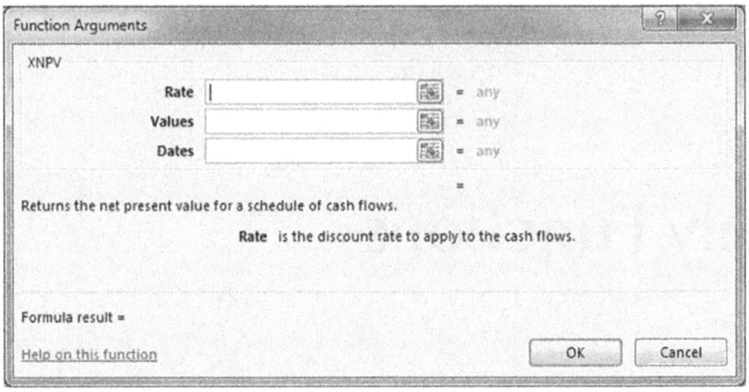

FIGURE 6.1   Ctrl+A function arguments.

MATCH, OFFSET, INDIRECT, MAX and MIN, and IF, COUNTIF and SUMIF. At a technical level they are memory intensive as each instance of the formula needs to be fully evaluated (using the BODMAS rules); at a practical level they can be difficult to audit (F2 and Ctrl+[may provide little information). In this chapter we will look at techniques which illustrate the power of such functions, and alternative approaches where they may help simplify our work.

ERROR HANDLING

A major objective of this and the previous chapter is to help you to think about writing formulas without resorting to the much over-used IF. We are about to develop a strong case to avoid the use of this function and to replace it with masks and other techniques instead. But there is one particular argument for including IF in our models and that is to handle errors. A formula either works, or it doesn't, and so in this context there is nothing better. As an example we might have a debt cover ratio calculation in which the cash available is divided by the debt service. At some stage the debt will have been repaid, in which case the denominator is 0 and will produce the #DIV/0! error value.

Excel has a number of error identification functions. ISERROR(cell ref) returns TRUE or FALSE if a cell contains any error value. ISERR(cell ref) does the same but excludes the #N/A error – use ISNA(cell ref) to test for this error (see the LOOKUP and MATCH functions below). This approach is acceptable to manage errors that have occurred in other formulas, but it looks rather cumbersome with the debt cover ratio calculation:

```
=IF(ISERROR(cash available/debt service),"NA",cash available/
debt service))
```

Firstly the ratio calculation is duplicated, and secondly it is not clear what might cause the error. I always recommend that when handling errors this way, try to make sure that the test condition identifies the root cause of the error; in this example:

```
=IF(debt service=0,"NA",cash available/debt service)
```

Note the use of the string "NA" ('not applicable') in this formula – it is common to return the MIN or AVERAGE of the debt cover ratios and to use a 0 would affect these results. Although Excel doesn't normally like text in formulas, it will work here.

IFERROR **and** IFNA

Two new functions have appeared in recent versions of Excel: IFERROR and IFNA. Both of these require a reference to test and have a second argument, which is the value to show if there is an error. Using the debt cover ratio calculation above we could rewrite it as:

```
=IFERROR(cash available/debt service,"NA")
```

If there is no error then the result of the calculation is seen, and if there is, we see the "NA" string.

IFERROR **Problem**

A major problem with using the IFERROR function is that it is usually written to deal with a specific, anticipated error, but of course it will work with unintended errors too. We used it in the debt cover ratio calculation to manage potential #DIV/0! errors, but what happens if there is a #VALUE! error in the cash available pathway? A colleague memorably describes the use of ISERROR as the modelling equivalent of removing the bulb from a warning light!

GOOD OLD IF

Although simple in principle, the IF function is prone to both overuse and abuse, and is very prone to error. Experience from model auditing has shown that some modellers have a limited understanding of the use of logic and tend to generate unnecessarily complex formulas. This approach is unfortunately reinforced by the intellectual satisfaction which some modellers obtain through writing such code. For educational and perhaps entertainment purposes here are two genuine IF formulas from our archive:

```
=IF(AB$143<Assumptions!$D$654,Assumptions!$E$654,IF(AB$143=Assu
mptions!$D$654,Assumptions!$E$661*Assumptions!$E$655+Assumption
s!$E$660*Assumptions!$E$654,IF(AB$143=Assumptions!$D$655,Assump
tions!$E$661*Assumptions!$E$656+Assumptions!$E$660*Assumptions!
$E$655,IF(AB$143=Assumptions!$D$656,Assumptions!$E$661*Assumpti
ons!$E$657+Assumptions!$E$660*Assumptions!$E$656,IF(AND(AB$143>
Assumptions!$D$654,AB$143<Assumptions!$D$655),Assumptions!$E$65
5,IF(AND(AB$143>Assumptions!$D$655,AB$143<Assumptions!$D$656),A
ssumptions!$E$656,IF(AND(AB$143>Assumptions!$D$656,AB$143<Assum
ptions!$D$657),Assumptions!$E$657,Assumptions!$E$657)))))))+(As
sumptions!$E$681*Assumptions!$E$682)
```

Six IFs with a handful of ANDs. Note that whatever the result, we add Assumptions!E681*Assumptions!E682 to it. And another:

```
=IF(IF(IF(E117>250000,(IF(SUM($C$112:E112)>E117-250000,(E117-
250000)-SUM($C$119:E119),SUM($C$112:E112)-SUM($C$119:E119))),0
)<0,0,(IF(E117>250000,(IF(SUM($C$112:E112)>E117-250000,(E117-
250000)-SUM($C$119:E119),SUM($C$112:E112)-SUM($C$119:E119))),
0)))<250000,0,IF(IF(E117>250000,(IF(SUM($C$112:E112)>E117-
250000,(E117-250000)-SUM($C$119:E119),SUM($C$112:E112)-
SUM($C$119:E119))),0)<0,0,(IF(E117>250000,(IF(SUM($C$112:E112
)>E117-250000,(E117-250000)-SUM($C$119:E119),SUM($C$112:E112)-
SUM($C$119:E119))),0))))
```

This has 11 IFs, along with hard-coded value of 250,000 repeated 13 times.

In the previous chapter we looked at the *Order of Operations* or *Rules of Arithmetic Priority* – BODMAS or PEMDAS. There is an interesting technical aspect to IF which is worth understanding in this context. The basic format of the IF function is:

```
=IF(test condition, outcome if TRUE, outcome if FALSE)
```

The question is, if Excel follows the BODMAS rules, what is the calculation order? Intuitively one would assume that Excel runs the test condition first, and then jumps to either the true or the false outcome, effectively ignoring the invalid outcome.

This is not correct. We have already considered the concept of the 'late-binding formula' above: Excel in fact calculates *all* the elements in an IF, following the BODMAS rules, and only after all the formulas have been evaluated does it perform the final step based on the original test condition. Looking at the two examples above, it is clear that a huge amount of calculation is taking place: in the first, you will see that the true outcome is simply to show the contents of Assumptions!$E$654 – the rest of the formula is the false outcome, but is still calculated by Excel. Try working out the calculation order in the second example.

To return to IF basics, you know that the test condition operators are:

= equality (equals to)	<> inequality (not equal to)
< less than	<= less than or equal to
> greater than	>= greater than or equal to

The tests and the outcomes can use values, text (in "quotes") cell references, formulas and functions.

Let us consider some common examples:

=IF(E10>0,E10,0) If the content of E10 is greater than 0, show that value, otherwise show a 0.

=IF(E10>0,E10*E5, "") If the content of E10 is greater than 0, multiply E10 by E5, otherwise show nothing. Caution: the lazy empty quotes "" technique returns a text string, although the cell will look empty. Any dependent formulas will now return the #VALUE! error. A much better solution is to return a 0 and use appropriate formatting (Chapter 7).

=IF(E10=0,E10,E10*E5) If the content of E10 is equal to 0, show 0, otherwise multiply E10 by E5. Caution: E10 must be *exactly* 0 for this to work.

Using AND and OR

At this stage we will look at techniques for building more complex conditions. If we need to specify that two conditions must be satisfied (e.g. E10>0 and E5>10) we can write an AND function:

=IF(AND(E10>0,E5>10),E10*E5,0)

The AND function returns TRUE if both arguments evaluate to TRUE. If either or both return FALSE, the AND returns FALSE. AND will allow up to 30 individual tests to be evaluated.

If we require either argument to be true, rather than both, we can use the OR function:

=IF(OR(E10>0,E5>10),E10*E5,0)

In this case, OR will return TRUE if either test is TRUE. Only if both tests are FALSE will it return FALSE. As with AND, up to 30 tests can be evaluated. Occasionally the product of the AND/OR test may be opposite to the result you actually need. Imagine that should both E10 be greater than 0 and E5 greater than 10, the FALSE outcome of the IF test should be followed. This can be done using the NOT function:

=IF(NOT(AND(E10>0,E5>10)),E10*E5,0)

A MAX/MIN Solution

Now let us extend this using an example that requires us to split positive (cash) and negative (overdraft) values from a cash flow (net cash):

Cash	=IF(NetCash>0,NetCash,0)
Overdraft	=IF(NetCash<0,0,NetCash)

I hope you can spot the mistake. The cash formula tests to see if net cash is positive and shows the value if it is. The overdraft formula tests to see if net cash is negative and shows a *zero* if it is. I correctly changed the direction of the test from > to <, but inadvertently switched the true/false arguments as well. The second formula is in fact a cash formula.

Let's consider an alternative solution for this problem. Instead of using an IF, let us try MAX and MIN:

Cash	=MAX(+NetCash,0)	or	=MAX(0,+NetCash)
Overdraft	=MIN(+NetCash,0)	or	=MIN(0,+NetCash)
(or alternatively,	=MAX(0-NetCash,0)		

The MAX function works by returning the largest value from the arguments in the brackets. In this case, it compares the NetCash value to 0. The MIN returns the smallest value. MAX does not return positive numbers in itself, but in this case the comparator is 0 so it returns any value greater than that. I have written each formula in two ways to show that the order of the arguments doesn't matter, unlike the IF. MAX and MIN can evaluate up to 30 arguments and they are described as array functions: the purpose of the + in front of the range name is to prevent Excel from evaluating the largest value in the whole NetCash range (Chapter 4). If this isn't clear, try writing the range name with and without the +, and note the results. If using cell references only, the plus sign is not required.

STARTING AGAIN

I have deliberately avoided going into too much detail with these last examples because in my opinion we are moving into dangerous waters and we are clearly not following the Principle of Error Reduction, and I am going to suggest some alternative ways of composing this logic that should be more readable and therefore less prone to error. Let us go back to the original IF test:

=IF(E10>0,E10,0)

As we saw in the previous chapter we could write just the test condition itself into a cell:

=E10>0

Excel will evaluate the formula and return TRUE or FALSE. These are referred to as the logical or boolean operators. If you rewrite the formula:

=(E10>0)+0 or =(E10>0)*1

Excel will return a 1 or a 0; 1 being TRUE, 0 is FALSE. The addition of the 0 or the multiplication by 1 forces Excel to return the value of the logical operator. Some people, and some formulas, prefer the values to the operators.

The Logical Mask

This functionality offers an alternative approach to building logic into models; instead of constructing long, cumbersome IF formulas we can break the underlying logic into individual steps, with each step carrying out a single logic test. This links back to the concept of the mask, introduced in the previous chapter.

Breaking down the =IF(E10>0,E10,0) formula into steps, we have

Mask	=E10>0
Calculation	=Mask*E10

This is a very simple illustration, and you are probably thinking that it seems redundant to split a one cell formula into two cells. But now let us extend it with the same multiple conditions used above:

=IF(AND(E10>0,E5>10),E10*E5,0) can be expressed as:
Line 1	=E10>0
Line 2	=E5>10
Mask	=AND(Line 1, Line 2)
Calculation	=E10*E5*Mask

And similarly,

=IF(OR(E10>0,E5>10),E10*E5,0) can be expressed as:
Line 1	=E10>0
Line 2	=E5>10
Mask	=OR(Line 1, Line 2)
Calculation	=E10*E5*Mask

Finally,

=IF(NOT(AND(E10>0,E5>10),E10*E5,0) is:
Line 1	=E10>0
Line 2	=E5>10
Line 3	=AND(Line 1, Line 2)
Mask	=NOT(Line 3)
Calculation	=E10*E5*Mask

The mask technique can be very useful for identifying events. For example, the accounting rules relating to depreciation generally specify that assets are depreciated when they are put into use, which may be some time after they were purchased. If we can find a driver that indicates that the asset is in use, we can build a simple mask to control the depreciation formula (Figure 6.2).

Mask	=Production>0
Depreciation	=(depreciation formula)*Mask

▲ A	B	C	D	E	F	G	H	I	J	K
1				2016	2017	2018	2019	2020	*Year*	
2										
3	Production									
4	units			0	10,000	10,000	10,000	10,000	*Production*	
5										
6	**Mask**			FALSE	TRUE	TRUE	TRUE	TRUE	*Mask*	
7										
8	Fixed assets									
9	asset life		4	years						
10	opening balance			0	100,000	75,000	50,000	25,000		
11	capex			100,000	0	0	0	0		
12	**depreciation**			0	25,000	25,000	25,000	25,000		
13	closing balance		0	100,000	75,000	50,000	25,000	0		
14										

FIGURE 6.2   Simple depreciation mask.

This approach can be too simplistic. If the driver is not directly associated with the asset, we could end up with the mask returning the wrong value and suspending depreciation, which is not acceptable. The test of `Production>0` only returns information about the current level of production, rather than the more important fact that the event of production starting (and therefore depreciation) has taken place. Let us change the routine and add an additional line:

Production is happening=`Production>0`
Production has started =`OR(previous cell, +ProductionHappening)`

`Previous cell` is a reference to the cell immediately to the left of the formula cell, and this new line needs a FALSE in the base column to start it off. The formula looks at the previous result and compares it to the current production level. The OR returns TRUE if either cell contains a TRUE. What makes this interesting is that when the new `ProductionStarted` line flips over to TRUE, it *cannot* revert back to FALSE ever. If production is halted, the formula still returns TRUE because the previous cell reads TRUE. If we make the depreciation formula read off the second line, we find that depreciation will now continue regardless of what subsequently happens to production.

We can also write this routine without the OR. The formula can be written as:

`=previous cell+ProductionStarted>0`

This produces the same result (Figure 6.3).

Even with these trivial examples, we are trying to set out our work in a way that can be easily followed. Each line contains only one action, be it a logic test, a mask or a calculation. One criticism is that apparently simple logic is now spread over several lines, but I think the ease with which we can revisit and understand what can be complex logic sequences more than repays the extra effort in setting up these routines.

⊿	A	B	C	D	E	F	G	H	I	J	K	L
1					2016	2017	2018	2019	2020	Year		
2												
3	Production											
4		units			0	10,000	10,000	10,000	0	Production		
5		is happening			FALSE	TRUE	TRUE	TRUE	FALSE	MaskProductionHappening		
6		has started		FALSE	FALSE	TRUE	TRUE	TRUE	TRUE	MaskProductionStarted		
7												
8	Fixed assets											
9		asset life		4	years							
10		opening balance			0	100,000	75,000	50,000	25,000			
11		capex			100,000	0	0	0	0			
12		depreciation			0	25,000	25,000	25,000	25,000			
13		closing balance		0	100,000	75,000	50,000	25,000	0			
14												

FIGURE 6.3   A combined mask.

Putting it into Practice

An example should help. Let us consider commercial bank loan. We will imagine that we can negotiate a repayment holiday, which means we can draw down the funds and simply pay the interest until the repayment period starts. At this stage we are not sure how long the repayment period lasts, nor are we sure about the duration of the loan.

The modelling problem is in two parts: we must identify a trigger to commence repayments and a trigger to stop repayments. Repayments therefore only take place in the time between the end of the repayment holiday and the completion of the repayment. The principle of left-to-right consistency demands that we can only have one formula for debt repayment.

To begin with, we will borrow 1,000,000 to be repaid over 10 years, with a 2-year repayment holiday at the start. We may want to defer the drawdown to the second year, and the duration of the loan and the repayment holiday are variables. Assuming equal repayments each year, the annual repayment will be:

```
=SUM(Amount)/(Duration - RepaymentHoliday)
```

that is, 8 annual payments of 125,000
We can set this up in the model (Figure 6.4):
We can set up a corkscrew to handle the debt (Figure 6.5):
Note that simply pulling in the annual repayment figure causes the debt to be overpaid. We need to suspend the repayments during the first 2 years. One solution is to set up a quick mask based on the year number or column number, along the lines of

```
=Number>RepaymentHoliday,
```
and on first pass this would do the trick (Figure 6.6).

But later on I shall consider the effect of deferring the loan drawdown, that is, borrowing the funds in year 2 or year 3. If this happens, and we assume that we are still entitled to the repayment holiday, then this mask will not work. If we consider a number sequence that has a one in the year in which the first

| AnnualRepayment | | f_x | =SUM(Amount)/(Term-RepaymentHoliday) |

	A	B	C	D	E	F	G	H	I	J	K	L	M	N	O	P
1					2016	2017	2018	2019	2020	2021	2022	2023	2024	2025		
2																
3		Business loan														
4		amount			1,000,000	0	0	0	0	0	0	0	0	0	0	*Amount*
5		term		10 *Term*												
6		repayment holiday		2 *RepaymentHoliday*												
7		annual repayment		125,000 *AnnualRepayment*												
8																

FIGURE 6.4 Setting up the loan.

	A	B	C	D	E	F	G	H	I	J	K	L	M	N	O	P
1					2016	2017	2018	2019	2020	2021	2022	2023	2024	2025		
2																
3		Business loan														
4		amount			1,000,000	0	0	0	0	0	0	0	0	0	0	*Amount*
5		term		10 *Term*												
6		repayment holiday		2 *RepaymentHoliday*												
7		annual repayment		125,000 *AnnualRepayment*												
8																
9		opening balance			0	875,000	750,000	625,000	500,000	375,000	250,000	125,000	0	-125,000	-125,000	*LoanBf*
10		drawdown			1,000,000	0	0	0	0	0	0	0	0	0	0	*LoanDrawdown*
11		repayment			125,000	125,000	125,000	125,000	125,000	125,000	125,000	125,000	125,000	125,000	125,000	*LoanRepayment*
12		closing balance		0	875,000	750,000	625,000	500,000	375,000	250,000	125,000	0	-125,000	-250,000	-250,000	*LoanCf*
13																

FIGURE 6.5 The loan corkscrew – note the overpayment.

	A	B	C	D	E	F	G	H	I	J	K	L	M	N	O	P
1					2016	2017	2018	2019	2020	2021	2022	2023	2024	2025		
2																
3		Business loan														
4		amount			1,000,000										0 *Amount*	
5		term		10 *Term*												
6		repayment holiday		2 *RepaymentHoliday*												
7		annual repayment		125,000 *AnnualRepayment*												
8																
9		number		0	1	2	3	4	5	6	7	8	9	10 *Number*		
10		mask			FALSE	FALSE	TRUE	TRUE	TRUE	TRUE	TRUE	TRUE	TRUE	TRUE	*Mask*	
11																
12		opening balance			0	1,000,000	1,000,000	875,000	750,000	625,000	500,000	375,000	250,000	125,000	*LoanBf*	
13		drawdown			1,000,000	0	0	0	0	0	0	0	0	0	*LoanDrawdown*	
14		repayment			0	0	125,000	125,000	125,000	125,000	125,000	125,000	125,000	125,000	*LoanRepayment*	
15		closing balance		0	1,000,000	1,000,000	875,000	750,000	625,000	500,000	375,000	250,000	125,000	0	*LoanCf*	
16																

FIGURE 6.6 A simple repayment mask.

repayment is due, we can write a formula such as = Previous + 1 where Previous is a cell reference to the preceding cell. If this is copied back to the start of the row, it does not work until you type −2 in the base column. You may recognise this as =0-RepaymentHoliday. At this point, the number sequence (or counter) is now driven by the input repayment holiday value, and the first repayment is due wherever the counter reads 1 (although this still does not solve the problem of the deferred drawdown) (Figure 6.7). The mask formula can be written as:

=HolidayCounter>0 and the repayment formula becomes
=AnnualRepayment*Mask

This now holds back the repayments until the end of the repayment holiday (as the mask changes from FALSE to TRUE), but it does not recognise that the loan will eventually get paid off, or could be paid off early. You should set up another counter, starting in the base column with =0-Term and incrementing by 1 each year. Set up a second mask which reads =DurationCounter<1. If you inspect this row it reads TRUE from the start. We should only make repayments when both lines read TRUE, so set up a repayment mask reading: =AND(+HolidayMask,+TermMask) and amend the repayment calculation in the corkscrew accordingly.

Note that AND and OR are grouped with the likes of MAX and MIN in that they require range names to be prefixed with a plus sign if they are to read from the same column and not the whole row Chapter 4 (Figure 6.8).

Test the operation of the masks by changing both the repayment holiday and duration values.

I mentioned previously that we might not be sure when we will actually drawdown the loan, but whenever this happens, we will still be entitled to the repayment holiday. This issue can be resolved by changing the existing mask. First, we need to identify when the loan is actually drawn down. Set up a row which tests for this: = Amount > 0. This returns TRUE in the year the drawdown takes place. We can create a flag to show that this event has occurred, and we can then replace the existing duration and holiday counters with a single loan repayment counter. On the line below the drawdown test put a 0 in the base column and then fill the row with =Previous+Above, where Previous is a cell reference to the previous cell in the row and Above is a cell or range reference to the drawdown test line. This row should read 1 from the point at which the drawdown takes place. In the next row, we can set up the loan counter using a neat trick to carry out a rolling sum:

=SUM($start of counter:start of counter).

The first reference in this formula must be absolute, the second part relative. When you copy this formula across the row, you should find that the numbers accumulate. The value of 1 occurs in the year in which the debt is drawn down (Figure 6.9).

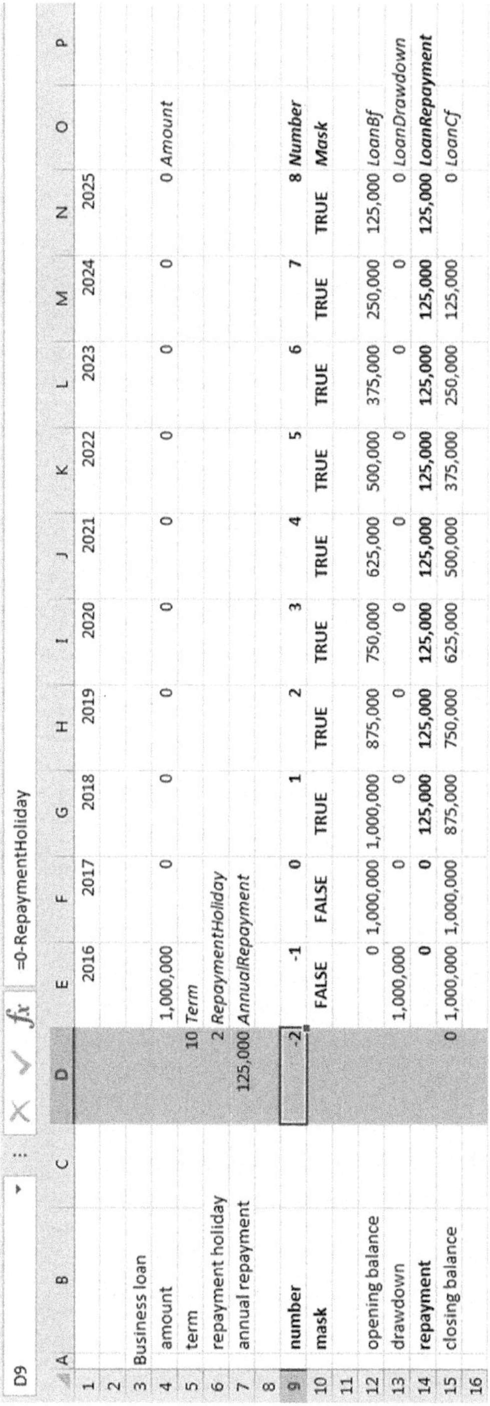

D9 =0-RepaymentHoliday

	A	B	C	D	E	F	G	H	I	J	K	L	M	N	O	P
1					2016	2017	2018	2019	2020	2021	2022	2023	2024	2025		
2																
3		Business loan														
4		amount			1,000,000	0	0	0	0	0	0	0	0	0	*Amount*	
5		term		10	*Term*											
6		repayment holiday		2	*RepaymentHoliday*											
7		annual repayment		125,000	*AnnualRepayment*											
8																
9		**number**		-2	-1	0	1	2	3	4	5	6	7	8	***Number***	
10		**mask**			FALSE	FALSE	TRUE	TRUE	TRUE	TRUE	TRUE	TRUE	TRUE	TRUE	***Mask***	
11																
12		opening balance			0	1,000,000	1,000,000	875,000	750,000	625,000	500,000	375,000	250,000	125,000	*LoanBf*	
13		drawdown			1,000,000	0	0	0	0	0	0	0	0	0	*LoanDrawdown*	
14		**repayment**			**0**	**0**	**125,000**	**125,000**	**125,000**	**125,000**	**125,000**	**125,000**	**125,000**	**125,000**	***LoanRepayment***	
15		closing balance		0	1,000,000	1,000,000	875,000	750,000	625,000	500,000	375,000	250,000	125,000	0	*LoanCf*	
16																

FIGURE 6.7 Revising the counter.

		2016	2017	2018	2019	2020	2021	2022	2023	2024	2025	
Business loan												
amount		1,000,000	0	0	0	0	0	0	0	0	0	Amount
term	10											Term
repayment holiday	2											RepaymentHoliday
annual repayment	125,000											AnnualRepayment
holiday counter	-2	-1	0	1	2	3	4	5	6	7	8	HolidayCounter
holiday mask	FALSE	FALSE	FALSE	TRUE	TRUE	TRUE	TRUE	TRUE	TRUE	TRUE	TRUE	HolidayMask
term counter	-10	-9	-8	-7	-6	-5	-4	-3	-2	-1	0	TermCounter
term mask	TRUE	TRUE	TRUE	TRUE	TRUE	TRUE	TRUE	TRUE	TRUE	TRUE	TRUE	TermMask
repayment mask	FALSE	FALSE	FALSE	TRUE	TRUE	TRUE	TRUE	TRUE	TRUE	TRUE	TRUE	RepaymentMask
opening balance	0	0	1,000,000	1,000,000	875,000	750,000	625,000	500,000	375,000	250,000	125,000	LoanBf
drawdown		1,000,000	0	0	0	0	0	0	0	0	0	LoanDrawdown
repayment	0	0	0	125,000	125,000	125,000	125,000	125,000	125,000	125,000	125,000	LoanRepayment
closing balance	0	1,000,000	1,000,000	875,000	750,000	625,000	500,000	375,000	250,000	125,000	0	LoanCf

FIGURE 6.8   The finished repayment mask.

#	A	B	C	D	E	F	G	H	I	J	K	L	M	N	O	P
1					2016	2017	2018	2019	2020	2021	2022	2023	2024	2025		
2																
3		Business loan														
4		amount		0	1,000,000	0	0	0	0	0	0	0	0	0	0	Amount
5		term		10	Term											
6		repayment holiday		2	RepaymentHoliday											
7		annual repayment		125,000	AnnualRepayment											
8																
9		loan drawdown		FALSE	TRUE	FALSE	FALSE	FALSE	FALSE	FALSE	FALSE	FALSE	FALSE	FALSE	FALSE	DrawdownMask
10		flag		0	1	1	1	1	1	1	1	1	1	1	1	Flag
11		counter		0	0	1	2	3	4	5	6	7	8	9	9	LoanCounter
12																
13		repayment mask		FALSE	FALSE	FALSE	FALSE	TRUE	TRUE	TRUE	TRUE	TRUE	TRUE	TRUE	TRUE	RepaymentMask
14																
15		opening balance			0	1,000,000	1,000,000	1,000,000	875,000	750,000	625,000	500,000	375,000	250,000	250,000	LoanBf
16		drawdown		0	1,000,000	0	0	0	0	0	0	0	0	0	0	LoanDrawdown
17		repayment		0	0	0	0	125,000	125,000	125,000	125,000	125,000	125,000	125,000	125,000	LoanRepayment
18		closing balance		0	1,000,000	1,000,000	1,000,000	875,000	750,000	625,000	500,000	375,000	250,000	125,000	125,000	LoanCf
19																

FIGURE 6.9   The loan drawdown Thtasdfasdfas.

To complete this routine, we need to know when the repayments should start, assuming that the repayment holiday still applies. We also need to identify when the repayments finish, although to get the logic the right way round we should actually identify the period during which the repayments have not finished (Figure 6.10).

```
>Repayments due        =LoanCounter>RepaymentHoliday
Repayments not finished =LoanCounter<=Term
```

This is a tidier solution than the previous version, in that only one counter is required. You may find alternative solutions.

REVOLVING CREDIT

A further example of the use of masks is in the concept of revolving credit. This is a financial instrument similar to the personal credit card, in which a loan facility is agreed and funds drawn down and repaid as required. Once the full amount is borrowed, no further funds are available. In reality we would need to recognise arrangement fees, interest and often a minimum repayment, but we can start with a basic corkscrew and mask combination. We will also recognise that the finance director wishes to maintain a minimum cash balance.

Before worrying about the code, let's consider the issues.

1. We generate cash each period.
2. We are required to have a minimum cash balance.
3. If the cash flow is less than the minimum, we can draw down funds to this level.
4. We can do this as often as we need to, provided we don't exceed the total credit limit.
5. If we have sufficient cash in a period, we can use it to repay any amount from the previous periods, subject to maintaining the minimum balance.

We can set up the following headings in the worksheet (Figure 6.11).

1. Enter the inputs: the credit limit and the minimum cash balance.
2. Enter test values for the cash flow (for this example I am assuming it will not go negative), and calculate the shortfall between the actual cash balance and the minimum balance required – use `=0-MIN(0,CashFlow-MinimumCashBalance)`. This will drive the drawdown in the corkscrew.
3. The mask is fairly straightforward: it will identify when we are able to make repayments. This will happen when there is a cash surplus when no funds are drawn down:
   `=AND(+CashFlow>0,+Shortfall=0)`
4. Set up a corkscrew to show the opening balance, the amount of credit used, the amount repaid and the closing balance. The opening balance (brought forward, bf) is a link to the previous closing balance (carried forward, cf). Leave the used and repaid lines blank for the moment; the closing balance cf is the bf plus the used, less the repaid.

	B	C	D	E 2016	F 2017	G 2018	H 2019	I 2020	J 2021	K 2022	L 2023	M 2024	N 2025	O	P
3	Business loan														
4	amount		0	1,000,000										0	*Amount*
5	term		8	*Term*											
6	repayment holiday		2	*RepaymentHoliday*											
7	annual repayment		166,667	*AnnualRepayment*											
9	loan drawdown		0	FALSE	TRUE	FALSE	FALSE	FALSE	FALSE	FALSE	FALSE	FALSE	FALSE		*DrawdownMask*
10	flag		0	0	1	1	1	1	1	1	1	1	1	1	*Flag*
11	counter		0	0	1	2	3	4	5	6	7	8	9	9	*LoanCounter*
13	repayments due			FALSE	FALSE	FALSE	TRUE	TRUE	TRUE	TRUE	TRUE	TRUE	TRUE		*RepaymentDueMask*
14	repayments not finished			TRUE	TRUE	TRUE	TRUE	TRUE	TRUE	TRUE	TRUE	TRUE	FALSE		*RepaymentUnfinishedMask*
15	repayment mask			FALSE	FALSE	FALSE	TRUE	TRUE	TRUE	TRUE	TRUE	TRUE	FALSE		*RepaymentMask*
17	opening balance			0	0	1,000,000	1,000,000	833,333	666,667	500,000	333,333	166,667	0		*LoanBf*
18	drawdown		0	1,000,000	0	0	0	0	0	0	0	0	0		*LoanDrawdown*
19	repayment			0	0	0	166,667	166,667	166,667	166,667	166,667	166,667	0		*LoanRepayment*
20	closing balance		0	0	1,000,000	1,000,000	833,333	666,667	500,000	333,333	166,667	0	0		*LoanCf*

FIGURE 6.10 The finished mask, with a term of 8 years and the loan drawdown in period 2. The loan is completely and exactly repaid.

	A	B	C	D	E	F	G	H	I	J	K	L	M	N	O	P
1					2016	2017	2018	2019	2020	2021	2022	2023	2024	2025		
2																
3		Revolving credit														
4		limit		10	*CreditLimit*											
5		minimum cash balance		5	*MinimumCashBalance*											
6																
7		Cash flow			10	5	4	0	1	1	20	12	12	12	*CashFlow*	
8		shortfall													*Shortfall*	
9																
10		Credit														
11		cash surplus													*Mask*	
12																
13		opening balance													*Bf*	
14		used													*Used*	
15		repaid													*Repaid*	
16		closing balance													*Cf*	
17				0												
18		New balance													*CashBalance*	
19																

FIGURE 6.11 Setting up the revolver.

5. The used amount will be the shortfall in funds, provided this, plus any previous amount used (bf), does not exceed the credit limit. This can be written using a MIN function:

`=MIN(+Shortfall,CreditLimit-Bf)`

6. The repaid amount is the smaller of the cash flow, the accumulated debt and the minimum cash balance, subject to cash being available, calculated as:

`=MIN(+CashFlow,Bf+Used,MinimumCashBalance)*Mask`

7. Finally, we introduce the idea of a simple cash cascade. We have analysed our original cash flow and drawn down or repaid our revolving credit facility to derive a new balance (Figure 6.12):

`=CashFlow+Used-Repaid`

Try changing the cash flow, minimum cash balance and credit limit values. You should find that this routine will prevent breaching the limit or overpaying. You may wish to extend this example by considering the effects of a negative cash flow, and instead of a minimum cash balance, a maximum overdraft facility. You might also consider flagging up periods in which the minimum cash balance cannot be maintained.

The cash cascade concept can be extended to include other financing components, and in order of priority, such that senior debt interest and principal are repaid ahead of subordinated debt interest and principal, ahead of dividends and so on.

LOOKUP

Good Old VLOOKUP and HLOOKUP

The lookup table is a well-established spreadsheet tool. As an organised structure, it contains reference information that can be retrieved for calculation purposes. It allows me, for example, to quote the current share price of a company, or to return the hourly rate for a consultant, or even to run scenarios (see Chapter 8). In the right circumstances it is robust and reliable, but it doesn't lend itself to all types of modelling. Considered by many to be a legacy from Lotus 1-2-3 the two basic flavours are VLOOKUP and HLOOKUP – with the former the information is arranged in rows, in the latter it is in columns.

The basic syntax of the VLOOKUP is:

`=VLOOKUP(item, lookup table, column, match type).`

Excel displays the prompts:

`=VLOOKUP(lookup_value,table_array,col_index_num,[range_lookup])`

You can enter an item into a cell, the VLOOKUP looks for it in the first (left-hand) column of the lookup table, reads across to the appropriate column, and returns the corresponding entry.

Item is the cell reference or range name containing the search item. The search item must occur in the first (index) column of the lookup table (in HLOOKUP the search item must occur in the first row).

		D	E (2016)	F (2017)	G (2018)	H (2019)	I (2020)	J (2021)	K (2022)	L (2023)	M (2024)	N (2025)	O
3	Revolving credit												
4	limit	10	CreditLimit										
5	minimum cash balance	5	MinimumCashBalance										
7	Cash flow		10	5	4	0	1	1	10	10	10	10	CashFlow
8	shortfall		0	0	1	5	4	4	0	0	0	0	Shortfall
10	Credit												
11	cash surplus		TRUE	TRUE	FALSE	FALSE	FALSE	FALSE	TRUE	TRUE	TRUE	TRUE	Mask
13	opening balance		0	0	0	1	6	10	10	5	0	0	Bf
14	used		0	0	1	5	4	0	0	0	0	0	Used
15	repaid		0	0	0	0	0	0	5	5	0	0	Repaid
16	closing balance	0	0	0	1	6	10	10	5	0	0	0	Cf
18	New balance		10	5	5	5	5	1	5	5	10	10	CashBalance

FIGURE 6.12 The completed revolver. The cash balance is maintained at 5 until the credit facility is used up. This is subsequently repaid.

| D5 | | | ▾ | ⋮ | ✕ | ✓ | *fx* | =VLOOKUP(D3,B10:G16,2,0) | |

▲	A	B	C	D	E	F	G	H
1								
2								
3			Enter ticker:	GHI				
4								
5			Company name	GHI Inc				
6			Current share price	11				
7								
8								
9		Ticker	CoName	Price	Hi	Lo	P/E	
10		ABC	ABC Ltd	13	23	7	8%	
11		DEF	DEF plc	13	22	11	6%	
12		GHI	GHI Inc	11	16	9	7%	
13		JKL	JKL Ltd	16	20	12	7%	
14		MNO	MNO plc	12	21	16	8%	
15		PQR	PQR Inc	19	22	13	10%	
16		STU	STU Group plc	15	24	11	9%	
17								

FIGURE 6.13   A lookup table.

Lookup table is the range in which the information is arranged. This can be cell references or a range name.

Column is the number of the column which contains the item you wish to return. This is normally a value. The left-hand column is column 1.

Slightly confusing match type is FALSE or 0 if an *exact* match is required. If TRUE or 1, Excel will match the lookup item with an item from the range which is less than or equal to the test item, but with the assumption that the first column has been sorted into ascending order. Be aware that if this argument is omitted, Excel assumes that the match type is TRUE.

We need one VLOOKUP formula for each item of information we wish to obtain. VLOOKUP is not case sensitive in terms of the search item and its corresponding entry in the index column. Look at the following example (Figure 6.13).

A well-constructed lookup table can be very reliable. However, there are problems and limitations. The index column must not contain duplicates; VLOOKUP will only handle the first match. One of the commonest problems is when new data are appended to the table and the formulas are not updated, although a simple workaround for this is to use a range name for the table and to rename the table after updating (or use the expanding range name trick on p 127). As the formula requires you to specify the column from which you want to return the result, a further structural problem occurs if columns are inserted or deleted. The hard-coded column number can also cause problems if the formula is copied, as can the failure to set absolute references for the lookup table – this latter problem is often missed. If the match type argument is omitted, the formula will return an approximate match rather than an exact match, which can be misleading as there will be no indication of this. Only if the item does not appear in the index column will Excel return the #N/A error. Lastly, it should be obvious but lookup does not work in reverse: with my share portfolio above, I cannot find out the company name of my lowest priced stock.

It should be apparent that VLOOKUP requires an organised table structure, with a column or row by which the information is arranged. Although we might identify the dates across the top of the forecast period as both unique and in ascending order and therefore suitable, the rest of our cash flow models does not conform to a formal lookup table structure.

There is also the Excel LOOKUP function. This comes in two forms, using vectors or arrays. Although subject to the same structural and organisational constraints as the V and H LOOKUPs, the vector form is worth a brief description as it leads into the MATCH and INDEX functions below.

If we have a row of dates across the top of a spreadsheet, and a series of periodic cash flows, we could use a MAX to return the largest cash flow. To relate this to its date, we could write a formula such as: =LOOKUP(max cash value, cash flow range, date range)

Excel will identify the position of the maximum cash value in the cash flow range and return the date from the same position in the date range. Except it doesn't, because Excel assumes that the cash flow values are in ascending order. Which they aren't. Let's develop this further.

LOOKUP WITHOUT USING LOOKUPs

In the example below, we can see a typical lumpy cash flow and the resulting cash balances of a project. Being prudent financial planners, we wish to avoid going into overdraft and so it would be helpful to flag up cash shortfalls. However, I do not want to keep scrolling across the screen on the off chance that this scenario might happen; it would be more useful if Excel could warn us of the event. Firstly we will identify the lowest cash flow. This is easily done with a MIN: =MIN(CashFlow). We will call this CashFlowMinimum. Next, we need to identify the year in which this occurs. The row of years is called YearCounter (Figure 6.14).

Let us solve this problem with a simple mask. We can put in a line that tests if the minimum cash value corresponds to the cash balance value for that year.

=CashFlowMinimum=CashFlow Call this row Mask.

As CashFlowMinimum is the name of a single cell, it is inherently absolute and can be copied across the row. We should see a TRUE value in the year in which this value occurs. Now multiply by the YearCounter.

=YearCounter*Mask Call this row CashFlowMinimumYear.

To finish off, put a SUM in the base column:

=SUM(CashFlowMinimumYear).

Change the numbers to prove that this works (Figure 6.15).

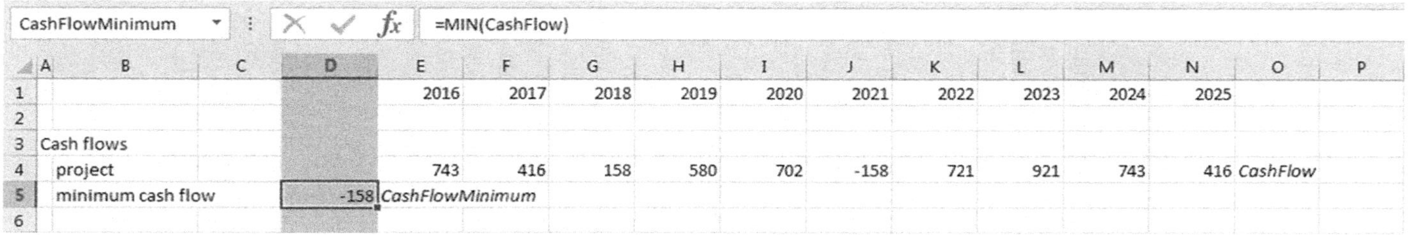

CashFlowMinimum   ·   ∶ | X ✓ *fx* | =MIN(CashFlow)

◢	A	B	C	D	E	F	G	H	I	J	K	L	M	N	O	P
1					2016	2017	2018	2019	2020	2021	2022	2023	2024	2025		
2																
3	Cash flows															
4	project				743	416	158	580	702	-158	721	921	743		416	CashFlow
5	minimum cash flow			-158	CashFlowMinimum									2025		
6																

FIGURE 6.14 Cash flow forecast.

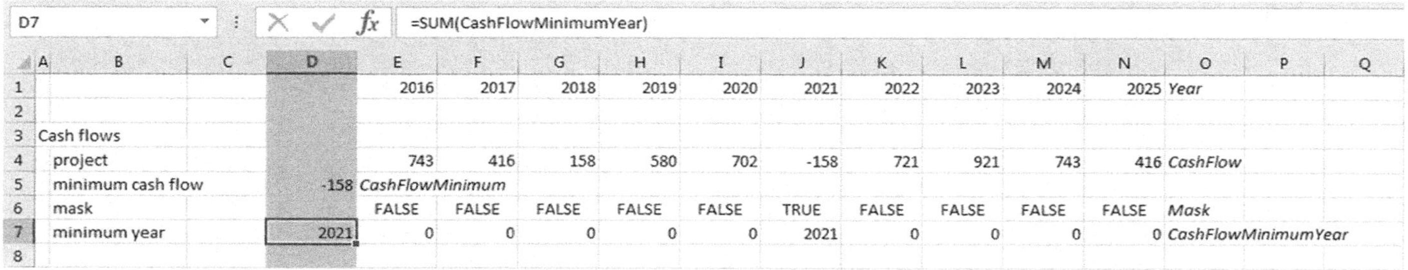

D7   ·   ∶ | X ✓ *fx* | =SUM(CashFlowMinimumYear)

◢	A	B	C	D	E	F	G	H	I	J	K	L	M	N	O	P	Q
1					2016	2017	2018	2019	2020	2021	2022	2023	2024	2025	Year		
2																	
3	Cash flows																
4	project				743	416	158	580	702	-158	721	921	743		416	CashFlow	
5	minimum cash flow			-158	CashFlowMinimum									2025			
6	mask				FALSE	FALSE	FALSE	FALSE	FALSE	TRUE	FALSE	FALSE	FALSE	FALSE	0	Mask	
7	minimum year			2021	0	0	0	0	0	2021	0	0	0	0	0	CashFlowMinimumYear	
8																	

FIGURE 6.15 Cash flow minimum value and year using a mask.

INDEX

This is a powerful function which we can use on its own or in combination with other functions and techniques. In essence it will look at a range and return a value from the position specified within that range, as:

```
=INDEX(range, position)
```

In Excel-speak it is written as follows:

```
=INDEX(array, row_num,[column_num])
```

In the examples that follow, we will assume that our range (or array) is one-dimensional, that is a single row, in which case we need only provide the column number as the position (Figure 6.16). Consider a row of cash flow values. To return the 4th number from the range, we would write:

```
=INDEX(cash flow, 4)
```

What then is the source of the '4'? This is where we return to the counter mechanism introduced in the previous chapter. We could add a row which counts the columns, and then change the INDEX formula to:

```
=INDEX(cash flow, column counter)
```

This doesn't really illustrate the power of INDEX. Now we can develop the counter idea further. Imagine we need to look ahead to the cash flow in four periods' time. We need another counter: write the 4 into the base column and in column E we add 1 to the previous cell and copy across the row. Reflect for a moment on the significance of the counter: the value tells us which column to look at. In the first column (column E) we want to show the value from column I; in the second column the value from J and so on, reading ahead 4 years each time. If you are testing this using cell references you will need to make the range reference absolute. There is also a risk that the last formulas in the row are reading off the end of the range, which we can solve with a nested MIN/MAX in the counter, where the counter stops when it reaches the value corresponding to the largest value in the column count range (Figure 6.17).

```
=MIN(previous+1,MAX(column counter))
```

We can also use the INDEX and counter mechanism to look backwards. If we switch the sign of the base number (using =0-value) the counter sequence now reads back four periods. In this case the INDEX in the first column attempts to look back to period −3 (Figure 6.18). Clearly this

10	Cash flows						
11	project		743	416	158	580	702 *CashFlow*
12	look at position	4					
13	value in position	=INDEX(CashFlow,D12)					
14							

FIGURE 6.16 A first look at INDEX.

E8 =INDEX(CashFlow,LookAheadCounter)

A	B	C	D	E	F	G	H	I	J	K	L	M	N	O	P
1				2016	2017	2018	2019	2020	2021	2022	2023	2024	2025	2025	Year
2																
3	column counter		0	1	2	3	4	5	6	7	8	9	10	10	ColumnCounter
4																
5	Cash flows														
6	project			743	416	158	580	702	-158	721	921	743	416	416	CashFlow
7	look ahead counter		4	5	6	7	8	9	10	10	10	10	10	10	LookAheadCounter
8	cash flow value			702	-158	721	921	743	416	416	416	416	416	416	
9																

FIGURE 6.17 INDEX using a look-ahead counter.

I8 =IF(LookBackCounter<1,0,INDEX(CashFlow,LookBackCounter))

A	B	C	D	E	F	G	H	I	J	K	L	M	N	O	P
1				2016	2017	2018	2019	2020	2021	2022	2023	2024	2025	2025	Year
2																
3	column counter		0	1	2	3	4	5	6	7	8	9	10	10	ColumnCounter
4																
5	Cash flows														
6	project			743	416	158	580	702	-158	721	921	743	416	416	CashFlow
7	look back counter		-4	-3	-2	-1	0	1	2	3	4	5	6	6	LookBackCounter
8	cash flow value			0	0	0	0	743	416	158	580	702	-158	-158	
9																

FIGURE 6.18 INDEX using the look-back counter.

is not possible, and so we need to manage the error by embedding the INDEX in an IF:

```
=IF(counter<1,0,INDEX(cash flow,counter))
```

MATCH

You may have noticed that the INDEX function is like the second part of a LOOKUP: it looks in the range at a specified position. If we look at the MATCH function we see that it acts as the first part of a LOOKUP: it looks for an item in a range and returns its position. It has the following syntax:

```
=MATCH(item, range, match type)
```

Item is the cell reference or range name of the value we wish to look for.

Range is the row or column where this item can be found.

Match type is 0 if an exact match is required. If 1, Excel will return an item from the range which is less than or equal to the test item, but with the assumption that the range is in ascending order. Using the value of −1 it will return a value greater than or equal to the test, assuming the range is in descending order. If this argument is omitted, Excel assumes that match type is TRUE.

Using the cash flow example above, we can write this formula:

```
=MATCH(CashFlowMinimum,CashFlow,0)
```

Important – do not miss out the 0. Call it CashFlowPosition.

The formula tells us that the lowest cash balance is in position 6. Now we need to find out the corresponding value from the year counter row. Although this is not entirely dissimilar to the LOOKUP function, remember that the cash flow line is in no particular order, as it simply reflects the cash flows generated each year (Figure 6.19).

MATCH **and** INDEX

Staying with the problem of looking up information in the financial model, where the values themselves are not organised and could occur anywhere in a given range, we can look at combining MATCH and INDEX, which together provide the lookup functionality we need. Returning to our minimum cash flow example, the MATCH function tells us that the lowest value is in position 6 of the cash balance row. We now use the INDEX to return the corresponding year.

```
=INDEX(YearCounter,CashFlowPosition)
```

If you feel confident you could omit the first step and simply nest the two formulas:

```
=INDEX(YearCounter,MATCH(CashFlowMinimum,CashFlow,0))
```

Again, do not forget the 0 (Figure 6.20).

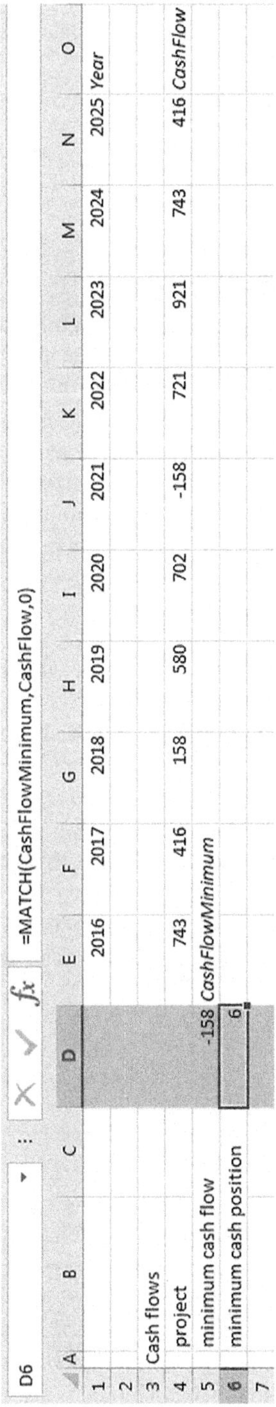

| D6 | | | fx | =MATCH(CashFlowMinimum,CashFlow,0) |

	A	B	C	D	E	F	G	H	I	J	K	L	M	N	O
1					2016	2017	2018	2019	2020	2021	2022	2023	2024	2025	Year
2															
3		Cash flows													
4		project			743	416	158	580	702	-158	721	921	743	416	CashFlow
5		minimum cash flow		-158	CashFlowMinimum										
6		minimum cash position		6											
7															

FIGURE 6.19 Using MATCH to locate the position of the minimum cash flow value.

D6			▾	:	×	✓	*fx*	=INDEX(Year,MATCH(CashFlowMinimum,CashFlow,0))		

▲	A	B	C	D	E	F	G	H	I	J	K
1					2016	2017	2018	2019	2020	2021	2022
2											
3	Cash flows										
4		project			743	416	158	580	702	-158	721
5		minimum cash flow		-158	*CashFlowMinimum*						
6		minimum cash year		2021							
7											

FIGURE 6.20 The nested `INDEX`/`MATCH`.

Straightaway there are a couple of caveats to consider. First, we must recognise that the search item is unique. Given that even in a formatted cell Excel can calculate to 15 decimal places, it may be considered unlikely that two cash balances are exactly the same – but it is not impossible. Second, the `MATCH` range must have a one-for-one correspondence with the `INDEX` range – there is no value to the exercise if they are of different sizes or are in a different order.

Although a nested `INDEX...MATCH` formula might look rather complex, it is a powerful combination that greatly exceeds the functionality of the `LOOKUP`s.

THE CONCEPT OF THE POOL

Now let's explore `INDEX` further. We can explore this in the context of the loan repayment schedule we looked at in the previous section. Although we have effectively solved the timing issues using the mask technique, we can use it to explore the concept of the pool as a timing mechanism. For the moment we'll take out the repayment holiday, and delete the loan and repayment masks. We'll borrow the money for five years. The basic idea is that we will make repayments for the period that the loan is in the pool. Set up new lines as shown, ignoring the negatives (Figure 6.21).

We add in the debt as it is drawdown. Once this has occurred, repayments will start and continue until the debt is paid off. The timing and duration of the loan are still variables.

The corkscrew is straightforward:

Opening balance bf	`=previous closing balance(cell reference)`
Add to pool	`=Amount`
Remove from pool	let us leave for a moment
Closing balance cf	`=PoolBf+PoolAdditions-PoolRemovals`

Delete the existing debt repayment formulas from the debt corkscrew. Repayment is now the `PoolCf/Term`. Do not worry about the overpayment that now follows.

The `PoolRemovals` line should show the debt dropping out after `duration` number of years. As the closing balance reaches 0, the repayment formula also reads 0. Prove this by typing in the loan amount in the appropriate cell. Note the effect on the repayments (Figure 6.22).

Business loan

Label	Value	Name
amount	1,000,000	Amount
term	5	Term
repayment holiday	0	RepaymentHoliday
annual repayment	200,000	AnnualRepayment

amount (schedule): 0 0 0 0 0 0 0 0 0

Loan pool

	E	F	G	H	I	J	K	L	M	N	Name
opening balance											PoolBf
add to pool											PoolAdditions
remove from pool											PoolRetirements
closing balance	0										PoolCf

Loan

	E	F	G	H	I	J	K	L	M	N	Name
opening balance	0	800000	600000	400000	200000	0	-200000	-400000	-600000	-800000	LoanBf
drawdown	1,000,000	0	0	0	0	0	0	0	0	0	LoanDrawdown
repayment	200,000	200,000	200,000	200,000	200,000	200,000	200,000	200,000	200,000	200,000	LoanRepayment
closing balance	800,000	600,000	400,000	200,000	0	-200,000	-400,000	-600,000	-800,000	#######	LoanCf

FIGURE 6.21   Setting up the loan pool.

Loan pool

	E	F	G	H	I	J	K	L	M	N	Name
opening balance	0	1000000	1000000	1000000	1000000	1000000	0	0	0	0	PoolBf
add to pool	1,000,000	0	0	0	0	0	0	0	0	0	PoolAdditions
remove from pool	0					**1000000**					PoolRetirements
closing balance	0	1,000,000	1,000,000	1,000,000	1,000,000	1,000,000	1,000,000	0	0	0	PoolCf

FIGURE 6.22   Adding detail.

Of course we need a calculation for this. Think back to the description of the INDEX function: it looks in a range at a specified position. The range we are interested in is the PoolAdditions line, and specifically position 1. We want the loan amount to appear in this cell. We could write =INDEX(PoolAdditions, 1) but that would be hard-coded. As with the mask treatment, the 1 and related values should be set up above the pool as a separate counter line. In the base column, type in =0-Term. In the rest of the row type =previous+1, where previous is a cell reference to the adjacent cell. This should result in a number sequence in which the value of 1 appears now in the required column. Name this row as PoolCounter (Figure 6.23).

Now we can write the PoolRemovals formula as:

```
=INDEX(PoolAdditions,PoolCounter)
```

Copy the formula to the other cells in the row. Remember that the position value for INDEX must be a positive whole number, so the negative and zero index values generate #VALUE! errors. We can protect against this by rewriting the formula once more with an error trap:

```
=IF(PoolIndex<1,0,INDEX(PoolAdditions,PoolCounter))
```

That is, if the PoolCounter is not a positive whole number, return 0.

Now, having proved that it works, let us find out why. It should be clear that the loan drops out where it does because the instruction in the INDEX formula is to look in the PoolAdditions row at the position specified in the PoolCounter row, in this case a 1, so return the value from position 1 in the PoolAdditions range. The next index value is 2, and the instruction in the formula is to look in the PoolAdditions range at position 2, and so on. We can test that the mechanism works if you delete the debt in year 1 and instead put the debt in year 2. Now change the loan duration and prove that the repayments are correct. Finally, split the loan so that the first tranche is drawn down in the first year and the remainder in the second. Does this work?

If you are still struggling with this you are in good company. Having taught this technique for several years I still find that this is the most frequent post-course enquiry I receive, which either suggests that I am not very good at teaching it, or that people have found it useful but did not quite grasp the issues the first time around. The usual question picks up on the formula's structure, in that the range element is an absolute reference (so make sure you have the $ signs if you are using cell references), and that the position element is a relative reference. It doesn't matter where you are in relation to the PoolAdditions line, but the position value is taken from the PoolCounter in the same column. Also, the PoolCounter is the driver of this mechanism – whatever value is used as the duration, the PoolCounter recalculates. The INDEX function simply does what it is told (Figure 6.24).

Note that in this example the first repayment occurs in the drawdown period. We could add a mask to control this, and likewise, if you want to include the

Figure 6.23 — Cell D10, formula bar: `=0-Term`

Loan pool	D	E	F	G	H	I	J	K	L	M	N	O	P
counter	-5	-4	-3	-2	-1	0	1	2	3	4	5		**5 *PoolCounter***
opening balance		0	1000000	1000000	1000000	1000000	1000000	0	0	0	0		0 *PoolBf*
add to pool		1000000	0	0	0	0	0	0	0	0	0		0 *PoolAdditions*
remove from pool		0	0	0	0	0	1000000	0	0	0	0		*PoolRetirements*
closing balance	0	1,000,000	1,000,000	1,000,000	1,000,000	1,000,000	0	0	0	0	0		0 *PoolCf*

FIGURE 6.23 Adding the counter.

Figure 6.24 — Cell E19, formula bar: `=PoolCf/Term`

	D	E	F	G	H	I	J	K	L	M	N	O	P
		2016	2017	2018	2019	2020	2021	2022	2023	2024	2025		*Year*
Business loan													
amount		1,000,000									0		*Amount*
term		5											*Term*
repayment holiday		0											*RepaymentHoliday*
annual repayment		200,000											*AnnualRepayment*
Loan pool													
counter	-5	-4	-3	-2	-1	0	1	2	3	4	5		**5 *PoolCounter***
opening balance		0	1,000,000	1,000,000	1,000,000	1,000,000	1,000,000	0	0	0	0		0 *PoolBf*
add to pool		1,000,000	0	0	0	0	0	0	0	0	0		0 *PoolAdditions*
remove from pool		0	0	0	0	0	1,000,000	0	0	0	0		0 *PoolRetirements*
closing balance	0	1,000,000	1,000,000	1,000,000	1,000,000	1,000,000	0	0	0	0	0		0 *PoolCf*
Loan													
opening balance		0	800,000	600,000	400,000	200,000	0	0	0	0	0		0 *LoanBf*
drawdown		1,000,000	0	0	0	0	0	0	0	0	0		0 *LoanDrawdown*
repayment		200,000	200,000	200,000	200,000	200,000	0	0	0	0	0		0 *LoanRepayment*
closing balance	0	800,000	600,000	400,000	200,000	0	0	0	0	0	0		0 *LoanCf*

FIGURE 6.24 The completed pool. The repayment line in the corkscrew is now the PoolCf/Term.

repayment holiday you can set up the mask we used previously. I will leave you to do this. If you want to extend this repayment schedule to look at semi-annual repayments rather than annual, the rule is that the model should be set up according to the shortest time period it will use. Instead of the PoolCounter values representing whole years, they will now represent periods and you can factor this in accordingly.

This INDEX and pool mechanism is very useful in modelling. There are many examples when a pool comes in handy, such as straight line depreciation. In this case you can set up a pool that picks up the capital expenditure as it is incurred and holds it for the life of the asset. While it is held in the pool it is available for the depreciation calculation, which can be as simple as PoolCf/AssetLife. As seen above, this pool can handle any number of assets, provided they share the same life. I could therefore have one depreciation pool for my 5-year assets, another for my 10-year assets and so on.

Other examples include corporate bonds, such that whilst the bond is in issue we pay a coupon (interest). Or venture capital, which has the features of debt to begin with and therefore drives an interest calculation, but at some stage we might want to convert to share capital and add the amount to the share capital corkscrew. We could also consider the retirement of tax losses, in which a company incurs a tax loss and can carry it forward over time to set against future profits. This period is defined by the tax authorities and is not unlimited. Another example is the commercial disposal or resale of fixed assets – they are depreciated while in the pool, but when retired they drop out into the fixed assets disposals routine (multiplied by some revaluation factor) and then into the cash flow.

Fixed Schedules

The INDEX and mask combination also allows to handle issues such as accelerated depreciation (or capital allowances in the UK). The problem is that the values to use for the depreciation charge differ each year, with higher charges in the first years. If we are not sure when the capital expenditure will take place it is often difficult to apply the correct rate for the year/column. Look at the following (Figure 6.25).

I have put a SUM in the base column at the start of the Capex line. The DepSchedule row lists the annual depreciation charges and I have included additional zero values to complete the forecast period. Make sure this row adds up to 100% by putting a logical check in the base column.

D5			✕ ✓	f_x	=SUM(DepSchedule)=1							
▲ A	B	C	D	E	F	G	H	I	J	K	L	M
1				2016	2017	2018	2019	2020	2021	2022	Year	
2			CapexAmount									
3	Capital expenditure		1,000	0	1,000	0	0	0	0	0	Capex	
4												
5	Depreciation schedule		TRUE	40%	30%	20%	10%	0	0	0	DepSchedule	
6												

FIGURE 6.25   Depreciation schedule.

We then add a mechanism to count the number of charges in the depreciation schedule, in case they are varied. This is expressed as =(DepSchedule>0)+0, with a SUM in the base column.

Next we need a flag to identify that the capital expenditure has occurred. The CapexHappening line captures the capex event =Capex>0, and the line below, CapexNumber, converts this to a value.

We now need to create a number sequence which counts off from the event of the capital expenditure. This number sequence will be used in an INDEX formula very shortly. The Counter row recognises the CapexHappening event (=previous+CapexNumber), and the Cumulative row creates the number sequence (=previous+Counter), with appropriate zero values in the base column.

We need a mask which will identify that the capex has taken place and is ready for depreciation, and we will need another to ensure that we only apply the depreciation for the correct number of periods. Mask A tests that Cumulative>0, and Mask B tests that the Cumulative≤=Count (the count of the number of depreciation charges in the schedule). The final Mask returns TRUE only when both Mask A and Mask B are TRUE, using an AND (Figure 6.26).

Finally we can set up the depreciation corkscrew. The depreciation rate row uses an INDEX formula to align the appropriate rate with the capital expenditure event:

```
=INDEX(DepSchedule,Cumulative)*Mask
```

DepSchedule is the set of rates in the depreciation schedule, Cumulative is the number sequence beginning in the capex year, and Mask ensures that the formula only works in the number of years specified in the depreciation schedule (Figure 6.27).

The rest of the corkscrew is straightforward. The depreciation formula is:

```
=CapexAmount*DepRate
```

Test that this routine works by changing the timing of the investment, or the depreciation schedule. Don't push it too far, because it will not handle more than one capex, but it is otherwise very robust. Think about creating an error trap based on ScheduleCheck in case the depreciation rates do not add up to 100%. Another audit check is that the total depreciation should equal the original capital expenditure amount.

OFFSET

Before moving on from the lookup functions, we will take a quick look at the OFFSET function. OFFSET is one of those functions like IF, which tend to be over-used and abused. In simple terms it has the following syntax:

```
=OFFSET(starting point, rows, columns)
```

Starting point is the cell from which you wish to navigate. It is not necessarily the current cell. If you are using cell references you should decide if this reference should be absolute or relative.

E15   fx   =AND(+MaskA,+MaskB)

	A	B	C	D	E	F	G	H	I	J	K	L	M
1					2016	2017	2018	2019	2020	2021	2022	Year	
2				*CapexAmount*									
3		Capital expenditure		1,000	0	1,000	0	0	0	0	0	Capex	
4													
5		Depreciation schedule		TRUE	40%	30%	20%	10%	0	0	0	DepSchedule	
6		count		4	1	1	1	1	0	0	0	DepCount	
7				*Count*									
8		capex happening			FALSE	TRUE	FALSE	FALSE	FALSE	FALSE	FALSE	CapexHappening	
9		as number			0	1	0	0	0	0	0	CapexNumber	
10													
11		counter		0	0	1	1	1	1	1	1	Counter	
12		cumulative		0	0	1	2	3	4	5	6	Cumulative	
13		mask A			FALSE	TRUE	TRUE	TRUE	TRUE	TRUE	TRUE	MaskA	
14		mask B			TRUE	TRUE	TRUE	TRUE	TRUE	FALSE	FALSE	MaskB	
15		mask			FALSE	TRUE	TRUE	TRUE	TRUE	FALSE	FALSE	Mask	
16													

FIGURE 6.26   The depreciation schedule counters and masks.

	A	B	C	D	E	F	G	H	I	J	K	L	M
1					2016	2017	2018	2019	2020	2021	2022	Year	
2				CapexAmount									
3	Capital expenditure			1,000	0	1,000	0	0	0	0	0	Capex	
4													
5	Depreciation schedule			TRUE	40%	30%	20%	10%	0	0	0	DepSchedule	
6	count			4	1	1	1	1	0	0	0	DepCount	
7				Count									
8	capex happening				FALSE	TRUE	FALSE	FALSE	FALSE	FALSE	FALSE	CapexHappening	
9	as number				0	1	0	0	0	0	0	CapexNumber	
10													
11	counter		0	0	0	1	1	1	1	1	1	Counter	
12	cumulative		0	0	0	1	2	3	4	5	6	Cumulative	
13	mask A				FALSE	TRUE	TRUE	TRUE	TRUE	TRUE	TRUE	MaskA	
14	mask B				TRUE	TRUE	TRUE	TRUE	TRUE	FALSE	FALSE	MaskB	
15	mask				FALSE	TRUE	TRUE	TRUE	TRUE	FALSE	FALSE	Mask	
16													
17	Depreciation												
18	rate				=INDEX(DepSchedule,Cumulative)*Mask				10%	0%	0%	DepRate	
19	opening balance				0	0	600	300	100	0	0	Bf	
20	capex				0	1,000	0	0	0	0	0	DepCapex	
21	depreciation				0	400	300	200	100	0	0	Depreciation	
22	closing balance		0		0	600	300	100	0	0	0	Cf	
23													

FIGURE 6.27   The completed depreciation routine.

Rows is a value or cell reference to a cell that contains a value that represents the number of rows you wish to read down (positive value) or up (negative value) from the starting point.

Columns is a value or cell reference to a cell that contains a value that represents the number of columns you wish to read to the right (positive value) or left (negative value) of the starting point.

The immediate point to note is that this is an indirect referencing technique: in effect we are giving Excel directions to a cell, rather than addressing it specifically.

If we look back at the loan pool removals routine in the previous exercise, it reads

```
=IF(PoolCounter<1,0,INDEX(PoolAdditions,PoolCounter))
```

INDEX asks Excel to read across a row to a particular position. We can achieve the same result using OFFSET. We need to type a 0 in the base column on the PoolAdditions row, which will act as our starting point. Call it PoolAdditionsBase.

Write the retire from pool formula as:

```
=IF(PoolCounter<1,0,OFFSET(PoolAdditionsBase,,PoolCounter))
```

The additional comma is required because in this example the row argument is not required.

Excel interprets this as the instruction to start at the PoolAdditionsBase cell and read across (blank rows and) the number of columns specified by the PoolCounter. Test to see if it works (Figure 6.28).

Unlike INDEX the OFFSET function can use negative numbers. We used the IF in the INDEX routine to guard against negative counter values forcing the

	-5	-4	-3	-2	-1	0	1	2	
14 Loan pool									
15 counter	-5	-4	-3	-2	-1	0	1	2	PoolCounter
16	PoolAdditionsBase								
17 opening balance		0	1,000,000	1,500,000	1,500,000	1,500,000	1,500,000	500,000	PoolBf
18 add to pool		1,000,000	500,000	0	0	0	0	0	PoolAdditions
19 retire from pool		0	0	0	0	0	1,000,000	500,000	PoolRetirements
20 closing balance	0	1,000,000	1,500,000	1,500,000	1,500,000	1,500,000	500,000	0	PoolCf
21									

FIGURE 6.28 The loan pool using OFFSET.

INDEX to return the #VALUE! error; but here we use to prevent OFFSET reading back (to the left) of PoolAdditionsBase, rather than to the right. In this case it will attempt to read beyond the edge of the spreadsheet or return the text in the row heading. I do not think that the resulting formula is an improvement on the original IF ... INDEX.

We often find that people hard code the row and column references into their OFFSETs, and as a model develops and routines are moved around, there always remains a nagging doubt that it might not be reading what it should. Because of the indirect nature of the referencing, you will find that the usual audit techniques (F2, Ctrl+[) point to the start cell and the cells containing the row and column values, but not to the target cell. Try it writing the depreciation schedule using OFFSET. In conclusion, I might add that the use of OFFSET in my firm is considered a disciplinary offence!

DATES

Calculations involving dates are fairly straightforward if we understand that Excel will read dates as numbers, provided they are in written in a valid date format. We can prove this quite simply by entering a date such as 25/5/16 (for the UK; use 5/25/16 in the US or your local date convention). The date appears in the cell and should be right aligned, which shows that Excel is treating it as a number (if it is left aligned Excel is reading it as text and we will be unable to use the date for calculation purposes). Strip the formatting from the cell using Ctrl+Shift+~ or Ctrl+Shift+!. In this example we can see a date serial number of 42,515, which is the number of days which have elapsed since 1 January 1900 (unless you are an Apple Mac user, in which case day 1 was 2 January 1904. If this is an issue check under File, Options, Advanced and in the When calculating this workbook section and identify the 1904 date system check box). Reformat the cell using Ctrl+# (default date format). If we then enter another date such as 25/12/2016 we can calculate the number of days between the two dates. Note that the dates do not need to be in the same format.

There is a slight bug in Excel which is becoming increasingly significant: on entering a date such as 25/5/16 Excel will normally convert it to 25/5/2016. Looking ahead less than 15 years we have dates such as 25/5/30. Write this into a spreadsheet and you will see 25/5/1930 – for some reason Excel returns to the last century. This may be immediately apparent, but unfortunately if any date formatting has been applied to a cell you might find yourself looking at 25-May-30, without realising that anything is wrong. I would consider this a risk factor for audit purposes and I now check if the model contained dates extending beyond 2029.

NOW()

The NOW() function can be entered into the worksheet to return the current date and time according to the computer's internal clock. The result is subject to the normal recalculation rules, so that it will only update when a recalculation occurs, through editing or writing formulas or F9 manual recalculation. If you take off the date formatting, we see that the function is calculated to several decimal places, which implies that Excel is working to a split second level of accuracy. Because of this I do not normally use NOW() for routine date calculations, as the results change very slightly during the course of a day. It is useful as a time stamp, but we can achieve this just as easily in the page header or footer settings. A variation on the theme is to use the TODAY() function, which returns the date serial number without the decimals. Both techniques assume your PC's clock is correct.

A neat trick to insert the current date into the workbook is Ctrl+; (semicolon). This is a hard-coded value and will not update. Use Ctrl+Shift+: (colon) to insert the current time. Note that both of these shortcuts can be used in cell comments (Ctrl+F2).

DATE (Year, Month, Day)

The timeline of a model is one of the most important sections, particularly in project finance models where so many actions (construction, operations, loan drawdowns and repayments) are directly driven by dates; the model start date may be the only hard-coded date. It is vital therefore that dates are entered or calculated correctly. There are a couple of approaches, first using the DATE function, and the second using the EDATE function. In either case we want to maintain the flexibility to change the input date and the model periodicity by simply changing the input and without having to change any formulas. This example also uses the YEAR, MONTH and DAY functions to extract the information from the date to then calculate the subsequent date.

1. Enter the start date and months in period values and name them as DateStart and MonthsInPeriod.
2. In the base column write a formula to subtract 1 from the start date (as =DateStart-1).
3. In the next column and row above link to this value and add 1, copying across the row. Name this row PeriodFrom (this is a modified corkscrew).
4. The start date has information about the year, month and day, but we want to increment the month by the months in period value. The formula is: =DATE(YEAR(PeriodFrom),MONTH(PeriodFrom)+MonthsInPeriod,DAY (PeriodFrom))-1
5. Copy this across the row and name it PeriodTo.
6. Check for spurious dates (30 February!), and change the start date and the months in period value.

An audit check might be to confirm that the calculated start date matches the input start date (Figure 6.29).

The EDATE version of this routine is simple, provided you are working with months (not days). In step 4 above, use =EDATE(+PeriodFrom, MonthsInPeriod)-1

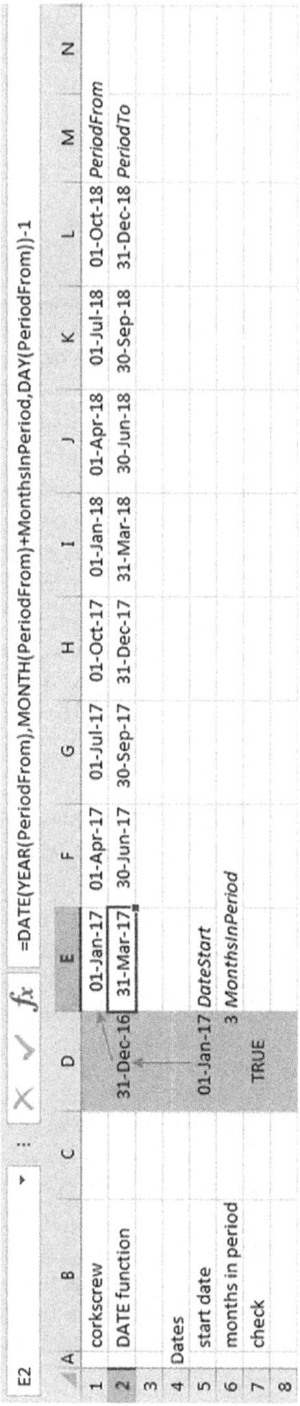

	A	B	C	D	E	F	G	H	I	J	K	L	M	N
E2					fx	=DATE(YEAR(PeriodFrom),MONTH(PeriodFrom)+MonthsInPeriod,DAY(PeriodFrom))-1								
1	corkscrew				01-Jan-17	01-Apr-17	01-Jul-17	01-Oct-17	01-Jan-18	01-Apr-18	01-Jul-18	01-Oct-18	*PeriodFrom*
2	DATE function			31-Dec-16	31-Mar-17	30-Jun-17	30-Sep-17	31-Dec-17	31-Mar-18	30-Jun-18	30-Sep-18	31-Dec-18	*PeriodTo*
3													
4	Dates												
5	start date			01-Jan-17	*DateStart*								
6	months in period			3	*MonthsInPeriod*								
7	check			TRUE									
8													

FIGURE 6.29   Calculating the timeline from the input start date.

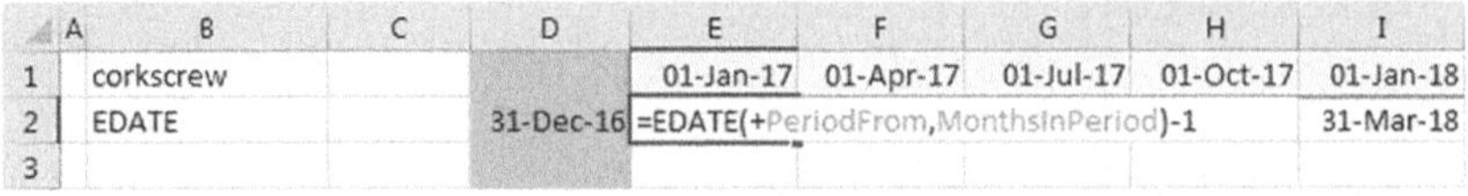

	A	B	C	D	E	F	G	H	I
1		corkscrew			01-Jan-17	01-Apr-17	01-Jul-17	01-Oct-17	01-Jan-18
2		EDATE		31-Dec-16	=EDATE(+PeriodFrom,MonthsInPeriod)-1				31-Mar-18
3									

FIGURE 6.30   The EDATE function.

In this example we add 3 months to the PeriodFrom date, and Excel works out the correct date (Figure 6.30).

Date Series

Although it would be better to calculate the date series used in a model, we might want to remind ourselves that Excel can help set up sensible date series as, for example, column headings. If we require a row of dates for the 'week commencing', we can type in the first two dates of the sequence and use the AutoFill method to copy the series across the row – select both cells, click and drag the little box (AutoFill handle) at the bottom right corner of the active range.

We can use the same functionality to put in month ends, by typing in the date of the first month end and this time right-click and drag the AutoFill handle. At the end of the operation Excel displays a shortcut menu from which we can select Fill Months. If you have entered a month end date (31/5/16) Excel is intelligent enough to recognise this and will give the appropriate month ends, rather than generating spurious dates such as 31/06/16.

FINANCIAL

If you ever have the opportunity to see one of the big project finance models used in a bank you might be surprised to see that there is little, if any, use of Excel financial functions. This is because these functions do not always work in the same way that you might have been taught at business school or in the textbooks. If you find yourself working for a bank or an accountancy firm you are likely to find that you are not allowed to use Excel's financial functions at all, and that you must write out your formulas arithmetically.

NPV

The concept of net present value (NPV) is based on the value of the cash flows into and out of an investment, discounted by the cost of capital or hurdle rate. If you have never looked at Excel's Help topic for NPV, you might assume we could enter the investment amount and list the expected cash flows, and then discount to their present values. But we must be careful about the timing of the investment and the returns: Excel assumes that the investment takes place at the end of period 1, rather than the present time 0 (and is actually a *present value* function). If the first cash flow (usually the investment) takes place in time 0 the formula should be written:

```
=NPV(DiscountRate, CashFlow 1 ... CashFlow n)+CashFlow 0
```

⊿	A	B	C	D	E	F	G	H	I	J	K	L	M	N
1	Period			0	1	2	3	4	5	6	7	8	9	10
2														
3	Cash flow			-1000	145	150	155	160	165	170	175	180	185	190
4														
5	Discount rate			10%	DiscountRate									
6														
7	NPV 1			4.93	=NPV(DiscountRate,D3:N3)									
8	NPV 2			5.42	=NPV(DiscountRate,E3:N3)+D3									
9														
10														

FIGURE 6.31   The NPV function.

This can be illustrated using the following example, where NPV 1 is the standard NPV formula and NPV 2 is the adjusted version (Figure 6.31).

If instead we calculate this arithmetically, using the period numbers 0, 1, 2, and write the following discount formula:

```
=CashFlow/(1+rate)^period
```

The SUM of this row, less the original investment is 5.42, and by showing the discounting of the cash flows it is much clearer. To make Excel agree with the time 0 investment NPV, rewrite the function as =NPV(Rate,E3:F3)+D3 (Figure 6.32).

The correct and full approach is to set out the discount factors explicitly, and to multiply the future cash flows by the relevant discount, and then to sum the discounted cash flows. A benefit of this technique is that it allows for changes to the discount rate over time, which the NPV function cannot handle (Figure 6.33).

A further refinement is to recognise that cash flows are normally treated as happening at the end of the period. In some circumstances we may need to consider them as midperiod cash flows, and this is easily done by changing the period row to 0.5, 1.5, 2.5 and so on.

Alternatively amend the discounting formula to =CashFlow/(1+rate)^(period+0.5)

A common source of confusion arises when calculating the quarterly or monthly NPV and failing to amend the discount rate appropriately. Remember that if we are calculating simple interest we can divide the annual rate by the number of periods, but if using compound interest we should use the following formula:

```
=(1+annual rate)^(1/period)-1
```

You can use this formula as an approximate audit check:

```
=(1+annual rate)=(1+monthly rate)^12-1
```

XNPV

In summary the NPV function requires us to know that the underlying algebra assumes that cash flows fall at the end of each period; that the first cash flow occurs at the end of period one and, importantly, the duration of each period is constant. When working with quarterly or monthly forecast periods this latter

E10		▸	⋮	× ✓	f_x	=E3/(1+DiscountRate)^E1									
▲	A	B	C	D	E	F	G	H	I	J	K	L	M	N	O
1	Period			0	1	2	3	4	5	6	7	8	9	10	
2															
3	Cash flow			-1000	145	150	155	160	165	170	175	180	185	190	
4															
5	Discount rate			10%	*DiscountRate*										
6															
7	NPV 1			4.93	=NPV(DiscountRate,D3:N3)										
8	NPV 2			5.42	=NPV(DiscountRate,E3:N3)+D3										
9															
10				5.42	131.82	123.97	116.45	109.28	102.45	95.96	89.80	83.97	78.46	73.25	
11															

FIGURE 6.32   Arithmetic NPV version 1.

E7		▸	⋮	× ✓	f_x	=D7/(1+DiscountRate)										
▲	A	B	C	D	E	F	G	H	I	J	K	L	M	N	O	P
1	Period			0	1	2	3	4	5	6	7	8	9	10	
2																
3	Cash flow			-1000	145	150	155	160	165	170	175	180	185	190 *CashFlow*	
4																
5	Discounting															
6	rate			10%	10%	10%	10%	10%	10%	10%	10%	10%	10%	10% *DiscountRate*	
7	factor			1	0.91	0.83	0.75	0.68	0.62	0.56	0.51	0.47	0.42	0.39 *DiscountFactor*	
8																
9	Discounted cash flows				131.82	123.97	116.45	109.28	102.45	95.96	89.80	83.97	78.46	73.25 *DCF*	
10																
11	Sum of DCFs			1,005.42 *SumDCF*												
12																
13	Net present value			5.42 *NPVDCF*												
14																

FIGURE 6.33   Arithmetic NPV version 2: with discount factors.

point is clearly not the case. The XNPV function allows very accurate discounting which takes account of the exact number of days in a period. To explore this we need to set up a worksheet with dates as shown. Note that Excel is quite intelligent when handling dates, so we can enter the first two dates and use AutoFill to fill the row.

If we then set up a cash flow we could calculate the NPV. If we were using the original net present value approach (NPV or arithmetical) we would need to adjust the annual rate to a quarterly rate, using =(1+annual rate)^0.25-1; but because we are providing the dates Excel is able to calculate the appropriate periodic discount rate. Now write the XNPV function, which has the syntax =XNPV(annual rate, cash flow, dates). Note the difference in the results. If we repeat this exercise arithmetically we will be able to see how XNPV works.

1. Calculate the days in each period, as the current date less than the previous date (keep an eye on period ending March 31 2016, as this includes the leap year February 29).
2. Calculate the periodic discount rate as =(1+quarterly rate)^(days in period/365)-1. Despite the previous comment about the leap year the 365 will work in this example.
3. Set up a discounting row with a 1 in the base column and =previous cell/ (1+periodic discount rate)
4. Multiply the cash flow by the periodic discount factor.
5. Put a sum of the discounted cash flows in the base column.

The XNPV and the arithmetical NPV do not agree. Overtype the first discount factor with a value of 1. Now they do agree. XNPV assumes that the cash flows take place on the dates specified, and so the first cash flow is NOT discounted (unlike NPV). If we replicate this in the arithmetical version we get the same result. Note that with XNPV we can be very flexible with dates – if we change from quarterly to semiannual the formulas still work, with Excel using the dates to derive the correct periodic discount rate (Figure 6.34).

Having shown that the arithmetical approach is the one generally to be adopted, the internal rate of return (IRR) calculation is the exception. If you have covered IRR at business school or in your finance studies, you will be aware that we use an iterative technique to calculate the IRR and we can safely use the Excel IRR function. The IRR function uses a default guess of the interest rate at 10%. If the cash flow does not begin with the investment as a negative amount, Excel gives up on the iteration and returns the #NUM! error. Also, you should know that if the cash flow changes signs more than once, there will be another IRR – Excel will not return this unless you change the guess:

```
=IRR(CashFlow, myguess%)
```

As with NPV the IRR also assumes equal time periods. Note that it will return a periodic IRR – if the cash flow is quarterly, the IRR is quarterly, and you will need to convert it back to an annual rate =(1+IRR(cash flow))^4-1

E17			▼	⋮	✕ ✓	*fx*	1				

	A	B	C	D	E	F	G	H	I	J	K	L
2	Period to:			31-Dec-15	31-Mar-16	30-Jun-16	30-Sep-16	31-Dec-16	31-Mar-17	30-Jun-17	30-Sep-17	31-Dec-17
3												
4	Cash flows				136	110	128	169	129	131	106	114
5												
6	Discount rate											
7	annual			10.0%								
8	quarterly			2.41%								
9												
10	NPV			922.48	=NPV(D8,E4:L4)							
11												
12	XNPV			944.62	=XNPV(D7,E4:L4,E2:L2)							
13												
14	Days in period				91	91	92	92	90	91	92	92
15												
16					2.40%	2.40%	2.43%	2.43%	2.38%	2.40%	2.43%	2.43%
17				1	1.00	0.98	0.95	0.93	0.91	0.89	0.87	0.85
18				944.62	136.00	107.42	122.03	157.29	117.27	116.29	91.87	96.46
19												
20	Audit check			TRUE								
21												
22												

FIGURE 6.34   XNPV function and arithmetical XNPV. Note the hard-coded 1 in E17 to align the arithmetic to the function.

And as with the XNPV the XIRR function can be used when dates are provided in the cash flow. The syntax is simple: =XIRR(cash flow, dates) but note that Excel is able to use the dates to convert the result to an *annual* return automatically.

OTHER USEFUL FUNCTIONS

LARGE and SMALL

I rather like the LARGE and SMALL functions primarily because they are generally overlooked and offer functionality that is very difficult to reproduce using other techniques. We have looked at MAX and MIN and recognised that they return the largest and smallest values from a range, respectively. But what about other values? Look back at the minimum cash balance routine earlier in this chapter. We briefly considered that it might be that there might be two or more years in which this balance occurred. We can pick out these values using SMALL, the syntax for which is:

```
=SMALL(range, value)
```

A value of 1 is the first smallest value (=MIN), 2 is the second smallest and so on. You can work out how LARGE works. Unfortunately SMALL and LARGE do not help with duplicate values, because if there are 2 years in which the cash balance is 0, SMALL will only identify the value itself. However, as previously noted, cash flow calculations are calculated to several decimal places and duplicates may be unlikely to occur.

I've used LARGE to set up a dynamic sorting system. We needed to show the exposure to a number of liabilities the value of which changed frequently. I should point out that the sort command was not an option – this runs the risk of changing the layout of the model. We used LARGE, MATCH and INDEX to solve the problem. Excel's RANK function is of little use (Figure 6.35).

We can combine SMALL with COUNTIF and COUNT to tackle a common modelling problem. In this example we will consider a series of annual debt service cover ratios (DSCR) over a long forecast period, during which the debt will be fully paid off. For financial management purposes we need to identify any periods in which the DSCR falls to critical levels, that is, potentially in breach of the loan covenant. Simply put, we need the lowest DSCR. Unfortunately, because of the zero values which follow the repayment of the loan, we cannot use the MIN function. We start by using COUNT to return the number of values in the DSCR row. Then we use the COUNTIF function to tell us how many values above 0 are in the DSCR row.

```
=COUNTIF(DSCR,">0")
```

This then returns a value of 6. We then subtract 6 from 10 to identify that there are four cells containing zero values (Figure 6.36). The MIN of this range would be 0, so we would like to know the next biggest number after 0, so the following formula would do the trick:

```
=SMALL(DSCR,DSCRBlanks+1)
```

RAND

I often find myself having to create sequences of numbers in order to demonstrate or test a routine, and this can be rather time-consuming. The RAND function generates random numbers between 0 and 1 at up to 15 decimal places, which in itself is moderately useful. You can multiply by 10 or 100 to generate more meaningful numbers, but this usually results in a wide range of values. To generate numbers within a particular range, say between 10 and 20, try the following:

```
=RAND()*(20-10)+10
```

This formula generates a random number between 0 and 1 and multiplies it by 10, and adds 10 to the result. The value therefore cannot be below 10 or above 20. Substitute in your own values.

The random numbers change every time Excel recalculates, so you may want to convert the formulas to values by using Copy and Edit, Paste Special, Paste Values.

The nice people at Microsoft have obviously read this section in the previous edition, because we now have the RANDBETWEEN function that does exactly this.

ISTEXT

Cell comments (Shift+F2) are a useful means for storing additional information in the spreadsheet. However, under Tools, Options, View, Comments they can be disabled and the user may not realise they are there. In the old days of Lotus 1-2-3, we were able to write comments directly into formulas, and we can still

Live data			Sorted data		
Label	*Values*	*Order number*	*LARGE* =LARGE(Values,Order)	*MATCH* =MATCH(LargeResult,Values,0)	*INDEX* =INDEX(Label,MatchResult)
A	-46	1	-22	5	E
B	-24	2	-24	2	B
C	-43	3	-37	6	F
D	-42	4	-42	4	D
E	-22	5	-43	3	C
F	-37	6	-46	1	A

FIGURE 6.35 LARGE, MATCH and INDEX for dynamic sorting.

DSCRsmallest   =SMALL(DSCR,DSCRBlanks+1)

	A	B	C	D	E	F	G	H	I	J	K	L	M	N	O
1	Year				1	2	3	4	5	6	7	8	9	10	
2															
3	DSCR				0	1.25	1.86	1.35	1.47	1.53	1.19	0	0	0	DSCR
4															
5		count of DSCR		10	*DSCRCount*										
6		DSCR greater than zero		6	*DSCROverZero*										
7		count of blank DSCRs		4	*DSCRBlanks*										
8		smallest DSCR value		1.19	*DSCRsmallest*										
9															

FIGURE 6.36 Debt service cover ratios minimum test.

do it using Excel. The trick here uses the ISTEXT function. This is one of the IS family of functions which return a logical TRUE or FALSE depending on the test. The syntax is simple:

```
=ISTEXT("text string") returns TRUE
=ISTEXT(calculation) returns FALSE
```

As we saw previously, TRUE has a value of 1, FALSE of 0. We can therefore write an annotated formula such as:

```
=NPV(DiscountRate, CashFlow)*ISTEXT("DiscountRate is the
company's real terms cost of capital, and CashFlow is the
project cash flow in real terms")
```

In this case, the ISTEXT formula multiplies the NPV by 1.

N

Comments can also be written into formulas using the N or Number function, which will convert a non-number to a number value, dates to their serial numbers, logical TRUE or FALSE to 1 or 0. More importantly it will return a value of 0 for text. For example, using the NPV example above, I might want to directly comment on the formula in the following way:

```
=NPV(DiscountRate, CashFlow)+N("DiscountRate is the company's
real terms cost of capital, and CashFlow is the project cash flow
in real terms")
```

Concatenation

Concatenation is the method of linking together a series of text strings, cell references and/or values. It can be used for reporting results, as in the following:

```
="The NPV of the project is" & NPVResult & "using a" & DiscountRate
& "discount rate"
```

The & ampersand character is referred to as the concatenation operator and each element of the formula needs to be prefixed with this symbol. Note that each text string must be enclosed in quotes, and spaces should be included for readability.

Alternatively, we can use the Excel CONCATENATE function:

```
=CONCATENATE("The NPV of the project is", NPVResult, "using a",
DiscountRate, "discount rate")
```

Needless to say, concatenation should be thought of as generating a text string and so should not be used for calculations. This is not strictly true, as you can prove using

```
=CONCATENATE(1, 2, 3)*10
```

TEXT

The concatenation example above does not actually look very tidy when complete, because Excel loses the number formatting of the original cells. To apply the number format within the concatenation formula, we can use the TEXT function, which has the following syntax:

```
=TEXT(number, "format text")
```

Number is the value or cell reference containing a value to be formatted; 'Format text' is one of Excel's number formats written in quotes (see Chapter 7).

With the NPV example above, I would like to format the NPV value in £000s, with no decimal places, and the cost of capital as percentage, two decimals. Assuming that we are not going to use the usual formatting techniques, we could write the individual formulas as:

```
=TEXT(NPVResult, "#,##0"); and
=TEXT(DiscountRate, "0.00%")
```

Combining this with the concatenation routine we get:

```
=CONCATENATE("The NPV of the project is", TEXT(NPVResult, "#,##0"),
"using a", TEXT(DiscountRate, "0.00%"), "discount rate")
```

Is this worth the effort? And just in case it isn't obvious, the result of the formula is now text and cannot be used for subsequent calculations.

INT and MOD

INT or integer rounds a number *down* to the nearest integer, or whole number*. MOD returns the modulus or remainder when one number is divided by another. When I am not teaching or writing about financial modelling I like to run marathons, and I wrote a neat little marathon calculator to help me work out my predicted time when running at a particular rate.

If I run an 8-min mile (apologies for the nonmetric units), it would take me $26.2 * 8 = 209.6$ min to run the full marathon, which I would like to express in hours and minutes.

1. Use the INT function to divide 209.6 by 60, which is 3 (hours).
   ```
   =INT(TotalMinutes/60).
   ```
2. Use the MOD function to return the remainder, which is 30 (minutes).
   ```
   =MOD(TotalMinutes, 60).
   ```
Note that we do not need the division operator in the MOD function.

---

* There is also the ROUND(value, number of places) function, which will round a number up or down to the specified number of decimal places. You might also look at the Excel ROUNDUP and ROUNDDOWN functions.

3. To show off, we can concatenate the two results together and format the output by writing:

```
=CONCATENATE(Hours,":", TEXT(Minutes,"#,#00"))
```

This gives the result 3:30.

Another use of MOD is seen in models which use a quarterly periodicity and in which annual totals are required. If we set up a row PeriodNumber for numbering the columns 1, 2, 3, 4 … and assume that the year end is every fourth column, we could write =MOD(PeriodNumber,4). This will show the remainder when dividing PeriodNumber by 4, as 1, 2, 3, 0. Using the logical mask technique from the previous chapter we could amend this to =MOD(PeriodNumber,4)=0 to return FALSE, FALSE, FALSE, TRUE. The relevant totals can now be multiplied by the mask to show only the annual totals.

Chapter 7

Model Use

INTRODUCTION

The test of a good model is ultimately how the users respond to it. Back in Chapter 3 we recognised the need to engage with the users at the outset to find out exactly what their requirements are, and this may involve both discussion and iteration to refine the purpose and function of the model. We must also ensure that expectations are realistic and that the limitations of the model – and the modeller – are known. The users must be able to comprehend how the model works but without getting overwhelmed with detail, and neither should they be able to edit/amend calculations without permission. As model developers we may be quite confident about examining a workings sheet that contains several hundred rows of code, or perusing the structure of the pro forma financial statements covered with telephone number-sized figures, but our users may not feel quite the same way. Have you ever watched someone looking at a model for the first time? See how long it is before they check their email, or their mobile phone, or fetch a glass of water, or engage in any other form of displacement activity before actually getting down to the task at hand.

RISK CONTROLS

In Chapter 1, we introduced the idea of risk controls. As we are now beginning to think about how our users are going to use the model we may/should remind ourselves of the key controls:

Access Control

The lowest level of control allows or restricts access to the model and its results. At its simplest this could be through the use of passwords to open the file. Sheet protection would further restrict the ability of users to interfere with the model.

Input Control

This level of control would allow users to enter/amend/delete values on the inputs sheet only. Further control would be through the use of data validation, drop-down lists, combo and list boxes, and protected/unprotected cells.

Change Control

This is the basic level of access for the model developers, in which calculations can be written and edited in the workings sheet. Sheet-level password protection could be applied. This should allow access to the audit sheet.

Version Control

This is for the manager of the model development team, responsible for model testing, validation and auditing, with full access to all components of the model.

PROTECTION

Workbook and worksheet protection allows us to prevent users from opening files or changing the contents of a sheet, unless they have the password. You should be aware that if you forget or lose the password not even Microsoft will be able to help you. There are third party codebreakers who may be able to help, but their services are at a premium. I prefer to use the techniques described further on in this chapter to restrict the way users can interact with my models and I only use protection as a last resort. Even then, I make sure that the password is known, and I have even written it in the model documentation. If the user knows that they are not supposed to change anything and yet they go ahead and unprotect the worksheet, it suggests that they are acting wilfully and deliberately and must therefore take the responsibility if anything goes wrong.

Sheet Protection

With sheet-level protection there are two steps. The first is to identify those cells which will remain unprotected when protection is switched on, and then there is the protection command itself.

1. Select the cells which will be unprotected. The use of a fill colour may be appropriate as there are no visible differences between protected and unprotected cells.
2. Use Ctrl+1 Format Cells and go to the Protection tab (Figure 7.1).
3. Uncheck the Locked box. Note that this has no effect until the worksheet is protected.
4. Use the Review, Protect Sheet command. The options are far more extensive, but remember this is at the sheet level only, note the workbook. You will need to repeat these steps for each sheet (Figure 7.2).

If you now attempt to edit a protected cell Excel will respond with a dialog box notifying of the protection.

There is also a slightly unethical option at step 3 in Excel, in which the other option is that the cell content is Hidden when the worksheet is protected. If this is applied the user cannot see the formula on the formula bar, although the cell

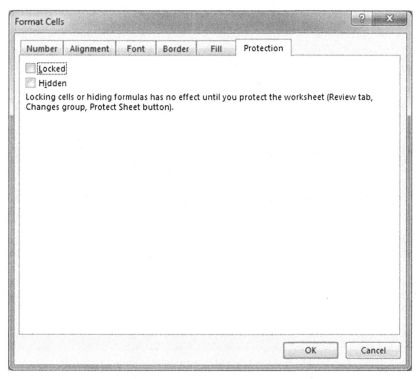

FIGURE 7.1   Protection#1: unprotect the cells.

FIGURE 7.2   Protection#2: protect the worksheet.

FIGURE 7.3   Protection #3: workbook protection.

value remains visible. It is probably worthwhile deselecting the Hidden box while setting up protection. We can prevent the user even selecting the cell.

Workbook Protection

Workbook protection is used to prevent structural changes to the file. Users will not be able to move, delete or insert sheets, but they will be able to insert and delete columns and rows, write, edit and delete values and formulas unless worksheet protection has also been applied. A protected workbook does not require a password to open it, but a password may be required to disable the protection (Figure 7.3).

Workbook protection is a one-step process, using the Review, Protect Workbook command. Use the Review, Unprotect Workbook command to unprotect.

Password Protection

A different way of managing workbook protection is to save the file and set up a password for the workbook to be opened or modified (Figure 7.4).

1. Run the File, Info, Protect, Encrypt with password command.
2. Enter a password (up to 255 characters).
3. Choose OK.

Alternatively, to allow users to open the workbook but to require them to enter a further password before they can save changes, use the following:

1. Run the File, Save As command (F12).
2. Click on Browse, and in the Save as dialog box select Tools and then General Options.
3. Enter a password to open, and/or a password to modify.
4. Click OK and re-enter the password(s) when prompted (Figure 7.5).

FIGURE 7.4   Password protection using the Encrypt dialog box.

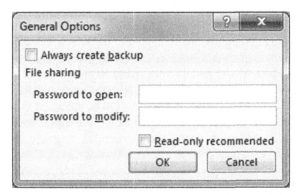

FIGURE 7.5   Password protection using Save As.

Note that the password to open uses encryption and cannot be recovered if lost. The password to modify restricts users but does not prevent them from subsequently disabling the password and other protections.

With the modelling methodology and structure proposed in Chapter 3 and the risk controls at the start of this chapter, it would be appropriate to protect the workings and outputs sheets because there should be no reason for the user to modify the calculations or the results. The inputs sheet would remain unprotected so that the users can run sensitivities and generally flex the assumptions. But given such a clear layout, the use of protection is practically redundant.

GROUPING AND OUTLINING

Even a relatively simple model may contain many rows of detail which serve to distract or confuse (or intimidate) the user; the use of the inputs/workings/outputs structure is helpful in this context, as the results are set out clearly and it should be easy to identify the inputs. Although it is possible to simply hide the appropriate rows, columns or sheets, it is more helpful to allow the user to expand or contract the detail as required through the use of grouping and outlining. For a model that has been laid out in a sensible and meaningful way this is fairly straightforward. I shall refer to rows but the same principles apply equally to columns.

1. Select the rows to be grouped. You should decide if the heading should appear above or below the group when the outline is collapsed. Keep the headings at the top if using grouping just to manage the worksheet, but at the bottom if you have data, for example, totals, to display.
2. Use the Data, Group, Group command. The left-hand edge of the screen expands to show the outlining buttons.
3. Repeat as necessary (Figure 7.6).

It is possible to get Excel to Auto Outline your work, but Excel will assume that the summary rows are at the bottom of the group; to amend this, use the Data and the Outline dialog box launcher.

We can create up to eight levels of grouping within a section, each one being numbered on the outlining toolbar to the left of the screen. Clicking the outline level buttons will expand and collapse individual groups, and clicking on the outline number buttons will collapse or expand all groups at that level. Use the Data, Ungroup, Clear Outline command to clear the outlines if not required.

The benefit of outlining is that information can be collapsed and expanded as needed. In large models, this can be very reassuring as the amount of information on screen is much reduced, but can be easily revealed. Be aware that audit techniques (F2, Ctrl+[etc.) may point to cells in collapsed ranges. If the outline symbols are not shown, the collapsed rows are hidden and can be revealed by selecting the rows above and below and using File, Format, Hide & Unhide, Unhide Rows, but note that rows and columns can be hidden independently of outlining. If outline symbols are restored, these rows are still grouped and can be collapsed or expanded as before. The disappearance of the outline symbols is the commonest source of difficulty so make sure that the worksheet contains appropriate documentation to advise users to use File, Options, Advanced, Display options for this worksheet, Show outline symbols if an outline is applied, should this happen.

As might be expected, there are a number of keyboard shortcuts in relation to outlining:

Group rows (or columns)	Alt+Shift+right arrow
Ungroup rows (or columns)	Alt+Shift+left arrow
Display or hide outline symbols	Ctrl+8
Hide rows	Ctrl+9
Unhide selected rows	Ctrl+Shift+(
Hide columns	Ctrl+0
Unhide columns	Ctrl+Shift+)

Do not use the number keypad for these shortcuts.

1 2	⊿	A B	C	D	E
	1	Period from	Base	01 Jan 17	01 Apr 17
	2	Period to		31 Mar 17	30 Jun 17
	3				
	4	Is iteration on?	FALSE	*Switch*	
	5				
+	6	PROJECT TIMING			
	34				
−	35	INFLATION			
	36				
	37	CPI			
	38	rate (% pa)		3%	3%
	39	index	1	1.01	1.01
	40				
	41	Building Materials Index			
	42	rate (% pa)		4%	4%
	43	index	1	1.01	1.02
	44				
+	45	REVENUE			
	68				
+	69	OPERATING COSTS			
	80				
+	81	WORKING CAPITAL			
	96				
+	97	PROPERTY, PLANT AND EQUIPMENT			
	130				
+	131	SALES TAX			
	141				
+	142	PARTNERS EQUITY			
	151				
+	152	PARTNERS CASH RETURNS			
	156				
+	157	CASH FLOW			
	187				
+	188	SENIOR DEBT			
	216				
+	217	INTEREST			
	223				
+	224	MMRA			
	263				
+	264	DSRA			
	287				
+	288	SUBORDINATED DEBT			

FIGURE 7.6   Grouping sections of the model to make them more manageable.

DATA INPUTS

Once a model has been developed and tested it can be handed over to the users. Assuming we have put in appropriate protections for the workings calculations and the output reports, we may still need to restrict the data being used to drive the model. There are several techniques we can use to restrict data entry to the model.

Data Validation

We can set constraints on the values that the user has to enter. This is a simple exercise.

1. Select the cell(s) for which the validation will apply.
2. Use the Data, Data Validation, Data Validation command.
3. Under the Validation criteria we can specify the constraints to apply – whole number, decimal, etc.
4. In the Data section we can identify the criteria to use (between, not between, equal to and so on).
5. If you have chosen the between criterion, you then specify the lower and upper values. With the other criteria you must identify the threshold value.
6. You may wish to enter an Input message or prompt to guide the user. This will appear when the user selects the cell or cells with the validation. There is no other visual indication in the worksheet that validation is in use.
7. You can also set up an Error Alert or warning if the user attempts to enter invalid data. There are three styles of alert: Stop, which offers the user the opportunity to Retry or Cancel; Warning, which does allow the user to continue with the invalid data; and Information, which gives the options to OK or Cancel.

Custom Validation

We may wish to set the unit price of our product as being between 10 and 20, which is easily done with the data validation options of Whole Number, Between, etc.

We would also like to restrict prices to even numbers.

1. Select the range.
2. Use Data, Data Validation, Data Validation, and choose Custom.
3. Enter the following formula:

```
=MOD(first cell in range, 2)=0
```

The MOD (modulus) function returns the remainder after a value has been divided by a number, in this case 2. The data validation requires that each number entered in the specified range must be exactly divisible by 2.

4. Test that the data validation works.

In the depreciation masking exercise in Chapter 5, it was noted that the technique only worked if there was only one investment, regardless of when it occurred. We can use data validation to ensure that only one value is typed in a range.

1. Select the range.
2. Use Data, Data Validation, Data Validation, and choose Custom. Enter the following formula, using the appropriate absolute cell references (not range names):

```
=COUNTIF(Investment,">0")=1
```

The COUNTIF function counts the number of values in the range which have a value greater than zero. If the count exceeds 1, then the validation restricts further entry.

3. Test that the validation works. Note that zero values and negative numbers could be entered without comment – amend the formula as required.

Problems with Validation

If a user copies or fills values from cells outside the validation range, no error is generated if the values breach the validation rule. If validation is applied to existing formulas, and these formulas subsequently evaluate to invalid numbers, the validation mechanism will not activate. Validation should therefore be restricted to data entry (inputs) only.

Cells and ranges that have validation applied to them have no distinctive markings and it may be appropriate to highlight them in some way if you are using this feature. If there are validation cells in the worksheet they can be located using the F5 Go To, Special technique, which can select all validated cells in the sheet, or cells which have the same validation rule as the selected cell. Tip: while these cells are selected apply a fill colour for reference.

The validation rules applied to a cell or range can be copied and pasted to other cells and ranges using the Validation option in the Paste Special dialog box.

Drop-Down Lists

There is one useful feature of validation which fixes the problem about the numbers themselves. We can provide a list of values (e.g. the prices as even numbers) which will then be listed in the validation cell. Either type these values into the same worksheet or enter them directly into the dialog box. My own preference, as always, is to have the values accessible in the worksheet for inspection and review. Note that the values should be listed on the same sheet, which makes sense if we are using the inputs sheet approach. If you need to refer to a list of values on another sheet you will have to use a range name, because data validation will not accept cell references to other sheets.

1. Select the cell for validation.
2. Choose the Allow List option in the Data Validation dialog box.
3. Specify the source cells; if using a range name prefix it with the equals sign, for example, =PriceList.
4. Make sure the In-cell drop-down check box is ticked.
5. Enter any input message and error alert as required – they may be redundant with this technique as we have more control over what the user is doing.
6. Choose OK (Figure 7.7).

Click on the validated cell. The drop-down list indicator should appear, from which we can select the value. It is still possible to type in a different value, at which point the error alert will appear, but the user is fairly restricted now and

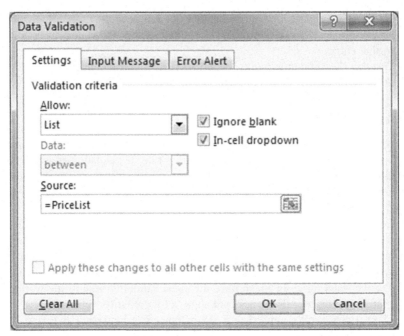

FIGURE 7.7 Setting up simple drop-down list functionality with Data Validation.

may not consider typing in values of their own. Note that with the validation list, the value selected from the list is the value that is entered in the cell, and is used in the dependent calculations, unlike the information returned from the list and combo boxes, below. The width of the drop-down list is controlled by the width of the cell which contains the source data.

List and Combo Boxes

A more sophisticated form of controlled data entry can be achieved using list and combo boxes. Most people associate these with macros, but they can be directly embedded in the worksheet. They are not too dissimilar to data validation lists, but instead of entering the selected value into the cell, they enter the position number of the value that was selected. We can explore this using the price list mentioned previously, and again I recommend that the source data is written into the worksheet. Unlike validation lists, these data can be on any sheet, and we can also use text rather than just values. The data shown in the list and combo boxes cannot be edited.

The difference between a combo box and a list box is that the combo box produces a drop-down list and if not active only shows one value from the list. The list box can be sized so that the full list is permanently visible, and even if reduced in size will always show two values from the list, the others being accessed using the spin controls. Which value is currently being used in the model?

A little thought needs to be given to the set-up of the box. Both combo and list boxes require an input range, which contains the source data, and a cell link – a

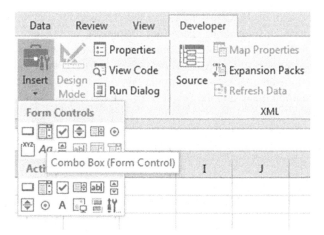

FIGURE 7.8   The Combo box tool in the Form Control list.

reference to the cell in the workbook which will contain the result of the selection and which can be anywhere in the workbook. Range names are useful in this context. The box itself is a workbook object and sits on top of the workbook, rather than in it. Both types of box are set up in the same way.

1. We will need to make sure that the Developer tab appears on the Ribbon: use File, Options, Customize Ribbon, and make sure the Developer tab check box is selected.
2. The Combo and List box tools appear in the Developer, Insert group. Click on the tool and click and drag in the workbook to draw the box. Tip: hold down the Alt key while dragging to force the box to snap to the worksheet gridlines.
3. The box then appears with edit handles, and the box can be resized or repositioned at will.
4. Right-click on the box and choose Format Control.
5. In the dialog box, enter the input range (the source data) and the cell link (where the information will be placed) (Figure 7.8).

The Input range contains the source information, the Cell link is where the result is to be stored in the worksheet (Figure 7.9).

6. With the Combo box you can specify how many lines you want to show when the box is selected, and with both boxes you can specify if you want 2-D or 3-D effects.
7. Choose OK (Figure 7.10).

Click in the worksheet to take the selection off the box. Test the box by selecting an item in the list, using either the drop-down list (combo box) or the spin control (list box). Note that a number appears in the cell identified as the cell link. This number corresponds to the position of the selected item in the list, and is not the item itself. This number can then be used for look-up and other types of function, or for running scenarios (Chapter 8).

If you need to edit the boxes you must right-click on them first. It is good practice to name the boxes, which can be done by selecting the box and typing a name into the Name Box on the formula bar. As worksheet objects you can group and ungroup them, and the Select Objects tool from the Drawing toolbar is useful in this context.

We will extend the list and combo box techniques in the context of sensitivity analysis and scenario management in the next chapter.

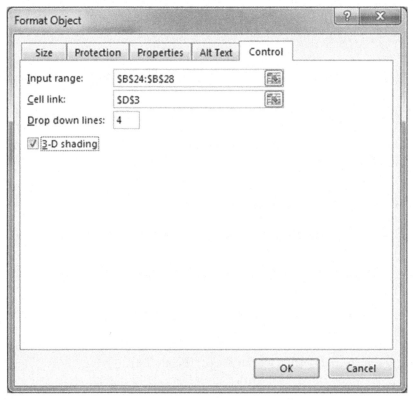

FIGURE 7.9   Formatting the combo box controls.

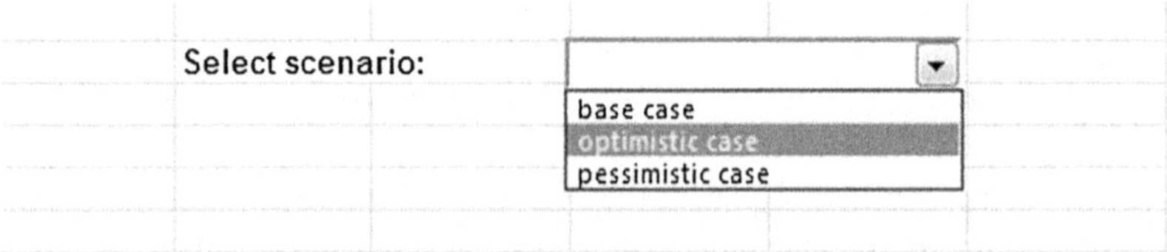

FIGURE 7.10   The combo box in the worksheet.

CONDITIONAL FORMATTING

The ability to change the appearance of cells based on logical conditions is a very useful feature of Excel, although in my experience few modellers get beyond a trivial implementation of conditional formatting, mainly because we don't need it that much. Conditional formatting functionality seems to increase with each new release of Excel and is mostly self-explanatory; I'm afraid that Sparklines and Data Bars, Color Scales and Icon Sets aren't, and are not likely to be, features in my models. We can be reasonably certain that if we are required to set up a conditional format it won't be one of the predefined formats.

To understand how to make the most of conditional formatting we can use a simple method to change the fill colour of all negative numbers, which we can very quickly review before looking at how we can really benefit from this feature.

1. Select the range to which the conditional format will apply.
2. Use the Home, Conditional Formatting, Highlight Cells Rules, Less Than command.
3. Enter 0 as the threshold value and select from the list of predefined formats.
4. Choose OK.

Inspect your range and note the appearance of the cells containing negative numbers. Prove that the formatting is dynamic by changing the values (Figure 7.11).

Now let us do something sensible. In the audit sheet section of Chapter 3, we saw how we could use F5 Edit, Go To, Special to locate cells containing errors. We can also use conditional formatting to highlight these cells. The basis for this is the ISERROR function.

1. Select the range to be audited. Make sure the active cell is the top left cell in the selection.
2. Use the Home, Conditional Formatting, New Rule command.
3. Select the 'Use a formula to determine which cells to format' option
4. Type in the test condition as =ISERROR(Cell reference). Make sure this cell reference is a relative address.

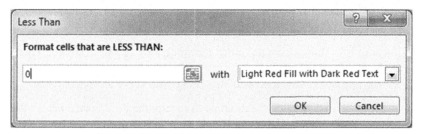

FIGURE 7.11   Simple conditional formatting.

FIGURE 7.12   Using the ISERROR condition. Note the relative cell reference.

5. Click the Format button and select the Fill tab.
6. Choose a colour such as red and choose OK, and OK again (Figure 7.12).

Now inspect the worksheet and note the appearance of the error cells. I suggest this makes them somewhat easier to locate. As the errors are corrected, the colour automatically disappears.

In Chapter 2, I suggested that we set up an audit summary cell that summarised all the checks on the audit sheet, and that this cell is linked to the output sheets. This meant that the outputs themselves document the audit status of the model, but in reality I might only want to know if the audit has failed, rather than that it has passed. This is easy to set up.

1. Select the output cell containing the link to the audit check cell.
2. In the conditional formatting dialog box, use the following formula (assuming the audit check cell is named AuditCheck)

```
=AuditCheck
```

Because AuditCheck contains either the value TRUE or FALSE, we don't need to specify further conditions.

3. Set the format to white text (unethical, but it will serve for this purpose).

To set up additional rules, for example to specify the FALSE outcome, we use the Manage Rules command from the Conditional Formatting menu (Figure 7.13).

The TRUE option applies a font colour of white, the FALSE option applies a bold, red font.

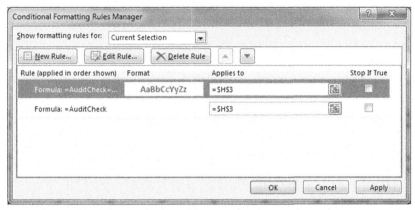

FIGURE 7.13   Setting up multiple rules with the Rules Manager.

We can use the last technique to good effect if we select the whole sheet and set the AuditCheck=TRUE outcome to have no format, and AuditCheck=FALSE to have text strike through. This means that the outputs sheets are unusable if the model has failed an audit check.

In Chapter 3, we considered the use of the base or initialisation column down the left-hand edge of the workings calculations. Its purpose is to handle initialisation and time-independent values, and I would normally recommend that it should be coloured, to distinguish it as having a different function to the adjacent calculations. We can use conditional formatting to do this. The condition formula is:

```
=COLUMN()=4
```

This assumes that column D is the base column. Amend as required, and set an appropriate fill colour.

We can extend this logic further in the context of the quarterly/annual modelling problem described in Chapter 3. The rolling sum and the corkscrew methods were both described, in which the annual figure appears in every fourth cell in the row. We can use custom formatting to emphasise this.

1. Select the sheet (Ctrl+A).
   Use Conditional Formatting command to set the following condition:

```
=MOD(COLUMN(),4)=0
```

   Choose an appropriate colour format.
2. Choose OK (Figure 7.14).

The COLUMN function returns the column number, and the MOD function divides this number by 4. If the remainder is zero, the format is applied. The sheet should now have coloured stripes every fourth column. When applied to the output sheets, we should be able to prove that the reports are based on the annual figures because if the quarterly columns have been hidden there should be no unformatted columns.

A visual differentiation of time periods.

FIGURE 7.14   A visual differentiation of time periods using conditional formatting.

Problems with Conditional Formatting

One of the issues with conditional formatting is that the condition is not explicit in the worksheet itself. Conditional formatting takes priority over any other formatting of the same type, so in the examples above, it would not be possible to apply a different fill colour to a column or cell.

Rule Priority

When using multiple conditions it is important to get the sequence right.

> Cell value Less than 10   Blue
> Cell value Less than 100   Green
> Cell value Less than 1000   Red

This sequence gives the expected results.

> Cell value Less than 1000   Red
> Cell value Less than 100   Green
> Cell value Less than 10   Blue

This sequence gives unexpected results – any value below 1000 is coloured red, and the subsequent criteria are not applied.

Multiple rules applying to the same range should be set up carefully using the Home, Conditional Formatting, Manage Rules dialog box. New rules can be created from within this dialog box and more importantly they can be arranged in order, and the 'Stop if true' option can be selected to prevent overlap or conflict of rules.

Excel allows any number of rules to be assigned to a worksheet, which would allow for a global set of conditions to be set up, covering everything from the trivial negative numbers example through to the complex logical formula tests. The Manage Rules dialog box can display the rules applying to the current selection, the current worksheet, or any worksheet in the workbook. The order in which the rules are listed is also their order of priority, and rules can be promoted or demoted over other rules. Rules can also be edited and deleted from this dialog box.

To find cells or ranges which have conditional formatting we can use the F5 Go To, Special command and select the 'Conditional formats' option.

CUSTOM FORMATTING

Excel offers a number of useful number formats and of course you have learnt the shortcuts for the most common:

Ctrl+Shift+!	Thousands, 2 decimal places
Ctrl+Shift+$	Currency, 2 decimal places
Ctrl+Shift+%	Percentage, 2 decimal places
Ctrl+Shift+^	Exponential format
Ctrl+Shift+~	General number format (only on US/UK keyboards)
Ctrl+1	Format cells dialog box

The number of decimal places can be changed using Alt+H, 9 (decrease) and Alt+H, 0 (increase).

You will know that having applied a format you can select the next cell or range and repeat the format command using the F4 function key.

In the following example, the results on the outputs sheet are some very big positive and negative numbers (Figure 7.15).

The accountants teach us that more than three digits tends to confuse, so it would be helpful if we could display the number in the format shown in the Figure 7.16.

It is not really worth the effort to simply divide all the results by 1,000,000, because Excel has enough work to do on the underlying calculations without worrying about these trivial divisions. Instead, we use a custom format. The cells will be formatted so that they are shown as decimal values, with negative numbers in parentheses and coloured red, and with zero values replaced with hyphens. We will build the format in steps:

1. Select the range to be formatted.
2. Use Ctrl+1 to launch the Format Cells dialog box.
3. Select the category of Custom and tab to the Type box.
4. Type in 0.0,, and choose OK. All the values in the range are now shown in decimal format. The commas in the format code are instructions to divide by a 1000, twice. Please note that this is the UK/US thousands notation: use the appropriate characters for your own regional style, so for example, when working in Germany I write 0,0..
5. At the moment the format does not clearly differentiate between positive and negative numbers. Return to the Format cells dialog box. After the existing 0.0,, type a semicolon ; and then the format for the negative numbers, which will be in red with parentheses. The code for this is:

```
0.0,,;[red](0.0,,)
```

The first part of the format code is for positive numbers, the second part for negative numbers. The colour is enclosed in square brackets, and again use the

	A B	C	D	E	F	G	H
1	Period from		01 Jan 14	01 Apr 14	01 Jul 14	01 Oct 14	01 Jan 15
2	Period to		31 Mar 14	30 Jun 14	30 Sep 14	31 Dec 14	31 Mar 15
3							
4	Revenue		0	0	0	0	4312138.086
5							
6	Operating costs		0	0	0	0	-1564020.498
7							
8	Working capital (increase) decrease		0	0	0	0	-1029505.96
9							
10	Capital expenditure		-20000000	-19000000	-18000000	-16000000	0
11							
12	Sales tax		-1400000	70000	70000	140000	1348685.617
13							
14	Project cash flow		-21400000	-18930000	-17930000	-15860000	3067297.245
15							
16	Interest on cash less overdraft		0	0	0	30029.90892	59803.46496
17							
18	Cash flow from (to) senior lenders						
19	interest		0	0	0	0	-1284992.714
20	principal		19400000	18930000	20333000	8381000	-1117400
21	total		19400000	18930000	20333000	8381000	-2402392.714
22							
23	Net transfer to						
24	major maintenance reserve		0	0	0	0	-76704.86255
25	debt service reserve		0	0	-2402392.714	-2381884.483	41016.46096
26	total		0	0	-2402392.714	-2381884.483	-35688.40159
27							
28	Cash flow from (to) subordinated lenders						
29	interest		0	0	0	0	-221204.1176
30	principal		0	0	0	9831294.118	-468862.3073
31	total		0	0	0	9831294.118	-690066.425
32							
33	Cash flow from (to) partners						
34	contributions		2000000	0	0	0	0
35	withdrawals		0	0	0	0	0
36	total		2000000	0	0	0	0
37							
38	Financing cash flow		21400000	18930000	17930607.29	15860439.54	-3068344.075
39							
40	Change in net cash balances		0	0	607.2864768	439.5435242	-1046.830001

FIGURE 7.15   'Good enough for government work'.

appropriate language to name the colour. Excel has eight named colours: black, blue, green, red, yellow, cyan, magenta and white. It is considered unethical to format values or text with white. Click OK to inspect the results in the worksheet.

6. On careful inspection you may note that the decimal points of the positive and negative values no longer line up. On the grand scheme of things, this may not be anything to worry about, but some people, usually fairly senior in the organisation, like to see everything lined up all neat and tidy. The problem here is that the closing bracket of the negative value has pushed the value into the cell, whereas the positive numbers are still hard up against the right-hand edge of the cell. We need to fix this, so select the numbers again and press Ctrl+1.

7. To allow for the bracket of the negative numbers, we need to move the positive numbers into the cell by the same distance. Amend the positive part of the format code with an underscore followed by a bracket:

```
0.0,,_);[red](0.0,,)
```

The underscore (_) character is the code to make the following character invisible. Click OK to see the very minor effect on screen, but verify that the

	A	B	C	D	E	F	G	H
1	Period from			01 Jan 14	01 Apr 14	01 Jul 14	01 Oct 14	01 Jan 15
2	Period to			31 Mar 14	30 Jun 14	30 Sep 14	31 Dec 14	31 Mar 15
3								
4	Revenue			.	.	.	.	4.3
5								
6	Operating costs			.	.	.	.	(1.6)
7								
8	Working capital (increase) decrease			.	.	.	.	(1.0)
9								
10	Capital expenditure			(20.0)	(19.0)	(18.0)	(16.0)	.
11								
12	Sales tax			(1.4)	0.1	0.1	0.1	1.3
13								
14	Project cash flow			(21.4)	(18.9)	(17.9)	(15.9)	3.1
15								
16	Interest on cash less overdraft			.	.	.	0.0	0.1
17								
18	Cash flow from (to) senior lenders							
19	interest			.	.	.	.	(1.3)
20	principal			19.4	18.9	20.3	8.4	(1.1)
21	total			19.4	18.9	20.3	8.4	(2.4)
22								
23	Net transfer to							
24	major maintenance reserve			.	.	.	.	(0.1)
25	debt service reserve			.	.	(2.4)	(2.4)	0.0
26	total			.	.	(2.4)	(2.4)	(0.0)
27								
28	Cash flow from (to) subordinated lenders							
29	interest			.	.	.	.	(0.2)
30	principal			.	.	.	9.8	(0.5)
31	total			.	.	.	9.8	(0.7)
32								
33	Cash flow from (to) partners							
34	contributions			2.0	.	.	.	.
35	withdrawals			.	.	.	.	.
36	total			2.0	.	.	.	.
37								
38	Financing cash flow			21.4	18.9	17.9	15.9	(3.1)
39								
40	Change in net cash balances			.	.	0.0	0.0	(0.0)

FIGURE 7.16   The effect of custom formatting.

decimal points of both positive and negative numbers do in fact line up. I am often asked if we could just use a space in the format code, rather than the nonsense of the invisible character, and indeed a space would do the trick just as well. The difficulties are that firstly the space is then difficult to see in the format code, and secondly that spaces do not have a fixed measurement – if you have ever tried to line up text on two different lines in Microsoft Word you will have discovered this (and French users of Excel often use the space as the thousands separator).

8. The results now look quite attractive in the worksheet, but we still have zero values displayed. These just clutter up the screen, and it would be helpful if they could be converted into hyphens. Select the cells and return to the Format Cells dialog box.

9. The first part of the format code is for positive numbers, the second part is for negative numbers, and the third part is for zero values. For neatness the hyphen needs to be in the same position as the decimal point. Type another semicolon and the following code:

```
0.0,,_); [red](0.0,,);-_0_)
```

The hyphen is the character to represent the zeros (if omitted, the cells would appear blank), the _0 hides the decimal value and the _) hides the bracket, the combined effect of which is to push the underscore into the same position as the decimal point. Click OK (Figure 7.17).

For completeness I will mention that there is a fourth component of the custom format which is for text. Type a further semicolon and, for example, a colour (in square brackets). Type the @ sign, and click OK. If you omit the @, Excel substitutes the word General into the code. I do not have much use for this format option.

We might also note that there is a rather unethical custom format based only on the semicolon separators: the format code of ;;; means that no formatting has been specified for positives, negatives or zero values, so the cell appears empty. Please don't use this in your own models.

At this stage you will probably want to stampede off to your other output sheets to format them as well. There are a couple of useful techniques here. You probably already know about the Format Painter tool, where you click on a cell containing the source format, click the Format Painter, and then click and drag over the destination cells. A little known trick is to double-click the Format Painter, after which the tool stays active as you repeat the click and drag action

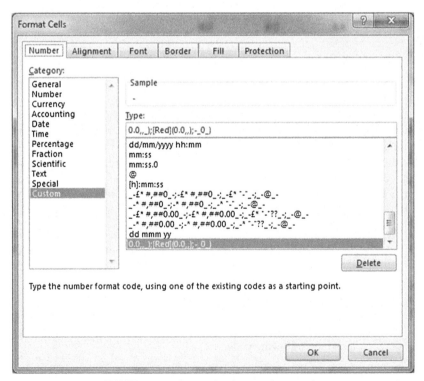

FIGURE 7.17 The completed custom format code.

over cells on different sheets (it normally switches itself off). You will lose any borders and colours on the destination sheets but they are easy to restore. If the format is to be applied repeatedly to different cells or sheets, try using the F4 (repeat last action) shortcut instead of the Format Painter.

Alternatively note that your custom formats will appear at the very bottom of the custom format list in the Format cells dialog box, while the formatted workbook is open.

Styles

A more sophisticated solution is to set up a Style.

1. Select a cell that contains the custom format, and run File, Cell Styles (J), New Cell Style.
2. Type in a style name, such as Millions. Switch off all options other than Number.
3. Choose OK.

To apply the format to other sheets, select the destination cells and use the Cell Styles (J) command and select the style from the list. You can also customise your toolbar with the Style drop-down list. To use the Millions style in other workbooks, you can use the File, Cell Styles (J), Merge Styles command (Figure 7.18).

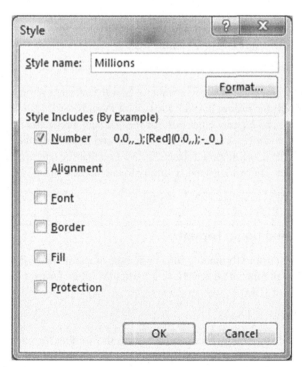

FIGURE 7.18   Clear the check boxes that do not apply to the Millions style.

Reporting

When using the Millions format we recognise that Excel is rounding the numbers quite shamelessly, so we should change the page footer to include the standard caveat 'Numbers may not agree due to rounding'. Also, Excel treats any value of 49,999 or less as zero – if this magnitude of number is significant for your purposes, amend the format code to 0.00, etc. I would also strongly recommend that you only use this formatting on your output sheets: the inputs sheet values must be in the same units as expressed in the data book or source documentation (Chapter 3). The workings values should be left as they are, with perhaps comma formatting to make them readable. Over the time you have spent developing your model, you have probably become quite familiar with some of the numbers and would recognise them easily. If you were to apply the millions format they become difficult to appreciate, particularly when Excel starts rounding them.

Currency

Another example of the use of custom formatting is to include a currency symbol in the cell, but showing the symbol on the left-hand side rather than immediately adjacent to the value. Using Ctrl+1 we enter the currency symbol followed by an asterisk * and a space, followed by the appropriate number format. This odd combination instructs Excel to show the symbol and then to repeat the space character as many times as possible before showing the value. Remember to include the currency symbol and the repeater on both sides of the format, otherwise negative values will be unaffected.

```
€* #,##0_);[red] €* (#,##0)
```

In some circumstances we might want to show the currency abbreviation rather than the symbol, for example, GBP for British Pounds, or USD for US dollars. We find that we can happily enter GBP as the currency prefix but not USD. This is because certain letters are reserved characters, and in this case the S is reserved for seconds in the date and time formats, so we find that the letters M, D, H and E are not available. The workaround is simply to enclose the string in quotes:

```
"USD"* #,##0_);[red]"USD"* (#,##0)
```

A Type of Conditional Format

We can also use custom formatting for a basic type of conditional formatting. If we need to flag up numbers that are above a particular value, for example, cash balances in excess of 100,000, we can select the range and apply the following format:

```
[blue][>=100,000]0;0
```

The 0 outside the square brackets represents the number format to be applied to values above 100,000. The 0 after the semicolon represents the formatting of numbers which are below 100,000. We can add a second condition, which in combination give three potential formats.

```
[blue][>=100,000]0;[green][>=50,000]0;[red]0
```

Values above 100,000 appear blue, above 50,000 green and below 50,000 red. Take care in putting the conditions in the correct order. Given the range of conditional formatting options now available I think this is of marginal interest.

CHARTING

One aspect of model use is the graphical presentation of results. Excel's charting features and the specific use of charts is beyond the scope of this book but there are some useful tricks we should be able to use.

F11 and Alt+F1

Every modeller should know the F11 shortcut for creating charts. Simply select the data and press the F11 key, and Excel prepares a chart on a chart sheet. Chart sheets are optimally laid out for printing, usually A4 landscape, and are more efficient in memory terms than charts embedded on the worksheet. Use Alt+F1 to create such an embedded chart.

You may find that the first time you use F11 you will create a bar chart, as this is the Excel default. If you want to use line or other charts, create a chart and use Design (JC), Change Chart Type, and select your preferred chart type in the dialog box. From the panel in the top of the dialog box select the subtype and right-click to choose Set as Default Chart. This will assign this chart type to F11 (Figure 7.19).

For most users, the combination of Excel, charts and printing is a great source of frustration and I routinely find that many prefer to dump their charts into PowerPoint to get the results they need. However, there is a little-known workaround in which we can place multiple charts on a single chart sheet and printing becomes very simple.

1. Select any cell in the workbook and press F11. This results in a blank chart sheet. Double-click the sheet tab and give the sheet a name, e.g. MultiChart.
2. Now select the first range to be charted and press F11 (or Alt+F1).
3. Right-click on the edge of the new chart and select Move Chart. Specify MultiChart as the destination, with the source chart as an object. If the Move Chart command does not appear, check that you are not accidentally clicking a chart component instead.
4. Move/resize the chart on the chart sheet.
5. Repeat as required. If the chart doesn't appear it may be underneath so move the existing chart around first.

Use text boxes to add additional information, and print when required. As noted above, the chart sheet is optimally set up for printing.

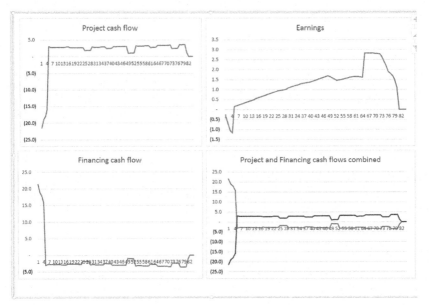

FIGURE 7.19   Multiple charts on a chart sheet.

Updating Charts

If a new data series needs to be added to a chart, the data can be selected and copied. If the chart is then selected, the data can be simply pasted (Ctrl+V) – Excel will assume that the values are a new data series and will plot them automatically.

See the dynamic range name section in Chapter 4 for an explanation of how to automatically include new values on a chart as they are added to an existing data series.

Chapter 8

Sensitivity Analysis and Scenarios

INTRODUCTION

Almost by definition, the purpose of any financial model is to explore the effects of changing the input assumptions. Sensitivity analysis, also referred to as what-if analysis, tends to refer to the process of adjusting one or two key drivers and observing or recording the results; scenario management refers to the process of changing several drivers to create specific operational or economic situations. A further refinement involves the assessment of likelihood or risk involved with a particular scenario. Building on the approach developed throughout this book it is worth emphasising that we should only use the one model for analysis. It is often tempting to develop scenarios in a series of copies of the original workbook, but this can lead to immense problems in the future if one of the common assumptions or calculation routines is then revised. Even a relatively trivial adjustment can then take several hours or days to distribute to the suite of scenario-specific workbooks, and even with the development of the change-tracking functionality in Excel it can be difficult to reconcile one workbook with another.

When describing the relationship between sensitivity and scenario analysis, we can define the former as the process for testing the model's reaction to the effects of changing a small number of model inputs, often independently of each other; and we might describe this using 'or': a 5% reduction in sales *or* a 10% increase in costs. Scenario analysis is concerned with multiple, simultaneous changes to economic or operational assumptions, where we would use 'and': a 5% reduction in sales *and* a 10% increase in costs.

In this chapter, we will look at a number of techniques for manipulating or flexing financial models, but before we start, backup your work first. It is not helpful to embark on a review of the model's assumptions and then to lose the original figures. For sensitivity and Goal Seek analysis, cell comments may be sufficient. We will consider other techniques for scenario management.

MODEL INTERROGATION

A topic which has become popular over the last couple of years is the idea of 'interrogating the model', a process of somehow challenging the results of the model without getting the hands dirty by understanding all the calculations.

Practical Financial Modelling.
231

This will involve some form of sensitivity or 'stress testing' in which the users are looking for patterns or connections in the results which result from specific changes to the inputs. The techniques for sensitivity and scenario analysis in this chapter will certainly help provide an understanding of the dynamics of the model and in a robust way. One particularly attractive feature is reproducibility: that a given set of inputs, either alone or in combination, will give the same results each time the model is run. We must understand, however, that it is the attention given to the relationships between the various inputs that makes the real difference to the validity of the results. The classic example is that of inflation rates and interest rates. They are very clearly related and yet we still see macroeconomic scenarios in which inflation is increased or decreased, but without any corresponding change or link to the interest rates.

Despite the fact that sensitivity and scenario analysis is one of the most important functions of a financial model, and that considerable time and effort is expended in developing, testing and auditing the model, the analysis is not often given the attention it deserves.

Give careful thought to the implicit relationships between the different components of the model. In the process of stress testing or 'flexing the numbers', keep your own commercial knowledge to the fore – for example, in a scenario of rising production, variable costs should rise too; but at higher levels, the management might be able to bring pressure on its supply chain and negotiate reduced costs. Do prices and costs really increase each year ('inflationary creep') or do they move in step changes due to other factors? What happens to all the cash that starts building up in the optimistic scenario? Do the loan covenants allow it to be released to shareholders if the lending ratios are covered? And more than anything, avoid implausible scenarios or combinations of factors: we have seen the example where the forecast rail passenger numbers (which generated the revenue) were in excess of the physical capacity of the trains supposed to carry them!

In a couple of examples in this book you may have noticed I've used the concept of the 'overdraft' (or 'bank indebtedness'). This does not indicate that my firm or project has an overdraft facility at the bank (not that common in these days), but it is simply a method of capturing the points at which expenditure exceeds income, resulting in a cash shortfall. If any numbers appear in this section it is incumbent on my or the model sponsor to consider alternative sources of short- or long-term finance to cover the predicted shortfall. The availability of such finance might well depend on the covenants attached to any existing loans and cover ratios. So we often find the base case model has been very carefully constructed so that the proposed financing works perfectly and sensible returns are shown for the various cover ratios and other metrics. Then the bank asks a simple question, for example, about the effect of a 10% reduction in revenues, and suddenly the model is producing nonsense, and no thought has been given by the modeller or sponsor about the actions which might be taken to mitigate the effects of the change. The result is that this simple stress test puts the model back several days or longer while these ramifications are considered. Most model auditors will now carry out a fixed number of such stress tests as a routine exercise in the audit process.

As shown in the previous chapter, charts can be very helpful in the analysis of complex numerical data. It can be very difficult to spot potential pinchpoints or hiccups over a 20-year forecast period, calculated quarterly, but the technique of simply highlighting a row and pressing F11 to view a line chart will convey this information very effectively. As each sensitivity or scenario is run, charts can be generated on the fly to validate the results of the analysis, and can (and should) be used with any of the techniques explained in this chapter. Useful lines to monitor include the operating cash flow, EBITDA, pre- and post-tax profits, cash available for debt service and the ratios. The competent modeller should always be able to explain the story behind the shape of the line (Figure 8.1).

SENSITIVITIES

We can think of sensitivity analysis as involving the testing of one or two key inputs, usually independently of each other. As previously mentioned, we can use the language of 'or' to describe this process: 10% decrease in revenues OR a 5% increase in costs.

Goal Seek

A good starting point is the Goal Seek tool. You have built your model and found that input *I1* generated the result, *R1*. Assuming you need result *R2*, what should input *I2* be in order to obtain this result? You can change the input manually and then inspect the result (which is fine if you are on billable time), but a more efficient way is to use Goal Seek.

Select the cell containing the result you wish to specify. This cell must contain a formula. Run the Data, What-If Analysis, Goal Seek command, and identify this result cell as the Set Cell. Next, specify the result you would like in the To value box. Finally, identify the By changing cell reference. This cell must contain an input value. Click OK (Figure 8.2).

Note the use of the singular throughout. We cannot specify the results for a range of cells, neither can we obtain the results by changing several inputs, although one workaround is to put link formulas on the inputs sheet, such that the value generated by Goal Seek is copied across the row. It does not matter which sheets contain the Set Cell or the Changing Cell.

Excel uses an iterative technique to obtain the result. If you recall the discussion concerning the use of iteration in Chapter 5, the File, Options, Formulas command offers the constraints of either 100 iterations, or until the maximum change is 0.001 (the defaults). Goal Seek therefore follows whichever of these constraints apply. Make sure that this is not obscured by formatting, and if needed retype the number generated by Goal Seek with appropriate rounding and common sense.

Project cash flow

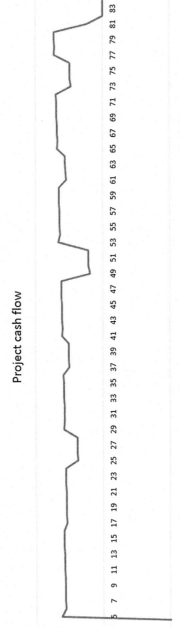

FIGURE 8.1 Interrogating the model: what is the cause of the dip in the line in periods 49–53?

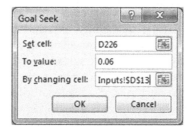

FIGURE 8.2   The Set Cell and changing cell can be on any sheet.

If you are also using iteration for circular code elsewhere in your model, Goal Seek can produce absurd results as it iterates its own iterations, even if the results under analysis are not involved in the circularity.

Data Tables

Data tables have been around since the earliest versions of Lotus 1-2-3 and Excel, and although they are very useful tools they contain several limitations which have never been resolved. These will be considered below. The concept of the data table is simple – Goal Seek offers the ability to specify one input variable and to see the effect on one formula. The data table allows us to provide a range of values for a particular input and the table will record the results as these values are run through the model. We can use either a one-way analysis, in which one variable is tested and the results of one or more formulas are recorded, or a two-way analysis, in which two variables are tested against each other and the results of a single dependent formula are displayed. Lotus 1-2-3 had the facility for three-way analysis using multiple sheets, but Microsoft has never pursued this.

The One-Way Data Table

The one-way or one-variable data table allows you to specify a range of values to be substituted into a single input variable cell, and to record the results of the analysis. On the inputs sheet (or equivalent), locate the cell which contains the variable to be tested. If this is at the start of a row or column, you should enter link formulas in the rest of the range.

Further down the sheet, either write the formula you wish to use, or put in a link to the formula if it is located elsewhere in the workbook (it can be helpful to split the screen or open a new window). With a one-way table you can test several formulas. In the row beginning in the cell above and to the right of the first formula cell, enter the list of values you wish to run through the model. If you have more than 255 of them, you will need to transpose the range such that the formula cell is above and to the right of the column of values. In either case there should be a blank cell in the top left position. Select the blank cell, the formula cell(s), the row (column) of inputs and the cells in which the results are to appear, and then run the Data, What-If Analysis, Data Table command.

In the dialog box, specify the Row input cell as the cell into which the row of numbers is to be placed (Excel is not asking you for the location of the data table – you have already done that). Click OK. Inspect the data table (Figure 8.3).

If the data table is showing the same result across the row (or down the column), press F9 (see below). If this has not helped, check that you have appropriate link formulas in the input row, that the input row actually feeds into the model, and that the formula under test is actually dependent on this particular input.

In routine use, it is normal to set up a data table for each sensitivity as, for example, the price sensitivity, the cost sensitivity and so.

The Two-Way Data Table

The two-variable data table allows us to test the interaction of two input variables, but we are restricted to one formula. The basic structure is as above, but the formula cell is placed at the intersection of the input row and the input column (Figure 8.4).

Observations

Once a data table has been set up, the values in the input row/column can be changed at will.

Unlike Goal Seek, data tables must be set up on the same sheet which contains the input variable under analysis. Several of the other modelling rules proposed earlier in the book are also redundant when using data tables. I had hoped that Excel 2013 would overcome this long-standing restriction, but cross-sheet functionality is still not available. Three-way data tables were a feature of Lotus 1-2-3 but Microsoft have never pursued this functionality.

The data table formula is an example of an array formula (Chapter 5). This type of formula is recognised by the curly brackets { }. Although an efficient way of writing code, problems arise if the user attempts to edit the formula. On pressing Enter, we are informed that 'That function is not valid'. The immediate solution is to press Esc. Array formulas can only be manipulated as a whole range, so any action such as inserting or deleting columns, or deleting cells, will generate the error message. The data table, or more specifically the results of the data table, must be deleted if other such actions are required. The TABLE function itself cannot be written manually.

Table Recalculation

We might ask how does the data table actually work? The workbook model has the original input value and will be reporting the original output value, so where do all the other data table results come from? In very simple terms we can recognise that an 'array' is a computer programming expression that describes

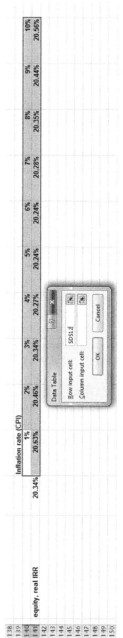

FIGURE 8.3   A one-way data table. The input cell is off screen but on the same sheet.

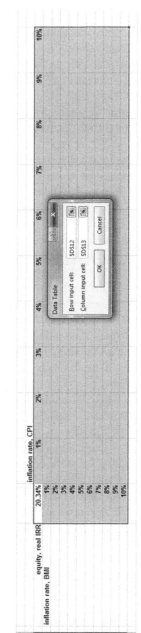

FIGURE 8.4   Two-way data table. The formula is at the intersection of the row and column input values.

a space in memory in which information is stored. Our routine formulas might be described as being located in the physical workbook in front of us, in the spreadsheet grid, or matrix. When we create the data table, Excel sets up a virtual copy of the entire model in memory – one for each of the input values. In each of these virtual models, the row or column input cell is populated by the individual inputs, which drives the virtual model and generates the result which is then shown in a physical cell in the worksheet.

If the model is, for example, 10 Mb in size, even a simple data table could consume very large amounts of memory in running all of the virtual models simultaneously, and recalculation can be drastically slowed as trivial changes to the physical model are replicated in the memory space. Data tables can be very memory intensive and potentially time consuming, so you can change the recalculation options by using File, Options, Formulas, Calculation Options (X), Automatic Except for Data Tables. This will allow the model proper to recalculate as before, and recalculation of the data table is forced by pressing F9 or Ctrl+= (Recalculate). This can lead to problems if, for example, the data table is printed without having been updated. The solution is to recognise that the formula driving the data table is not subject to the recalculation exception and calculates normally. You should make sure that the current model input for the data table (the value in the row or column input cell) also appears in the data table input row or column. The result underneath or next to this value should be the same as the driving formula. If it is not, press F9.

Bear in mind that recalculation options are persistent and remain in effect if other workbooks are opened in this session; they are also workbook attributes and will be saved in the file, to be put into effect automatically when the workbook is next opened.

As with Goal Seek, data tables only allow for one row input cell and one column input cell. If the variable is to be used across the forecast period, then make sure you have link formulas in the relevant row, otherwise the table will show only the sensitivity to changing the first value. A disadvantage of this limitation is that it is not possible to model trends or manipulate values in other ways. For example, if I were looking at the sensitivity of my new product to price, I could create a data table to show the effect of price change on net present value (NPV). I could put an escalator formula in the input row to increase the price by 2% each quarter, but would I actually want to pursue this strategy at the higher price end of my data table values? Likewise, the data table would not allow me to explore price skimming, curves and other techniques.

SCENARIOS

Scenarios are used for more sophisticated analysis, where the effects and interactions of multiple variables need to be explored; and again we use the language here of 'and', as in a 10% decrease in revenues AND a 5% increase in costs. These can be set up as formal, defined, scenarios – worst case/most likely/best case, in which the variables in each scenario have been chosen to represent a particular position. Alternatively the model can be used to test particular permutations of the variables, which can be either controlled, by using data validation/ drop-down lists to restrict the analysis to a specific set of variables, or uncontrolled, in which the user can change any and all variables.

Setting up a scenario requires some careful thought beforehand. The first point is that the values used in the base model must be documented, so that the user can always reverse or undo their changes. Second, how are the results to be used? It is difficult to display the results of two or more scenarios for comparison without using Paste Value techniques (although we will look at the delta sheet technique below). Third, make sure that the relationships between the variables are clearly understood and, if needed, fully documented. Inflation, for example, has a creeping effect over a period of time, but it tends to manifest itself in step changes – retail prices, for example, tend to go up in whole units (and the marketing types will be sensitive to the 9.99 barrier!). Similarly most wages are adjusted annually, and this would need to be addressed if using a quarterly model (see Chapter 5 and the use of masks). Make sure that linkages are recognised: the total variable cost should vary with changes in production levels, but the fixed costs should remain the same. And one that I still find slips through – interest rates are a function of inflation.

Finally, the user should be clear about the cells and ranges which are allowed to be changed. The inputs/workings/outputs structure would restrict the user to the inputs sheet only, and the sensible use of colour, cell comments, drop-down lists and the like, should guide the user into the safe use of the model. A further development of the model structure might be a variation on the usual layout – many models contain large numbers of inputs, of which only a few may be identified as key drivers for scenario analysis. In this case it might be worthwhile setting up a separate scenario inputs sheet which contains the relevant variables which then feed into the workings. A further development would be to link the key outputs back to this sheet, so that the results of the scenario can be seen alongside/underneath the assumptions. This can be quite effective if set up properly.

There are several techniques we can use to set up scenarios.

Scenario Manager

This is a tool that comes with Excel and lives under Data, What-If Analysis, Scenario Manager. It has some neat functionality, but is rather restricted in what it does and generally does not conform with the principles of good modelling practice. The Scenario Manager is restricted to a maximum of 32 changing cells, which can be worked around by using link formulas to copy the changing cells across the row. Furthermore, the Scenario Manager is strictly sheet specific which means that although we might expect all the inputs to be on one sheet anyway, we cannot run the scenario from an output sheet, for example. It is possible to produce summaries and pivot tables of scenarios, but this requires the results cells to be on the same sheet as well. Another point against the Scenario Manager is that the values used for the changing cells are stored in the dialog box itself and are not visible in the spreadsheet until the specific scenario is run (the 'black box approach') (Figure 8.5). This means that the significance of a particular value cannot be directly documented. A further dimension of this problem is that it can be difficult to identify the changing cells in the worksheet, although this can be easily solved by the use of cell colour while setting up the scenario in the first place. Is it worth mentioning that it is perfectly possible to create a group of scenarios which each have a different number of changing cells, or indeed use different changing cells? And in the absence of the scenario toolbar, which scenario is currently in use?

The key issue arising from the consideration of Excel's Scenario Manager is that the variables are stored in the dialog box and not in the workbook and therefore are not immediately available for inspection or audit. The need for such transparency is addressed by the use of other techniques, such as the CHOOSE function and the LOOKUP functions.

CHOOSE

This function is fairly widely used and might be described as a quick and dirty approach to scenarios. The syntax of the function is:

```
=CHOOSE(number, first item, second item, third item, ..., twenty
ninth item)
```

FIGURE 8.5   Excel's Scenario Manager – the black box.

Number is a value (or reference to a cell or formula which returns a value) representing the position of an item in a list.

First item is the item returned from the list if number is 1; and so on up to 29. The item could be a value, reference, formula or text.

In the following example, we will look at the use of the CHOOSE function to test three pricing scenarios: a constant price across the forecast period, a loss-leading scenario (low initial price then increase) and a price skimming scenario (high initial price, followed by a reduction).

For the original input variable on the inputs sheet, we can now add additional rows to reflect each scenario. Make sure each row is numbered so that we can crosscheck the scenario number against the scenario row (we will see this again in the lookup section further on). The assumptions underlying each scenario can also be documented (Figure 8.6).

We then set up a cell which will contain the scenario number. As this contains an input value it should be located on the inputs sheet, and documented as such. On the workings sheet the original formulas that linked to the input need to be updated (Figure 8.7). The CHOOSE function can be written:

```
=CHOOSE(PriceCell,PriceConstant,PriceLossLeading,PriceSkimming)
```

By changing the PriceCell value, each scenario can be run rapidly and reliably.

A further elegant touch is to set up an additional cell which returns the name of the scenario:

```
=CHOOSE(PriceCell,"Constant price", "Loss leading","Price skimming")
```

	A	B	C	D	E	F	G	H	I	J	K	L	M	N
1	Period				Q1	Q2	Q3	Q4	Q1	Q2	Q3	Q4		
2														
3	Price													
4	1 constant				18	18	18	18	18	18	18	18	PriceConstantIn	
5	2 loss-leading				14	14	16	16	18	18	18	18	PriceLossLeadingIn	
6	3 price-skimming				20	20	18	18	18	18	16	16	PriceSkimmingIn	
7														

FIGURE 8.6   The three scenarios as described on the inputs sheet.

E9   fx   =CHOOSE(PriceCell,PriceConstant,PriceLossLeading,PriceSkimming)

	A	B	C	D	E	F	G	H	I	J	K	L	M	N
1	Period				Q1	Q2	Q3	Q4	Q1	Q2	Q3	Q4		
2														
3	price scenario number			2	PriceCell									
4														
5	Price													
6	constant				18	18	18	18	18	18	18	18	PriceConstant	
7	loss-leading				14	14	16	16	18	18	18	18	PriceLossLeading	
8	price-skimming				20	20	18	18	18	18	16	16	PriceSkimming	
9	scenario price				14	14	16	16	18	18	18	18	Price	
10														

FIGURE 8.7   The corresponding workings sheet, with the PriceCell switch.

If the output sheets are linked to this cell, we can solve the problem of documenting the name of the scenario in current use.

Care is needed when using CHOOSE. If the user enters an invalid scenario number, #VALUE! errors are generated (hence the suggestion to use drop-down lists/data validation). If the order of the scenarios listed on the inputs sheet should change, or if a scenario is added or removed, the dependent CHOOSE functions will need updating. This is something we generally wish to avoid. However, it is very simple to use, and if set up sensibly can prove to be robust and reliable.

We can easily extend the use of CHOOSE such that each of the key drivers identified can have its own CHOOSE functionality. For each of these inputs we can prepare a scenario list and scenario cell. In this way, for example, we could test the price skimming scenario with corresponding high promotion/low promotion scenarios, with PriceCell set to 3 and PromotionCell set to 1, and so on into a number of permutations. Alternatively, with the example of best case/most likely/worst case, we could set up three scenario lines for each driver, such that on entering a 1 in the scenario cell the model assembles the best case scenario.

CHOOSE, and LOOKUP and INDEX in the next section, can be used to great effect with the List Box/Combo box techniques described in Chapter 7.

LOOKUP

Another way of running scenarios is to use the LOOKUP functions in place of CHOOSE. We can use the same example as before, but this time we recognise that the rows containing the price scenarios are effectively look-up tables. I suggested that the rows were numbered, but this technique works just as well with the row heading text. We keep the price cell as before. We will need to put a column number in each column so that the VLOOKUP can offset accordingly (see Chapter 6) (Figure 8.8).

Instead of the CHOOSE function, write:

```
=VLOOKUP(PriceCell,PriceTable,ColumnNumber,0)
```

This works by looking for the value (or text) in the PriceCell in the first row of the look-up table or scenario block. VLOOKUP then counts across ColumnNumber columns and returns the scenario price.

	A	B	C	D	E	F	G	H	I	J	K	L	M	N
1	Period				Q1	Q2	Q3	Q4	Q1	Q2	Q3	Q4		
2														
3		price scenario number		3	PriceCell									
4														
5		Price			5	6	7	8	9	10	11	12	ColumnNumber	
6	1	constant			18	18	18	18	18	18	18	18	PriceConstant	
7	2	loss-leading			14	14	16	16	18	18	18	18	PriceLossLeading	
8	3	price-skimming			20	20	18	18	18	18	16	16	PriceSkimming	
9		scenario price			=VLOOKUP(PriceCell,$A$6:$L$8,ColumnNumber,0)					18	16	16	Price	
10														

FIGURE 8.8 Using a look-up table. Note the numbering in column A, which forms part of the look-up table itself.

INDEX

INDEX was introduced in Chapter 6 and is probably the most efficient of the formula techniques for running scenarios. The CHOOSE function is cumbersome because it has to contain all the arguments, in the correct order, and the LOOKUP requires a look-up table structure. If we recall that the syntax of INDEX is simple, INDEX(range, position), we can set up a row of inputs for each scenario (as with CHOOSE and LOOKUP), a cell which contains the scenario number (such as PriceCell), and on the workings we can write a simple INDEX function to read the value from the (vertical) range, as shown in Figure 8.9.

INDEX can also use the values provided from list and combo boxes. As with the other techniques the assumptions underlying each scenario row should be documented.

Issues with the Function Approach

These techniques are reliable and easy to use if the number of scenarios is limited. We need to be careful about invalid scenario numbers (which we can control with the list and combo boxes), and we should hope that our users would not rearrange the scenario order.

INDEX, CHOOSE and VLOOKUP are limited in that the inputs sheet can fill up rapidly with row after row of scenario variables. Theoretically each one should be documented and with reference to the issue of linkages mentioned above, it may be necessary to advise that certain permutations of variables may not be valid (e.g. high interest/low inflation). Furthermore, the standard auditing checks (F2 Edit Cell, Ctrl+[Select Precedents) do not indicate which specific cells are used in each calculation. However, all the information is available in the workbook, and it should be fairly easy to see the differences between one scenario row and the next. The main problem is that particularly in the scenario which has been assembled from several different drivers (constant price, low promotion, low volume, etc.), it can be difficult to see the specific numbers being used in the scenario, and in some cases the scenario can be difficult to reconstruct. These methods are best used when the number of scenarios and their permutations are small. Of the three methods the INDEX is my preferred technique.

	A	B	C	D	E	F	G	H	I	J	K	L	M	N
1	Period				Q1	Q2	Q3	Q4	Q1	Q2	Q3	Q4		
2														
3	price scenario number			1	PriceCell									
4														
5	Price													
6	constant				18	18	18	18	18	18	18	18	PriceConstant	
7	loss-leading				14	14	16	16	18	18	18	18	PriceLossLeading	
8	price-skimming				20	20	18	18	18	18	16	16	PriceSkimming	
9	scenario price				=INDEX(E6:E8,PriceCell)		18	18	18	18	18	18	Price	
10														

FIGURE 8.9   The simplest option: INDEX(range, position).

Multiple Input Sheets

One solution to the problem of creating more complex scenarios is to model them separately on individual sheets. Each sheet contains just the assumptions related to that scenario, with appropriate documentation. This gives more control and reduces the potential for multiple and/or invalid permutations. I mentioned in the introduction to this chapter that we should use the original model when carrying out scenario analysis, rather than multiple copies of the workbook, and this argument extends to the use of a single workings sheet. The implication of this is that each of the scenario-specific inputs sheets should, at the user's request, feed into the workings sheet and through to the outputs. Multiple workings sheets, as with multiple workbooks, would be difficult to update, modify or audit.

I have used and taught the following technique for several years, but unlike the other techniques I have described in this book, I have never had any feedback about it. I can only assume either that my exposition of it is so clear and concise that analysts are able to instantly comprehend the elegance of the technique and apply it themselves, or alternatively that people prefer INDEX, CHOOSE or VLOOKUP. I rather suspect the latter.

There are two versions of this technique, one which uses cell references and one which uses range names. The former is the simplest and we will explore it first. Step 1 in either method is to copy the original inputs sheet within the same workbook. Use Home, Format, Move or Copy Sheet, (or Ctrl+click and drag the sheet tab). Give the copied sheet a sensible name.

The Cell Reference Method

If you have used the methods described in Chapter 3 you should have formulas on your workings sheet which link to the inputs, and you will have avoided calculations which combine references from different sheets, for example,

This...

| Cell E3 contains | =inputs!E4 | Link to inflation rate on inputs |
| Cell E4 contains | =D4*(1+E3) | Inflation index calculation |

Rather than this...

| Cell E3 contains | =D3*(1+inputs!E4) | |

If you have used this mixed referencing (three-dimensional or cross-sheet calculations) you can still use this technique but be careful. Also if you have the habit of prefixing all your formulas with a plus sign (=+inputs!E4) you should proceed with care.

To force the formulas to read from the new (copied) inputs sheet, we can simply run a Replace command on the workings sheet which will convert all references to the old input sheet name to the new input sheet name. Use Ctrl+H (Replace). My own preference is to use the exact sheet name-specific string =inputs! and replace with =BaseCase! If you have mixed referencing and/or the plus sign prefix then just use the sheet name! syntax itself – your need for care here is because sometimes the sheet name description may have been used legitimately as text elsewhere in the sheet and you may not wish to replace it. If this is likely to be the case, select all the calculations on the workings sheet, because Replace will then only work within the selection. Before considering the extended use and functionality of this technique, we will look at the rather more arcane range name method.

The Range Name Method

You may find it helpful to refer back to the treatment of range names in Chapter 4, especially the topic of sheet-level names. You should also ensure that you have not used any three-dimensional calculations, otherwise the following technique will not work:

So this...

Cell E3 contains `=InflationIn`   Link to inflation rate on inputs

Cell E4 contains `=D4*(1+InflationRate)`   Inflation index calculation

Rather than this...

Cell E3 contains   `=D3*(1+InflationIn)`

If you have the habit of prefixing your formulas with the + sign you may find it helpful to run a quick Ctrl+H (Replace) to convert all your `=+` formulas prefixes with the simple `=`.

When you created the copy of the original inputs sheet, you also copied all the range names on that sheet. The names on the original inputs sheet are global names and those on the copy are local, or sheet-level, names. If you inspect the formulas on the workings sheet, the references to original inputs still stand. To pick up the new inputs, the range name must be prefixed with the sheet name (Figure 8.10).

If we were to attempt the same Replace command used with the cell references, we are immediately struck by the problem of the search string – if you have used the conventions suggested in earlier chapters you may have differentiated your input range names using the suffix `-In` (`InflationIn` etc.). But the sheet name needs to prefix the formula. We don't have the time to waste on searching manually through the workings sheet to identify all formulas containing `In` (which might include inflation and interest!).

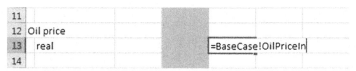

FIGURE 8.10   Switching scenarios with sheet-level (or local) names.

We need a method which will allow us to identify all cells which contain references to the inputs sheet. In Chapter 2, we looked at several techniques for locating cells and information, one of which was the Ctrl+] (Select Dependents) shortcut. However, we noted that it was formula driven: if an input value was selected and there was no dependent formula on that sheet, the shortcut would not work. This leads to the big step: we now select all the inputs on the original (global names) inputs sheet and Cut and Paste them onto the bottom of the workings sheet.

When named areas are cut and pasted the name moves with range. The global input names are now all located in the workings sheet, and at this stage should all be highlighted. If you now press Ctrl+] you should find that Excel highlights all formulas that contain references to these ranges.

Having differentiated input links from workings calculations, you can now run Ctrl+H (Replace), using the equals = sign as the search string. The Replace string is (e.g.) =Expansion! Test to see that it works.

The final step is to delete the (now blank) original inputs sheet, the pasted inputs at the bottom of the workings sheet, and the redundant names in the Ctrl+F3 or Name Manager dialog box.

Complete the sequence by making a copy of the new inputs sheet. Both of these contain sheet-level names.

Using Multiple Inputs Sheets

Whether you have used cell references or range names, you should now have a model with two inputs sheets. You should now change the content of each sheet to reflect the scenario it is intended to represent, and you can change the sheet tab name accordingly.

If you inspect the formulas on the workings sheet, you can immediately identify which scenario is being used, because the formulas contain the relevant scenario sheet names.

To flip from one scenario to the other, simply run the Ctrl+H Replace command again. If you want to set up multiple scenarios, copy one of the inputs sheets as many times as required. If you want to document the scenario name on the outputs, you can set up a cell on the workings which will read the scenario name from the appropriate inputs sheet.

```
=InputBestCase!ScenarioNameIn
```

This method is arguably better than the INDEX/CHOOSE/LOOKUP approach in that the workings formulas themselves describe the scenario being used. The Edit, Replace command is simple to run, and can be easily driven by macros (see Chapter 9).

As each input sheet has the same layout it may be difficult to see what is changing from one scenario sheet to the next, so the use of colour and cell comments is helpful in this context. The issue of rearranging, modifying and removing scenarios is far simpler to manage than is the case with the CHOOSE/LOOKUP functions.

Printing Scenarios

We are often required to print reports in which we compare two or more scenarios. The problem is that Excel can only calculate one scenario at a time, which is not much use. One option is to have multiple versions of the same file, but this is inherently unreliable as any amendments to one file then need to be replicated in all the others.

Before looking at possible solutions, make sure that the name of the scenario is embedded in the worksheet. Do not rely on putting it into the page header or footer, because in the heat of the moment, users forget to change the settings, and Excel still doesn't have the ability to link headers or footers to cells. We have previously introduced techniques which can be used here, using range names or concatenation, depending how the scenario is driven. With the CHOOSE, VLOOKUP or INDEX type routines, simply set up a formula that will return the appropriate scenario name depending on the input number or selection from the drop-down list, for example:

```
=CHOOSE(ScenarioNumber,"Best Case","Most Likely","Worst Case")
```

Give this cell a name, such as ScenarioName, and put a link to this on each of the outputs sheets/ranges.

The concatenation trick (Chapter 5) is used to set up the sheet title so that it includes the scenario name:

```
="Cash Flow:"&ScenarioName
```

If we are using the multiple input sheet scenario method, set up cells on each input sheet which contain the scenario name, and give each cell the same name, using the sheet-level name technique, for example, InputBase!ScenarioIn, InputMostLikely!ScenarioIn and so on. On the workings sheet set up the usual link to the current scenario, such that when the Edit, Replace command is run the range name picks up the correct scenario name.

The solution to the problem of printing scenarios is to decide if the results are to be stored permanently in the model or if they are to be discarded after printing. In the latter case it is then simply a process of running the scenario, printing, resetting and running the next scenario, a process that calls out for macro automation. In the former case, where the results are to be stored, or perhaps even displayed alongside each other, we need to think about copying sheets with pasted values. I would always be cautious when thinking about generating large numbers of sheets, for despite their apparent simplicity and limited content they can increase the size of the file quite considerably.

1. Set up the outputs as required, with appropriate sheet tabs and page settings.
2. Run the scenario.
3. Make a copy of each sheet, either by Ctrl+click and drag, or by grouping the sheets and right-click Move or Copy.
4. Use Ctrl+A to select the whole sheet, then Ctrl+C (Copy) and then Home, Paste (V), Paste Values over the formulas.
5. Repeat 2–4 for each scenario.

We can adapt the Paste Values technique if the key results from each scenario need to be presented on the same page.

Bear in mind that if the model is changed in any way the results are instantly outdated and the scenarios will need to be run again. This naturally points us towards setting up some macro functionality to achieve this.

DELTA SHEETS

One of the problems with running sensitivities and scenarios is to detect and monitor the impact of input changes not just on the headline results but on the individual components of the model. For example, a 10% fall in revenues would be expected to have an impact on the NPV, but what other effects might it have? We might think about the operating cash flow, which would lead us to the working capital and perhaps corporation tax. The fall in revenue might also affect debt service, including interest payments, and so. Operating cash flow effects will affect the NPV, but the debt service will not. Or will it? Interest payments are set against profits, on which tax is calculated, which is deducted from the operating cash flow. This is real model interrogation.

The delta sheet concept allows us to have two (or more) sets of results at the same time, with the delta sheet itself highlighting the differences. Delta (Δ) is the symbol for 'change' or 'difference'. The delta sheet approach will impact the structure of the model and so if you are doing this to examine another person's results you may need to seek permission to do so, or carry out the work on a backup copy of the original. In some cases we might consider using delta sheets in the audit workbook introduced in Chapter 2.

In the following example we will consider changing the unit price of a product and determining the effects of this on the elements of the cash flow, by comparing it with the original cash flow (base case).

1. Make a copy of the original cash flow (Ctrl+click and drag the sheet tab). Name the original sheet 'CashFlow Original' and the new sheet 'CashFlow Sensitivity'.
2. Make a further copy of the original cash flow and name it 'CashFlow Delta'. The sheets should be arranged in the order Original, Sensitivity, Delta.
3. On the original cash flow select all the formulas. Press Ctrl+A to select the whole sheet, then copy (Ctrl+C) and without removing the highlighting paste the values (Alt+H, V, V). This hard codes the original values.
4. Go to the delta sheet and press Ctrl+A to select the whole sheet. Now press F5 Go To, Special, and Formulas, OK.
5. With the formulas selected, type an equals sign in the active cell. Click on the corresponding cell in the original sheet, and then type a minus. Now click on the corresponding cell on the sensitivities sheet. The delta formula should be to the effect of =original value-sensitivity value. Now press Ctrl+Enter. This is the shortcut to fill the selected range with the content of the active cell.

The sheet should be full of zeroes. A quick audit check is that if the cells are selected the SUM on the status bar should be zero.

6. The original sheet contains the original values, hard coded. The sensitivity sheet contains live formulas. The delta sheet shows the difference between the two.

7. Now run the sensitivity by changing the price on the inputs sheet. Inspect the delta sheet.

This version of the delta sheet shows the differences as values. We can also set up the delta sheet to show percentage differences.

8. Copy the delta sheet, naming it as Cash Flow Delta Pc, and repeat step 4 to select the formulas.

9. As the denominator may be zero it can be helpful to use an IFERROR function; and we can use a sign switch to show the direction of the change, so the formula should read: =0-IFERROR(delta value/(original value + sensitivity value),0) (Figures 8.11–8.13).

Additional delta sheets can be added if further sensitivities or scenarios are being considered, with the base case sheet remaining the fixed point of reference and the sensitivity sheet retaining the links to the model calculations. Previous delta sheets can be copied and the values pasted for future reference.

	A	B	C	D	E	F	G
1	Period from			01 Jan 14	01 Apr 14	01 Jul 14	01 Oct 14
2	Period to			31 Mar 14	30 Jun 14	30 Sep 14	31 Dec 14
3							
4	Revenue			='Cash Flow Original'!D4-'Cash Flow Sensitivity'!D4			
5							
6	Operating costs			-	-	-	-
7							
8	Working capital (increase) decrease			-	-	-	-
9							
10	Capital expenditure			-	-	-	-
11							
12	Sales tax			-	-	-	-
13							
14	Project cash flow			-	-	-	-
15							

FIGURE 8.11   An extract from the Cash flow delta sheet at this point.

	A	B	C	D	E	F	G	H	I	J
1	Period from			01 Jan 14	01 Apr 14	01 Jul 14	01 Oct 14	01 Jan 15	01 Apr 15	01 Jul 15
2	Period to			31 Mar 14	30 Jun 14	30 Sep 14	31 Dec 14	31 Mar 15	30 Jun 15	30 Sep 15
3										
4	Revenue			-	-	-	-	(0.6)	(0.6)	(0.6)
5										
6	Operating costs			-	-	-	-	-	-	-
7										
8	Working capital (increase) decrease			-	-	-	-	0.2	0.0	0.0
9										
10	Capital expenditure			-	-	-	-	-	-	-
11										
12	Sales tax			-	-	-	-	(0.0)	(0.0)	(0.0)
13										
14	Project cash flow			-	-	-	-	(0.5)	(0.6)	(0.6)
15										

FIGURE 8.12   The Cash flow delta showing changes.

	A	B	C	D	E	F	G	H	I	J
1	Period from			01 Jan 14	01 Apr 14	01 Jul 14	01 Oct 14	01 Jan 15	01 Apr 15	01 Jul 15
2	Period to			31 Mar 14	30 Jun 14	30 Sep 14	31 Dec 14	31 Mar 15	30 Jun 15	30 Sep 15
3										
4	Revenue			=0-IFERROR('Cash Flow Delta'!D4/ 'Cash Flow Original'!D4+'Cash Flow Sensitivity'!D4 ,0)						
5										
6	Operating costs			.	.	.	.	.	.	.
7										
8	Working capital (increase) decrease			.	.	.	.	10%	12%	12%
9										
10	Capital expenditure			.	.	.	.	.	.	.
11										
12	Sales tax			.	.	.	.	2%	10%	10%
13										
14	Project cash flow			.	.	.	.	7%	10%	10%
15										

FIGURE 8.13   An extract from the Cash Flow Delta Pc sheet.

Remember the technique for pasting data series on to charts described in Chapter 7: this can be used to present the delta results graphically.

SOLVER

Excel has an add-in called Solver. This tool allows a Goal Seek functionality but with multiple input cells (up to 200) for which you can specify constraints, to calculate a single dependent formula. As my intention has been to offer modelling solutions using native Excel tools, I will not go further at this point, other than to offer the usual caveat that Solver is effectively a black box and that the assumptions underpinning the input cells are not documented in the worksheet. The precedent cells used by Solver must be on the same sheet as the target formula, which would breach the inputs–workings–outputs structure in the same way as do the data table and the Scenario Manager techniques.

The way I normally deal with Solver is to explain that if you do the sort of modelling that requires the use of Solver, you probably do not need me to explain how to use it; and therefore if you do not do this type of modelling you are unlikely to need it!

RISK

Risk is a topic that is much discussed in financial modelling and a proper exploration of the subject is outside the scope of this book. However, we do encounter the basic ideas of risk analysis in our modelling, and we should be able to understand why risk modelling is not as straightforward as it might seem. When carrying out sensitivity analysis, the presumption is that each of the values in the data table is equally likely. Using our professional judgement and experience we will of course recognise that this is not the case, and that within the population of values used in the table some are indeed more likely than others. When we start assigning probability to these values we are starting to think about risk. The exact definitions vary, but risk implies that all outcomes can be predicted and that we can predict the likelihood of one outcome over another. If a risk factor has a probability of 0 then it will never happen, and a factor with a probability of 1 is certain. When assigning risk to a set of values, for example, in a data table, the total of the probabilities must equal 1. If it is less than 1, then there is an outcome which has not been predicted, and this leads into the concept of uncertainty. If we have not identified all the outcomes that might arise, or we are not able to assess the likelihood of their occurrence, then we are dealing with uncertainty.

Where do we obtain the information from which to derive our probabilities? With operational factors we may be able to draw on significant previous experience, for example, that we incur a 3% wastage rate in the manufacture of a type of biscuit, but with financial factors this becomes much less precise – what exactly is the interest rate risk? The risk modellers refer to objective and subjective probability – the former is based on past experience, the latter on expert opinion. We can improve the wastage rate at the biscuit factory if the food scientists apply their knowledge of the interaction of flour, water, fat, sugar and temperature to the manufacturing process – the results will be measurable and reproducible. But what about the interest rates? In the United Kingdom, advertising for personal financial products always carries the strapline to the effect that 'investments may go down in value, as well as up'. What will the interest rate be next month? Next year? In 10 years? The global financial crisis provided a classic example of market movements that went off the scale. The cash flow forecasting models we saw were perfectly good models but had not been tested at such extremes; when revised estimates were entered the models still worked. As we saw in Chapter 1, models don't have any magical predictive powers and can only reflect the assumptions and operational parameters provided to the modelling analyst in good faith.

Another point is that certain sets of figures do not show the features of random variation and therefore are not subject to chance or probability. Staying with the biscuit factory for a moment, the production capacity does not fluctuate in itself. Capacity is a variable, described as deterministic, in that we can increase or decrease production levels by units of, say, 100 boxes, but we would not claim that there is a 10% chance of production exceeding 1000 boxes/day. It is the management who make this decision. Although the production capacity is deterministic, the appetite or demand for my biscuits is highly variable (described as stochastic), and in consultation with marketing colleagues we may be able to assign probabilities to the level of demand for the product over a particular forecast period.

When looking at carrying out any form of risk analysis careful thought needs to be given to relationships: if we are going to run a sensitivity or other analysis on a factor, are there any related factors which would be affected? The classic example is the relationship between interest rates and inflation, and we have seen models in which one has been tested independently of the other. Similarly, does inflation have an equal effect on revenues and on costs? Before carrying out any such analysis we must make sure that the correlations and dependencies of the elements of the model are fully understood if the results are to have any value.

Monte Carlo Simulation

For some analysts, Monte Carlo simulation is the epitome of the modelling process. We use third-party software to perform this analysis, the two leading products being @RISK from Palisade,[1] and Crystal Ball from Oracle.[2] The analysis requires the modeller to define each input in terms of a statistical population and there are many populations to choose from. When the simulation is run, the software generates a random number from within the population, enters it into the input cell, recalculates the model and stores the results. It then repeats the process up to several thousands of times, for each input specified. In this way the model can simulate the millions of permutations that can result from the interaction of the selected inputs. In my opinion this is fine for scientific and engineering purposes, but of little use for financial modelling. In simple terms, the financial variables we use in our modelling do not fit into the population distributions used by the software. Although they may have a stochastic appearance, with randomness of sorts, the only meaningful constraints that can be applied relate to the triangular distribution of lowest value–most likely value–highest value. Unfortunately, the very ease with which the software allows the modeller to set up the Monte Carlo simulation leads us into problems.

Most people have had little exposure to statistics other than at college or at university, and most such courses are based around the statistics of the normal distribution (Figure 8.14).

From this we learn expressions such as:

1. *Arithmetic mean*: The sum of all the observations in a sample, divided by the number of observations in the sample.
2. *Mode*: The most frequent, or common, value in a sample.
3. *Median*: The middle value of a sample.
4. The blanket expression 'average' is often used with reference to these three definitions.

FIGURE 8.14 Statistics 101: the normal distribution.

1. http://www.palisade-europe.com/.
2. http://www.oracle.com/us/products/applications/crystalball/overview/index.html.

5. *Standard deviation* is used to describe the spread of the numbers in the sample about the mean (or more correctly, the square root of the arithmetic mean of the squares of the deviations from the arithmetic mean). One standard deviation of each side of the mean will include 68% of the sample, two standard deviations cover 95% and three standard deviations cover 98% of the sample.

The moment we consider a different population distribution we realise that these terms no longer have the same meaning and must be used with much more care.

But when looking at models using the Monte Carlo technique we often find a casual disregard for what is very specific terminology and indeed we often find that the analyst has chosen the wrong population distribution, failed to identify the correlating factors or has assigned a distribution to what should be a deterministic element. Quite often we note that Monte Carlo analysis has been performed simply because the software was available, and the analyst thought that it would add value to the model. There are indeed certain kinds of model in which specialist risk techniques are required, and risk modelling is a specialism in itself, but our general recommendation is for the general modeller to be aware of the techniques but to use them with caution (Figure 8.15).

The UK HM Treasury *Appraisal and Evaluation in Central Government* (the *Green Book*) discusses the use of Monte Carlo simulation in project modelling and concludes that the triangular distribution is the preferred method, in which the spread runs from the lowest likely value to the highest likely value, with the apex as the most likely. In the United Kingdom, the public sector put a lot of reliance on risk modelling techniques with an apparent view that this provides some form of scientific confirmation or validation of the model's predictions.

A final observation concerning risk modelling is that it must always be a management tool; but the rôle of management in anticipating and, more importantly, in mitigating risks as they arise is not included in the risk metrics. The information that there is a 20% probability of a cost overrun by *x* amount fails to recognise that management will probably take early action once the first signs of this risk materialise, which takes us back to the model interrogation ideas from the start of this chapter.

FIGURE 8.15 The triangular distribution: lowest likely value, most likely, highest likely and a bit of 'noise'. If you must define a distribution, this is probably the easiest to justify.

45												
46	Data table	sum of p =1										
47	probability	TRUE	0.001	0.01	0.01	0.03	0.06	0.18	0.25	0.18	0.15	0.08	0.05
48	oil price		42	44	46	48	50	52	54	56	58	60	62
49	NPV @ 15%	(19.2)	(70.4)	(56.7)	(43.7)	(31.2)	(19.2)	(7.7)	3.8	15.3	26.8	38.3	49.8
50												

FIGURE 8.16   Triangular distribution applied to a data table.

54												
55	Data table	sum of p =1										
56	probability	TRUE	0.001	0.01	0.01	0.03	0.06	0.18	0.25	0.18	0.15	0.08	0.05
57	oil price		42	44	46	48	50	52	54	56	58	60	62
58	IRR	12%	-18%	-7%	0%	6%	12%	17%	22%	26%	31%	35%	40%
59												
60	Expected rate of return	23%	0%	0%	0%	0%	1%	3%	5%	5%	5%	3%	2%
61												

FIGURE 8.17   The expected rate of return.

Risk Analysis Using Data Tables

Following the observation about the triangular distribution above, we could use a one-way data table as a risk modelling tool. If it is set up so that the first value is the lowest likely value, and the last value the highest likely, the values in the data table represent the distribution. Easy read, and easy to explain (Figure 8.16).

If probability values have been assigned to each input in the data table, it is even possible to perform a very simple risk assessment: in this example the probability values have been written above the data table values (with an audit test that they sum to 1). We can add up the probabilities of the positive NPVs to identify that the probability of breaking even is 0.71.

If we repeat this exercise using the internal rate of return (IRR) we can take a further step by multiplying the table results against the probability values and adding these together, to give the expected rate of return (Figure 8.17).

Chapter 9

Automation

INTRODUCTION

Spreadsheets of any size or complexity may involve repetitive tasks, or tasks that need to be completed in a particular sequence. Sometimes developers or users find themselves looking for Excel functionality that simply doesn't appear to exist. Macros are predefined sequences of commands and events that the user can run as required, to automate and control spreadsheet use. They can either be recorded, which requires the user or developer to carry out the appropriate command sequence first, or they can be written using the Visual Basic Editor in Excel, which allows access to a wide range of additional techniques. Visual Basic for Applications (VBA) is the macro programming language used in Microsoft products.

In the early days of spreadsheets, the first macro commands were easily learnt and applied by the reasonably expert spreadsheet modeller. Lotus 1-2-3 release 3, for example, had some 80 commands. It was a straightforward task to both write and debug the code. With the introduction of Windows the situation grew rather more complex. Both Lotus and Microsoft introduced macro languages (Lotus Script and an early form of Visual Basic, respectively) which were considerably more advanced, and allowed for the creation and use of dialog boxes, as well as offering the ability to interrogate other applications for information. Although these languages and their successors could be learnt by the expert user, their inherent complexity meant that the writing of macro code became a task better suited to the programmer, rather than the modeller. It may also be worth noting that model auditors will not routinely inspect macro code.

However, some modellers believe that a model is not finished unless it has a library of macros. Certainly there are times when the use of macros is unavoidable, but using the principle of error reduction, their use should be limited. Programmers are trained to write code, and have systems and methodologies concerning specification, development, testing, documentation, implementation and quality control (not entirely dissimilar to the model development methodology we have explored in this book). Financial analysts and modellers tend not to have this discipline, and the archives of finance departments are full of half-finished macro modules which were begun with the best of intentions but the developers lacked the time or expertise to see the job through to completion.

The worst type of macro-driven model is what we call the 'black box'. On opening the file, the user is confronted with an attractive 'user input screen', from which selections can be made or data entered. On clicking the OK button, the screen freezes and after a few moments the nearest printer starts spewing out paper. In the meantime, the user suspects that the macro may have ground to a halt and starts hitting the Escape key. Up pops a dialog warning that 'Code execution has been interrupted'. Should you continue, end or debug? If you end, what has happened in the model so far – and what is the effect of Undo at this point?

VBA is a programming language and there are many books and courses on the subject. The purpose of including it here is to identify and demonstrate a small number of VBA techniques that are relevant to the type of financial modelling we have been using in this book.

We will need to use the Developer tab tools, so run File, Options, Customize Ribbon command and select the Developer check box. You may also notice that you can access macros, and record them, from the Macros button on the View ribbon.

Macro Security Settings

Microsoft has taken a very robust approach to the problem of malicious macro code and there are now several layers of security. To work through the examples given in this chapter, we will need to disable all security settings in the Trust Center. To disable these settings, run Developer, Macro Security and select Enable all macros. Note the warning that potentially dangerous code could be run, and remember to restore the security settings when done (Figure 9.1).

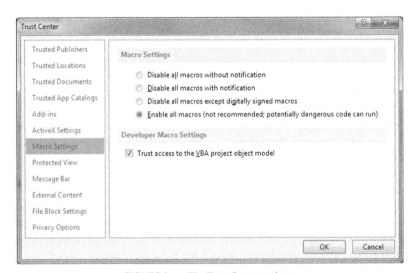

FIGURE 9.1 The Trust Center settings.

Personal.xlsb

As we will see in a moment, when we create macros they need to be stored somewhere, and one option is to keep them in your Personal Macro Workbook. This is actually a workbook called `personal.xlsb`. This file normally lives in your XLSTART folder and is loaded automatically, as a hidden workbook, when you start Excel. The location of this folder depends on your Excel version and any network or installation settings so if you can't find it try looking in:

```
C:\Program Files \Microsoft Office\Office15\XLSTART; or
C:\Program Files (x86)\Microsoft Office\Office15\XLSTART; or
C:\Users\[username]\AppData\Roaming\Microsoft\Excel\XLSTART
```

These paths can be typed into the *Search programs and files* box on the Windows Start menu.[1]

`Personal.xlsb` may not actually exist until you have saved a macro in it, but once created the macros stored there can be used in any of your spreadsheets. Note that if you attempt to edit any of these macros (see below), Excel will warn you that you cannot edit a macro in a hidden workbook. To view and edit the macro code we can unhide the workbook using View, Unhide.

If you are still unable to find your `personal.xlsb`, the simplest technique is simply to start the Macro recorder and in the dialog box choose the Store macro in option of Personal Macro Workbook. Choose OK, click on a cell in the spreadsheet and stop recording (see the next section for more information about the macro recorder). At this stage you should be able to go to the View tab and see that the Unhide button is now available; if you click on it you should finally see your Personal workbook.

RECORDED MACROS

The simplest way to get started with macros is to record a straightforward command sequence and then to inspect the resulting code in the Visual Basic Editor. The starting point, as always, is to decide what exactly the macro is supposed to do and then to write down the steps you will need to carry out. Remember the top-down methodology introduced in Chapter 3?

Recorded Macro Options

There are three ways to record a macro:

> View, Macros, Record New Macro;
> Developer, Record Macro;
> Record Macro button on the Excel status bar.

---

1. If you are familiar with the Immediate window in the VBA Editor (see below) you can type: `?application.StartupPath`.

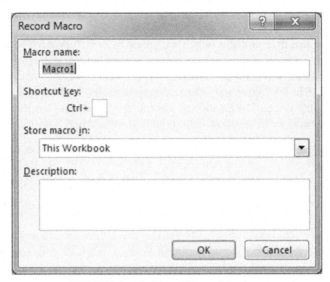

FIGURE 9.2   The Record Macro dialog box.

The dialog box contains the following options (Figure 9.2):

1. Name: use the range name convention of compound words – Excel will not accept spaces in macro names. Please develop the discipline of providing meaningful names, even if you are just experimenting.
2. Shortcut key: Ctrl+ – enter a keyboard shortcut used to run the macro. Hold down the Shift key for further permutations. Note that this shortcut will override any existing Excel shortcut in this workbook.
3. Store macro in: this offers three choices:
   a. This workbook (default): the macro can only be run whilst this workbook is open; it could be used in another workbook if both are open at the same time.
   b. Personal macro workbook: the macro will be stored in a workbook called personal.xlsb, as discussed above.
   c. New workbook: means exactly that.
4. Description: as with the macro name, develop the discipline of noting the purpose and function of the macro. You can use up to 255 characters. This information is stored in the macro header which you will see when we open the Visual Basic Editor shortly.

Iteration Macro

Let us revisit the Iteration command sequence used in Chapter 5. We used iteration to calculate a routine that involved a circularity, and we noted that it is not advisable to leave iteration switched on all the time as it masks any accidental circularity. We set up a mechanism such that if the iteration was on, we set

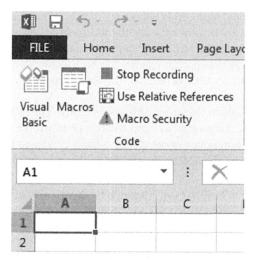

FIGURE 9.3   The Stop Recording button in the Code group on the Developer tab.

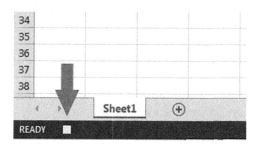

FIGURE 9.4   The anonymous Stop Recording button on the Status bar.

the Switch to TRUE and this activated the circular formula. When iteration was switched off, we set the Switch to FALSE and this suspended the circularity.

Let's identify the steps involved in switching the iteration on, and then switching it off:

1. Activate the sheet that contains the Switch cell.
2. Go to the Switch cell.
3. File, Options, Formulas, Enable iterative calculation, then click OK.
4. Enter TRUE into the Switch cell.

Next,

5. Activate the sheet that contains the Switch cell.
6. Go to the Switch cell.
7. Enter FALSE into the Switch cell.
8. Run File, Options, Formulas, click off the Enable iterative calculation check box, then click OK.

In both cases, the first step is to activate the sheet that contains the Switch cell. This is because the user may run the macro from any sheet in the workbook. If we have not identified the relevant sheet, the macro may run on another sheet, with unexpected results. We also select the Switch cell for a similar reason – we do not want the TRUE or FALSE dropping into the active cell if it is on another sheet.

I have also changed the order of events slightly. The ON macro switches on iteration before it changes the Switch cell contents. If the TRUE was entered first, Excel would complain about the circularity and generate an error message. Likewise, the OFF macro inserts the FALSE into the Switch cell before switching off the iteration. (In reality, the errors would not appear during macro execution, but it shows that we are thinking the matter through.)

Now we are in a position to carry out the command sequence and record it. In some cases it is worthwhile running through the sequence once or twice to rehearse it – bear in mind that any digressions or errors will also be recorded. This will lead to messy code, and it could slow down the execution of the finished macro.

1. Use any of the three methods to start recording the macro (View, Macros, Record Macro; Developer, Record Macro; or click the Record Macro button).
2. Give the macro a name such as IterationOn.
3. Assign a shortcut if you wish.
4. Store the macro in this workbook.
5. Write a description for the macro ('Recorded macro, for switching on the iteration to calculate a circular routine').
6. Click OK.
7. Press F5 (Go To) and type in the destination switch (assuming you have set up the appropriate name previously). Click OK.
8. Run File, Options, Formulas and switch on Enable iterative calculation. Click OK.
9. Type TRUE into the Switch cell and press Enter.
10. Stop the macro recorder using View, Macros, Stop Recording or Developer, Stop Recording or click the Stop Recording status bar button (Figures 9.3 and 9.4).

Repeat the process to record the macro to turn off the iteration.

1. Repeat step 1 above to start recording.
2. Give the macro a name such as IterationOff.
3. Assign a shortcut if you wish.
4. Store the macro in this workbook.
5. Write a description for the macro ('Recorded macro, for switching off the iteration to suspend a circular routine').
6. Click OK.
7. Press F5 (Go To) and type in the destination Switch (assuming you have set up the appropriate name previously). Click OK.

8. Type FALSE into the Switch cell, and press Enter.
9. Run File, Options, Formulas, switch off Enable iterative calculation, then click OK.
10. Stop the macro recorder with View, Macros, Stop Recording or Developer, Stop Recording or click the Stop Recording status bar button.

You can test the macros by using View, Macros, View Macros or Developer, Macros (or Alt+F8), and selecting them from the list, or by using your keyboard shortcut, if you assigned one. See below for running macros from buttons and the ribbon.

Note that while a macro is recording there is no visible indication on screen, other than the anonymous button on the status bar. This will disappear when you stop recording. A user once complained to me that his computer was running abnormally slowly – I discovered that he had used the macro recorder earlier that morning but hadn't switched it off – Excel had recorded some 4 h of work!

ASSIGNING MACROS

Macros can be run by using keyboard shortcuts, worksheet buttons or from the ribbon. Before deciding which technique to use, you should consider where the macro has been stored. If the macro is in your personal macro workbook it will be available in all workbooks and can be assigned to shortcuts and buttons. If the macro is stored in a specific workbook, it will be available if that workbook is open. A macro can be used in a new or different workbook if both the macro workbook and the target are open at the same time.

Keyboard Shortcuts

On recording a macro, you are invited to assign the macro to a shortcut before proceeding. The shortcut automatically includes Ctrl, and is followed by a letter. Further combinations are allowed, holding down Shift+letter (it is not necessary to press Ctrl). The use of Alt+ is not permitted.

If you recorded the macro without choosing a shortcut, or wish to assign new shortcut to an existing macro, use the View, Macros, View Macros or Developer, Macros command (or Alt+F8) and choose Options. This allows you to specify the shortcut required.

Note that the shortcut assigned to the macro takes precedence over the default Excel shortcuts; even if you are not a shortcut user your colleagues may be, and it can be frustrating (and dangerous) to find that a favourite shortcut such as Ctrl+P (print) or Ctrl+S (save) has apparently been hijacked for some other purpose. This especially applies to shortcuts for macros in your personal macro workbook, which are available for any and all subsequent workbooks.

It is good modelling practice to include a list of keyboard shortcuts in the documentation of your model. With a recorded macro the shortcut is included as a comment, but otherwise this should be added manually. To find out if a keyboard shortcut has been assigned to a macro, use the Alt+F8 shortcut to bring up the macros dialog box, select the macro from the list and choose Options.

Workbook Buttons

Workbook buttons are graphic objects stored in the workbook. The Developer ribbon has an Insert button which gives a dropdown list of Form and ActiveX controls. From the Form Controls identify the Button button (Figure 9.5).

The mouse pointer changes from the arrow to a crosshair: you can either simply click in the worksheet for a default button, or click and drag to draw a button of your own sizing. Hold down Alt while dragging to 'snap to' cell gridlines. On doing so, the Assign Macro dialog box appears, from which you can select the macro to assign to the button.

Note that the button is selected and has edit handles; whilst this is the case you can edit the button text and by right-clicking carry out other commands from the shortcut menu. If you lose the selection, perhaps by clicking back in the worksheet, do not left-click the new button – this will only run the macro. To work with the macro button, right-click it first.

Edit the button text as required, and use the edit handles to resize or reposition the button. It can be helpful to name the button. Use Ctrl+F3 (Define Name) or alternatively click in the Name Box and enter a name there.

If you have several buttons, it can be easier to manipulate them if they are grouped together. It is an awkward process in which you need to right-Shift+click on each button in turn. Edit handles should appear around all

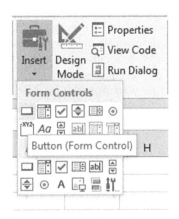

FIGURE 9.5   The Button button on the Controls group on the Developer tab.

selected buttons (note that Ctrl+clicking does not work in this context). Right-click on any button and choose Grouping, Group. The grouped buttons can now be edited and formatted together. Buttons can be ungrouped by right-clicking and using Grouping, Ungroup. Having been grouped previously, individual buttons can be regrouped using Grouping, Regroup.

Adding Macros to the Ribbon

We are now able to add macros to the Excel ribbon; as individual buttons stored in custom groups. These can be added to existing ribbons or by creating a new tab with your own custom ribbon. The procedure is reasonably straightforward:

1. Use File, Options and Customize Ribbon (or right-click on the ribbon) (Figure 9.6).
2. The dialog box contains the options to create New Tabs and New Groups. Regardless of how many macros you have, you must create at least one custom group. The new group option can be used to add macro buttons to any existing ribbon, by selecting the tab name first, then right-clicking the tab or group and choosing Add New Group. To set up a new tab in between, for example, Home and Insert, right-click the Home tab in the list and click Add New Tab in the shortcut menu.
3. Use the Rename... command to give a name to the new tab or group.
4. Making sure you have selected the new tab or group, select Macros from the Choose commands from dropdown list. Highlight the macro and click Add. This adds the macro to the target group.
5. Choose OK to return to the workbook and inspect the additions to the ribbon. Remember that macros stored in personal.xlsb can be used at any time, but if the macro is in a specific workbook Excel will attempt to open it if the button is clicked.
6. Macros assigned to the ribbon can be accessed using the keyboard, and Excel automatically assigns them the shortcuts Y1, Y2 and so on. For example, if we put the Iteration macro on the Formulas tab we would use Alt+M, Y1. The Yx is used on each tab, so another macro on the View tab would be Alt+W, Y1.
7. This process is much too simple and can easily get out of hand. The dialog box also contains the options to remove macro buttons, groups and tabs; and in the worst case scenario the specific ribbon tab can be reset to the defaults, or all customisation removed.

Bear in mind that custom tabs, groups and buttons will reappear when you next open Excel; unless the associated macros are stored in your personal macro workbook you are likely to experience errors if the menus or buttons are used in the wrong context.

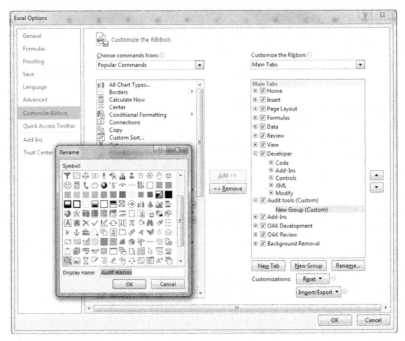

FIGURE 9.6   Setting up a new tab (Audit tools) and a new group (Audit macros).

WRITTEN MACROS

A basic understanding of macro code allows more complex macros to be written, and allows access to the many macro commands and routines that are simply not available through recording. However, writing Visual Basic code can be daunting and difficult; in this section we will consider some of the basic concepts which might then lead into more complex code.

Once you have recorded a few macros, you may find that the Visual Basic Editor serves as a useful introduction to writing code. Use the Developer, Visual Basic command or Alt+F11 to open the Visual Basic Editor application (Figure 9.7). This allows us to inspect the underlying code of the macro. If you chose to store the macro in your personal macro workbook, you will need to unhide this file first, View, Unhide command.

We can now examine the Iteration macro as recorded. The code should be:

```
Sub IterationOn()
    Application.Iteration = True
    Application.Goto "Switch"
    ActiveCell.Formula = "TRUE"
    Range("C3").Select
End Sub
```

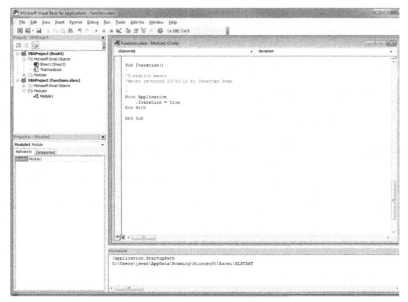

FIGURE 9.7 The Visual Basic Editor.

The final line of code is the action taken on pressing Enter after writing TRUE into the Switch cell. It can be safely deleted, as it is redundant.

You can learn a fair amount of VB using recorded macros and some trial and error. If you have cut out too much from the code, Excel will throw up error messages and return you from the workbook to the VB Editor. The error dialog box may not be particularly informative, but usually the Editor will highlight the offending code. If you can supply the correction, you can then press F5 to continue with the execution of the code. Alternatively, you may be able to cancel the macro using Ctrl+Break. If the macro does not appear to work in the manner you think it should, you can enter Step mode using F8. Each time you press the key, one line of the macro is carried out.

It is good practice to document your work. Comments can be inserted anywhere in and around the macro, as long as you use the single apostrophe ' prefix.

Branching Macros

The iteration exercise serves as a useful introduction to written macros – we might want to combine the functionality of the two separate macros into just one – if iteration is off, switch it on, and if it is on, switch it off.

We considered the use of the IF function in Chapter 6: we specify the test condition, the outcome to show if the condition evaluates to TRUE, and the outcome when the condition is FALSE. We can write the same functionality into the macro, using an IF... THEN... ELSE sequence.

As with the recorded macro, it is good practice to write down what you want the macro to achieve and the steps required. In this case:

1. If the iteration is OFF, then
    a. Switch iteration on;
    b. Set the Switch to TRUE, else
2. If the iteration is ON, then
    a. Set the Switch to False;
    b. Switch the iteration off.

As we will run this macro from a worksheet button, we will have the button itself confirm the iteration status, so in each case above we will have a third step in which the text on the button changes.

Writing the Macro

Open the Visual Basic Editor using Developer, Visual Basic (or Alt+F11). Use the Project Explorer window to check where the current module will be stored (current workbook or personal workbook). We will assume that the Switch cell has already been named (if not, do so now).

In the code window, write the following:

Command	Explanation
	Comments can be entered into the macro if they are prefixed with ' (single apostrophe)
Sub IterationSwitch()	'Name of macro
IterationStatus=Application. Iteration	'Returns and stores the current iteration setting
Application.Goto "Switch"	'Select the Switch cell
If IterationStatus = TRUE Then	'Test condition
ActiveCell.Formula = "FALSE"	'Enters FALSE in the Switch cell
Application.Iteration = False	'Switches off the iteration
Else	'If IterationStatus = False
Application.Iteration = True	'Switches on the iteration
ActiveCell.Formula ="TRUE"	'Enters TRUE in the Switch cell
End If	
End Sub	

Use the Developer, Macros (or Alt+F8) and Options to assign a keyboard shortcut (try Ctrl+Shift+I). Neither Excel nor VB will document this new short-cut, so add comment to your code.

Now test the macro and its operation in the workbook. If you have errors, use the F8 Step and F5 Resume commands as required.

Notice the definition of IterationStatus, in which VB returns the current iteration setting. Also note that regardless of a true or false outcome, the content of the Switch cell will change, so the Go To action is put at the start of the macro. Finally note the all-important End If command.

We can refine this macro further. If you run this macro using the keyboard shortcut and you are on a different sheet, the current code leaves you looking at the Switch cell. It would be helpful if the macro would return us to our starting position; and, while we are running the macro, we want to freeze the screen to prevent it flickering during movements. We can identify the current cell location at the start of the macro, and return to it at the end; and this also applies to the screen updating. Add these new commands to your code:

Command	Explanation
Sub IterationSwitch()	
Application.ScreenUpdating = False	'Freezes the screen display
IterationStatus=Application. Iteration	
CurrentSheet = ActiveSheet.Name	Returns and stores the current sheet
CurrentCell = ActiveCell.Address	Returns and stores the current cell address
Application.Goto "Switch"	
If IterationStatus = TRUE Then	
ActiveCell.Formula = "FALSE"	
Application.Iteration = False	
Else	
Application.Iteration = True	
ActiveCell.Formula ="TRUE"	
End If	
Sheets(CurrentSheet).Select	Activates the original sheet
Range(CurrentCell).Select	Selects the original active cell
Application.ScreenUpdating = True	Returns the screen display to normal
End Sub	

QUARTERLY/ANNUAL MACRO

In Chapter 5, we looked at techniques to set up our outputs in such a way so that we could either report on an annual or a quarterly basis. With either the rolling sum or the corkscrew technique we have to hide the Q1, Q2 and Q3 columns, which can prove rather time-consuming. We can automate this process with a simple written macro. The assumption is that the first Q1 is in column E.

Command	Explanation
| ```
Sub QuartersToAnnual()
'Quarterly to Annual Macro
'Macro written 16/01/2015 by
jswan
'Converts a quarterly report to an annual report
'by hiding each Q1-Q3 column,
'then unhides row headings
Application.ScreenUpdating =
False
For Each Col In
Worksheets("Sheet1").Columns
  If Col.Column Mod 4 <> 0 Then

  Col.Select
  Selection.EntireColumn.Hidden =
  True
End If
Next Col
  Range("A1:D1").Select
  Selection.EntireColumn.Hidden =
  False
  Range("A1").Select
End Sub
``` | 'Usual documentation<br><br><br>'Stops the screen flickering<br>while the macro runs<br>' Substitute sheet names as<br>required<br>'If the column number is not<br>exactly divisible by 4<br>'Select the column<br>'Hide the column<br><br><br>'Repeat for next column<br>'Select first four columns<br>'Unhide the columns<br><br>'Move active cell to A1 |

We can reverse the effects of this macro with some very simple code.

Command	Explanation
| ```
Sub AnnualToQuarters()
'Annual to Quarterly Macro
'Macro written 16/01/2015 by
jswan
'Restores the hidden columns
Cells.Select

Selection.EntireColumn.Hidden =
False
Range("A1").Select
End Sub
``` | 'Usual documentation<br><br><br>'Selects the worksheet<br>(equivalent of Ctrl+A)<br>'Unhides the columns<br><br>'Goes to A1 (Ctrl+Home) |

ERROR HANDLING

VBA is now a very robust tool and will trap errors as they are written, or on execution. As mentioned above, the Step mode and other debug features of the VBA editor are useful, provided you can understand what Excel is telling you! In some cases it can be helpful to build your own error-handling routine if you want to test your code for yourself. The Quarterly to Annual macro above is usually quite slow, and with the screen updating off it may appear that nothing is happening. What would happen if your user pressed Escape at this point? (Figure 9.8).

FIGURE 9.8   Error message box.

This example also introduces a call to a simple subroutine and uses a message box.

```
On Error GoTo Error_Report          'Code at top of macro,
                                    which will run the error
                                    subroutine
Application.EnableCancelKey =       'This recognizes the Escape
xlErrorHandler                      key
YOUR CODE                           'This is your macro
Exit Sub                            'This ends the macro if no
                                    errors occur
Error_Report:                       'Start of subroutine; note
                                    the colon :
MsgBox "Error: " & Err.Number & "   'Displays a message box
" &                                 with the concatenated error
Err.Description                     number and description
End Sub                             'The macro terminates
```

It is worth knowing that the Excel Undo (Ctrl+Z) has no effect when running macros. This means that should be a macro break, for whatever reason, all the actions taken up to that point remain in place. If we consider the Quarterly to Annual macro it makes substantial changes to the worksheet layout, but we also have a macro that will put it back together again. In this case we can amend our error-handling code then to call Annual to Quarterly macro if things go wrong. This simply needs the addition of the code:

```
Error_Report:
MsgBox "Error: " & Err.Number & "
" &
Err.Description
Call QuarterlyToAnnual              'This calls the other macro
End Sub
```

DEBT SCULPTING

As mentioned in the introduction to this chapter, most modellers try to avoid the use of macros unless they are really necessary, and this is reflected in my own teaching and practice. However, there is one particular topic that comes up time and again: debt sculpting. If we consider a simple bank loan, we might drawdown (borrow) the funds at time *a* and make a series of repayments over a fixed period of time, in which the repayments are constant. Interest is paid on the balance and will therefore decrease over time. This is often described as a term loan, and the repayment method is described as an annuity. The banks use techniques such as the various debt cover ratios to monitor the financial health of the borrower. If, in a particular period, we were required to pay back 10 and our cash for the period is 10, the ratio is 1; we could service the debt but would have no surplus funds for anything else. For commercial loans banks would be looking for a ratio of 1.2 or better, so 10 of repayment and 12 of cash (we will ignore interest for the moment). If we have 15 of cash then we are in a comfortable position.

The difficulty is that cash is difficult to predict (that's why we have financial modelling!) and we use the expression the 'lumpy cash flow' to describe the reality of a firm's cash position over a period of time. At times we could be comfortably off, at others we could be at risk of breaching the ratios.

Workbook Formulas

Consider the example below. It is a simple debt corkscrew that we have seen before. It forms the basis of the following exercise and we will make a few exceptions to normal practice. We will borrow 100 and repay it within 15 periods (Figure 9.9).

1. The brought forward (bf) is the corkscrew cell reference formula linking to the previous carry forward (cf). Copy it across the row, and set up the range names as shown.
2. The drawdown of 100 is hard-coded in column D. Fill the rest of the row with 0 values.
3. Leave the repayment line blank for the moment.
4. The cf is the bf plus the drawdown, less the repayment. Copy across the row.
5. Now add a line for the cash flow available for debt service (often known as CFADS), using the numbers shown.

	A	B	C	D	E	F	G	H	T	U
1	Debt sculpting			1	2	3	4	5		
2										
3	CFADS			-10	5	6	7	8	CFADS	
4										
9	Senior debt									
10	bf			0	100.00	100.00	100.00	100.00	SeniorBf	
11	drawdown			100	0.00	0.00	0.00	0.00	SeniorDrawdown	
12	repayment								SeniorRepayment	
13	cf		0	100	100.00	100.00	100.00	100.00	SeniorCf	
14										

FIGURE 9.9   The debt corkscrew. This is 16 columns wide, with the range names in column T.

6. Enter a value for the target minimum debt service cover ratio – use 1.5 for the moment.
7. The debt service cover ratio (DSCR) is simply the CFADS divided by the debt service (the repayment). Write it with an error trap:

```
=IF(SeniorRepayment=0,"NA",CFADS/SeniorRepayment)
```

8. This formula should be written in column E and copied across (although breaching our rule of left-to-right consistency, this keeps matters simple).
9. In column C write a MIN formula to return the lowest calculated DSCR. You may wish to add an audit check that this value is greater than or equal to the minimum permitted DSCR.
10. Now we can write a simple repayment formula of the drawdown (absolute reference) divided by 15 (hard-coded). Again this should go into column E and then copy across the row. Inspect the DSCRs (Figure 9.10).

Note that this repayment method ignores the CFADS and indeed in the first two periods the repayments exceed the cash available. The 1.5 DSCR minimum isn't satisfied until the sixth repayment period. Further on, however, the ratios are very healthy, but this surplus cash is of no use.

The concept of debt sculpting is to reverse the DSCR problem. Instead of calculating the debt repayment independently of cash availability, we instead calculate the repayment *based on* cash availability. In simple terms, if we had a repayment due of 10 and we have 9 of cash, we're in trouble. Instead we divide the cash by the minimum permitted ratio to return the payment that would satisfy the bank. With 9 of cash, a repayment of 6 would satisfy a 1.5 ratio requirement. Conversely, if we had more cash, we could increase the repayment, so with 20 of cash we could repay 13.333, instead of the 10 (and perhaps allowing us to pay off the loan sooner). This is where the term 'sculpting' comes in – we are shaping the repayments to match the cash.

E12	▾	:	✕	✓	*fx*	=$D$11/15					
	A	B		C	D	E	F	G	H	T	U
1	Debt sculpting				1	2	3	4	5		
2											
3	CFADS				-10	5	6	7	8	CFADS	
4											
9	Senior debt										
10	bf				0	100.00	93.33	86.67	80.00	SeniorBf	
11	drawdown				100	0.00	0.00	0.00	0.00	SeniorDrawdown	
12	repayment					6.67	6.67	6.67	6.67	SeniorRepayment	
13	cf			0	100	93.33	86.67	80.00	73.33	SeniorCf	
14											
15	DSCR										
16	target			1.50	DSCRTarget						
17	actual					0.75	0.90	1.05	1.20	DSCRActual	
18	minimum			0.75	DSCRMinimum						
19											

FIGURE 9.10   DSCR calculations.

We can replace the existing repayment calculations in the corkscrew with the sculpted routine:

1. Delete the existing repayment formula.
2. Replace it with CFADS divided by the DSCR target minimum value.

Note that the DSCRs are all at 1.5. Notice, as well, that the sculpted repayment formula continues to service the debt even though it has been paid off (the cf ends up negative). We could fix this with a mask, but there are more serious things to consider.

In this example we have ignored interest. In a complex model there may be features such as debt service reserve accounts and maintenance reserve accounts, and other financing instruments. We have a line of hard-coded values representing CFADS; in reality this would be a formula that almost invariably is linked to these other elements and we would now be looking at a deeply unpleasant circularity. The magnitude and complexity of this circularity is such that it would be unwise to use the iteration techniques considered in Chapter 5 or even with the Iteration macro in this chapter; remember that iteration solves both the circularities you know about – and those you don't!

Let's see if we can resolve the current problems with sculpted debt repayment. If you are doing this exercise in a real model you should delete the debt repayment calculations in the corkscrew to avoid any circularities. The first issue is that the repayment doesn't take into account the remaining balance, leading to the overpayments in the final two periods. Add the following section to the debt corkscrew example (Figure 9.11):

1. In anticipation of rounding errors which may occur we will use the usual rounding value, so enter 0.001 into a cell in column C and name it `Tolerance` (as seen in the audit sheet exercises).
2. The adjusted CFADS line is the original sculpted repayment: `CFADS/ DSCRTarget`.
3. The sculpted payment is the smaller of the adjusted CFADS and the senior bf, as `=MIN(+SculptedCFADS,+SeniorBf)`. We don't need to calculate a repayment if the loan has been repaid, so multiply this formula by `(SeniorBf>Tolerance)` (i.e. `TRUE` or `FALSE`).
4. If we link the payment target values into the corkscrew we again run the risk of circularities. Instead we will copy and paste values. If you haven't already done so, delete the existing repayments, which will return the sculpted payment values to the original adjusted CFADS values. It may be helpful to colour the sculpted payment and senior repayment rows.
5. Select the sculpted payment values and copy (Ctrl+C).

E9		▾	:	×	✓	*fx*	=MIN(+SculptedCFADS,+SeniorBf)*(SeniorBf>Tolerance)		

⊿	A	B	C	D	E	F	G	H	T	U
1	Debt sculpting			1	2	3	4	5		
2										
3	Tolerance		0.001	*Tolerance*						
4										
5	CFADS			-10	5	6	7	8	*CFADS*	
6										
7	Sculpted debt									
8	adjusted CFADS				3.33	4.00	4.67	5.33	*SculptedCFADS*	
9	sculpted payment				3.33	4.00	4.67	5.33	*SculptedPayment*	
10										
11	Senior debt									
12	bf			0	100.00	96.67	92.67	88.00	*SeniorBf*	
13	drawdown			100	0.00	0.00	0.00	0.00	*SeniorDrawdown*	
14	repayment				3.33	4.00	4.67	5.33	*SeniorRepayment*	
15	cf		0	100	96.67	92.67	88.00	82.67	*SeniorCf*	
16										

FIGURE 9.11   Adding the sculpted debt routine above the debt corkscrew.

6. Go to the first repayment cell and paste values (Alt+H, V, V). This will result in the overpayment seen before, with the negative cf balances. Note the ratios are satisfactory but that there are negative values in the last two cf cells.

7. Now repeat the copy, paste values. This time the debt should be completely and exactly paid off, with the DSCRs all on target, apart from the final one where we have surplus cash.

You may wish to delete the repayment line and repeat the exercise, watching the effects on the adjusted CFADS and observing the results as the debt is paid off. Try changing the target minimum DSCR to 1.2.

The final issue, which will lead us into the macro, is that we continue the iterations until the debt is paid off and the ratio requirements are satisfied. With a 16-column forecast period we can do this by inspection. With a 25-year forecast period, calculated quarterly, this would be very time-consuming. We will now add lines to identify the point at which we have achieved our result (Figure 9.12).

1. Add a further line to the DSCR section. This will test to see if the loan has been repaid, which is when the cf reaches 0. The test will return TRUE or FALSE, which we will coerce into 1 or 0 (for the MAX in the next step). Use
=AND(+SeniorCf>(0-Tolerance),+SeniorCf<Tolerance)+0
Copy across the row and name it RepaymentComplete.

2. Now add a test to see if the debt has been repaid and that the minimum calculated DSCR is greater than or equal to the target minimum. Use
=AND(MAX(RepaymentComplete)=1,DSCRMinimum>=DSCRTarget)
Name it SeniorRepaidFlag.

17	DSCR								
18	target		1.50	DSCRTarget					
19	actual				1.50	1.50	1.50	1.50	1.50	1.50
20	minimum		1.50	DSCRMinimum					
21	repaid = 1				=AND(+SeniorCf>(0-Tolerance),+SeniorCf<Tolerance)+0				
22	flag		TRUE	SeniorRepaidFlag					
23									

FIGURE 9.12 Completing the logic to control the sculpting mechanism.

Repeat the copy/paste value routine above to confirm that the logic and the flag work correctly.

We haven't included an interest calculation for this example, but should you have any interest it should be deducted from the CFADS to avoid a circularity.

The example we are using for this exercise is simple but allows us to understand the calculation and control mechanisms without the circularities normally associated with this type of repayment mechanism. As we have it now, the sculpting routine takes two iterations, but in a real model it can take many more. This is where we bring in the macro.

Debt Sculpting Macro

This macro is, in principle, reasonably straightforward. We have calculations in place to determine the sculpted debt, and by using copy/paste value we can avoid the inherent circularity associated with this method. Having done the exercise manually, the only issue is that we don't know how many times to repeat the operation, but we do have a control – the SeniorRepaidFlag – that will identify a successful conclusion. Be aware that in a real model this macro can take a while to run, so you may wish to include the error-handling code from above. You may also want to include the navigation code from the Iteration macro if you intend to run the macro from different locations in the spreadsheet.

```
Sub DebtSculpting()
'Debt Sculpting Macro
'Macro written 20/01/2015 by      'Usual documentation
jswan
Dim i as Integer                 'Optional - we can use this to
                                 count the number of iterations

Application.ScreenUpdating =
False
Application.Goto                 'Go to the existing senior
Reference:="SeniorRepayment"     repayments
Selection.ClearContents          'And delete them
Calculate                        'Force a recalculation if
                                 manual recalculation is used

Do Until                         'The start of the code that
Range("SeniorRepaidFlag").       will loop until the control is
Value = True                     True
```

```
i = i + 1                      'Optional: This will be used to
                               count the number of times we
                               repeat the loop

Application.Goto               'Go to the current sculpted
Reference:="SculptedPayment"   debt
Selection.Copy                 'Copy the content
Application.Goto               'Go to the repayment line in
Reference:="SeniorRepayment"   the corkscrew
Selection.PasteSpecial         'Paste the values
Paste:=xlPasteValues
Calculate                      'Force a recalculation
Loop                           'Return to the start of the
                               loop

Calculate                      'Force a final recalculation
Application.ScreenUpdating =
True
MsgBox("The number of          'Optional: shows a message box
iterations was: " & i)         with the number of iterations
End Sub
```

The Do...Loop approach is used here because we don't know how many times the macro will iterate. The optional counter *i* in this macro will record and display the number of iterative loops executed by the code. We could use the counter *i* to run the macro a fixed number of times. This would use a For...Next statement, in which we would replace the Do and Loop code with:

```
For i = 1 To 9                 'The start of the code that
                               will repeat a fixed number
                               of times, ten times in this
                               example
Application.Goto Reference:="SculptedPayment"
Selection.Copy
Application.Goto Reference:="SeniorRepayment"
Selection.PasteSpecial Paste:=xlPasteValues
Calculate
Next i                         'Return to the start and
                               increment i by 1
```

With both versions of the macro you could also use the MsgBox to pause the macro at the end of each iteration, in case you wanted to inspect the changes.

DEBUGGING

When writing code errors are inevitable but unlike the spreadsheet formula errors we have looked at in earlier chapters the VBA errors are more likely to force the macro to a halt and are more obvious. It is usually easy to realise something is broken, but it is much harder to work out why. The Tax Calculator user-defined function (UDF) example below worked beautifully until I used a gross salary of 35,000, when Excel returned a #NUM! error. I could see nothing wrong with the code, but eventually realised that I had described the Gross variable type as an `Integer`, which can have a value up to 32,767 – as you will see, it should be `Long`. There are several simple techniques we can use to debug code.

Step Mode

This mode allows us to run individual lines of macro in sequence. It may be helpful to rearrange the screen so that the worksheet window and the VB Editor window fit together. In the VB Editor, click on the macro to test. The Step commands are in the Debug menu, but the keyboard shortcut is so easy to use. Press F8 repeatedly to step through the code, noting any changes in the worksheet. The active line is coloured yellow in the VB Editor; this code is not executed until F8 is pressed.

If you are satisfied with a block of code and suspect that the problem lies just beyond it, you can click at the end of the block and press Ctrl+F8. This will run the code in the block up to the cursor, at which point you can use F8 again.

Use the Run, Reset to allow the macro to run (Alt+R, R, then F5 to run the code). Step mode is temporary and the coloured lines disappear (Figure 9.13).

Breakpoints

The breakpoint technique follows on from the Ctrl+F8 Run to cursor command. A breakpoint can be inserted in the macro code using the Debug menu or by

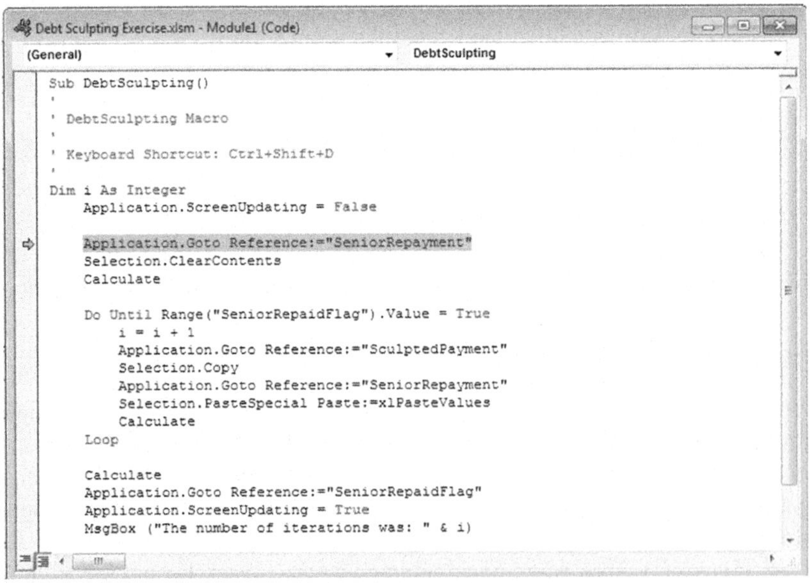

FIGURE 9.13   Step mode in the Debt Sculpting macro.

using F9. A brown dot appears in the margin and the code is highlighted in brown. F5 can be used to run the macro to the breakpoint, at which point the code is highlighted in yellow, as in Step mode. Use F5 to resume. Several breakpoints can be set, each of which allow code execution up to that point. Use Ctrl+Shift+F9 to remove all breakpoints when done.

Both Step mode and breakpoints are useful when inspecting code in someone else's work (Figure 9.14).

Locals Window

A further feature, to use in combination with the Step and Breakpoint tools, is the Locals window (View, Locals Window). In the Iteration macro we declared three variables: currentsheet and currentcell, to record the address of the active cell, and IterationStatus, for the current iteration setting. If the Locals window is open and we use F8 to step through the code, the window will show the values for each of these as the code is executed. The Values column Locals window allows you to manually edit these results if required.

The Immediate Window

The Immediate window is often considered to be an advanced VBA topic but it is a useful feature. Open the VBA Editor (Alt+F11) and run View, Immediate Window (or Ctrl+G). This window helps with macro design

```
Sub DebtSculpting()
'
' DebtSculpting Macro
'
' Keyboard Shortcut: Ctrl+Shift+D

Dim i As Integer
    Application.ScreenUpdating = False

    Application.Goto Reference:="SeniorRepayment"
    Selection.ClearContents
    Calculate

    Do Until Range("SeniorRepaidFlag").Value = True
        i = i + 1
        Application.Goto Reference:="SculptedPayment"
        Selection.Copy
        Application.Goto Reference:="SeniorRepayment"
        Selection.PasteSpecial Paste:=xlPasteValues
        Calculate
    Loop

    Calculate
    Application.Goto Reference:="SeniorRepaidFlag"
    Application.ScreenUpdating = True
    MsgBox ("The number of iterations was: " & i)
```

FIGURE 9.14   A breakpoint in the Debt Sculpting macro.

FIGURE 9.15 Testing VBA commands using the Immediate window.

and with debugging, and offers a different way of working with VBA code (Figure 9.15).

The value of any variable can be returned using the `debug.Print` command. For example, again using the Iteration macro we can type `debug. Print IterationStatus` to see the current setting (alternatively, simply `?IterationStatus` will work). Another example returns the number of range names in the active workbook:

`?ActiveWorkbook.Names.Count.`

Another use is to write code and test to see if it works, before adding to a macro. Typing `Application.Goto "Switch"` will select the `Switch` cell back in the worksheet. `Application.Iteration = TRUE` will switch on iteration without any need to go through File, Options, Formulas.

The location of the XLSTART folder is dependent on installation and network settings but can be easily found using `?Application.StartupPath`; and similarly the AddIns folder is at `?Application.UserLibraryPath`.

USER-DEFINED FUNCTIONS

With its various add-in packs and third-party add-ins Excel can offer several hundred functions, which is still not enough for some users and so Excel allows us to write our own. As with macros I am generally cautious about the use of UDFs as their management can be a problem, especially if the function does not reside in the workbook itself, although Microsoft have made the process less risky. I have seen too many models in which the UDF is resident on the analyst's PC back in the office. Do make sure that the UDF is stored in the workbook, and bear in mind that the recipient's macro security settings may not accept it. I have also noticed that writing UDFs can be addictive and that some people end up creating functions that effectively duplicate existing Excel functionality. Bear in mind from the outset that functions are customised calculations and return values – they cannot carry out instructions to perform tasks (that's what macros are for). In this section we will consider some very simple examples of UDFs, but without going into very much detail. There is a wealth of online help about UDFs and even the Microsoft VBA Help provides some reasonably useful functionality.

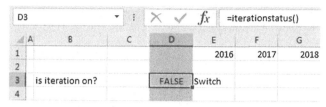

FIGURE 9.16   The IterationStatus UDF in use.

As a quick introduction consider the range name counter example, based directly on VBA code. In the VBA Editor this is written as a function:

```
Function CountNames()
        CountNames = ActiveWorkbook.Names.Count
End Function
```

This function can then be typed into the worksheet, as =countnames().

We have looked at iteration several times in this book and, whether writing the code or using a macro, we have used the Switch technique to control the circular formulas. In every case, we have had to switch on the iteration and then change the Switch to TRUE or FALSE. We could use a UDF:

```
Function IterationStatus()
Application.Volatile        'This forces Excel to recalculate
                           the function when the workbook
                           recalculates
        IterationStatus = Application.Iteration
End Function
```

If we write this function into the Switch cell it will automatically change with the iteration settings (Figure 9.16).

Tax Calculator

In previous editions I used an example of a UDF which created a random number between two other values, using the approach shown in Chapter 6 using the Excel RAND function. Microsoft was clearly so impressed by this that they brought out the RANDBETWEEN function. I now use a neat little function that allows us to understand some of the key features of the UDF.

In the United Kingdom, as elsewhere, there are a series of tax thresholds used to calculate tax on personal income. We will consider a three-tier system, in which the first x amount is zero-rated, the next y amount attracts tax at a basic rate and then any amount z above this is taxed at the higher rate. The arithmetic for this can be entered in a small number of cells, but we will write a UDF to do the whole calculation. Write the code first, then we will analyse it.

Open the Visual Basic Editor (Developer, Visual Basic command, or press Alt+F11).

1. Use the Insert, Module command if necessary.
2. Write (or copy) the following code:

```
Function PersonalTax(Gross As Long, ZeroBand As Long, BasicBand
As Long, BasicRate As Single, HigherRate As Single) As Long
    If Gross <= ZeroBand Then PersonalTax = 0 Else
        With Application.WorksheetFunction
            Basic = .Max(.Min(BasicBand - ZeroBand, Gross -
        ZeroBand), 0)
            Higher = .Max(Gross - BasicBand, 0)
        End With
    PersonalTax = (Basic * BasicRate) + (Higher * HigherRate)
    End Function
```

3. Alt+Tab back to the worksheet and enter the following into cells A1:A5
   A1 35000 Name this cell as Gross (note these names correspond exactly to the function arguments)
   A2 10000 Name this cell as ZeroBand
   A3 30000 Name this cell as BasicBand
   A4 20%   Name this cell as BasicRate
   A5 40%   Name this cell as HigherRate
4. In cell A7 write the function in a cell: =PersonalTax(A1, A2, A3, A4, A5)
5. Test the operation of the function. If you are using an older version of Excel you may find that the function does not recalculate automatically (or on pressing F9). If you want to fix this, insert the following line after the function definition: Application.Volatile True

Tip: After typing the function name, press Ctrl+Shift+A. Excel will bring up the Function Wizard to help you fill in the arguments; alternatively, if you have set up the range names you will find them substituted directly into the function (Figure 9.17).

The function name is PersonalTax, and we have specified the variable types of the required arguments: Gross, ZeroBand, BasicBand and PersonalTax deal

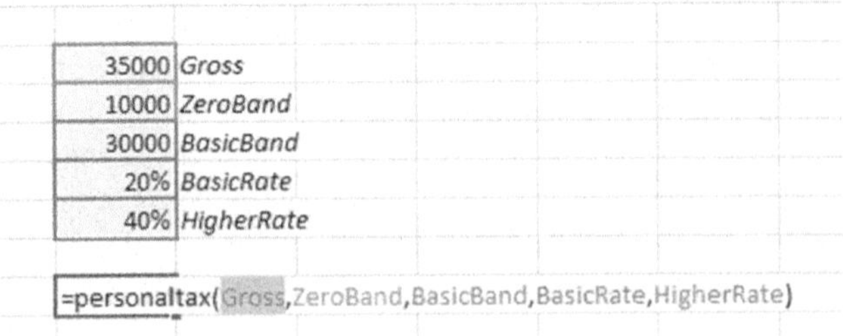

35000	Gross
10000	ZeroBand
30000	BasicBand
20%	BasicRate
40%	HigherRate

=personaltax(Gross,ZeroBand,BasicBand,BasicRate,HigherRate)

FIGURE 9.17   Writing the personaltax function using Ctrl+Shift+A.

with values in excess of 32,767 and are Long. BasicRate and HigherRate, although percentages, are Single.

We use an IF to test to see if the Gross is less than the taxable amount; if so the function returns 0. Notice the IF follows the VBA format of If...Then... Else. If Gross is above this, it could either be taxed at the basic rate, if it is below the basic band, but there could also be a proportion which falls into the higher band. We have used MAX and MIN many times before, but as with the IF we need to use the VBA versions, in which case they would be written as Application.WorksheetFunction.Max(...). To avoid having to write this out several times we use the With...End With as an instruction that if VBA sees a function such as .Max it will assume it is prefixed with the full statement. Finally we have the simple arithmetic to calculate the tax on each portion. We haven't done it here but you can add comments to your code in the usual way, with the ' apostrophe prefix.

You will have seen that despite the use of upper case in the function name in the VB editor, the worksheet uses lower case only. As you write the function Excel will attempt to fill in keywords and capitalise according to its own rules. As with macros, if you make errors you can use the F8 Step mode to run through the function. Remember to reset after debugging any mistakes.

Local Range Names

Here is another simple example of a UDF. One of the problems with using range names is when the user accidentally creates local names which conflict with existing global names. In the modelling methodology set out in the first part of this book, I suggested that names on the inputs sheet should have the suffix '...In' to differentiate the input names from those on the workings sheet. If, however, the 'In' is omitted, and the same range name is created on the workings sheet, the latter name becomes a local or sheet level name and can only be referenced on that sheet. To refer to the range from another sheet, we must include the sheet name along with the range name (e.g. =Workings!UnitPrice). This can lead to problems – the Paste Name and Go To commands do not identify conflicting names and list only the names on the current sheet, which may then be a mixture of global and local names. The following UDF attempts to resolve this, and is used with the Paste List command.

```
Function LocalNameCheck(TestName As String, Reference)
NameVerify = Names(TestName).RefersTo
If NameVerify = Reference Then
   LocalNameCheck = 0
Else
   LocalNameCheck = NameVerify
End If
End Function
```

The function is written into the worksheet alongside the list of names. The TestName is the cell reference of the range name in the list, and the Reference is the range reference. NameVerify returns the global name reference, and the IF checks that it matches with the reference from the list in the worksheet. If they are the same, the function returns 0, but if they are different (because the name in the worksheet references a local range name) the function returns the conflicting global range reference. The function works reliably in the inputs/workings model structure if the check is run on the workings sheet, but is less reliable in other model layouts.

Managing UDFs

If you save the file which contains your UDFs with a name such as functions.xls and keep the workbook open, you can access these functions from your other models by prefixing the function name with the (path and) filename:

```
=functions.xls!personaltax(...)
```

You can also write the function by using the Formulas, Insert Function command and equivalent techniques, where it will be listed in the User-Defined category (if there are no available UDFs this category will not be listed). It will not contain a description, but you can fix this by using Developer, Macros (Alt+F8). The dialog box only lists macros, but if you type the function name you should be able to click on the Options button. Write the appropriate description for the function, and close the dialog box.

As with macros, it is possible to store UDFs in the personal.xlsb so that they are available to all your models but they will still require the filename prefix. Follow the steps in Section Personal.xlsb and use the VB Editor to write your UDF.

It is now possible to manage UDFs by saving them as add-ins. Write the UDF code in the usual way, but when saving the workbook choose the Excel Add-In option towards the bottom of the file types list. This will automatically put the file into the AddIns folder, so give the file a meaningful name (do make sure that the UDFs are fully documented in the VBA code or in the workbook itself).

The add-in workbook needs to be enabled, either through File, Options, Add-Ins and the Add-Ins manager, or the Developer tab, Add-Ins. In the Add-Ins dialog box select Browse. This should show you the AddIns folder, from which you can select the workbook. On returning to the Add-Ins dialog box make sure there is a tick next to the workbook, and choose OK. From this point onwards the UDF can be typed directly in the worksheet, with no filename required.

Add-Ins should be removed if not required, and Excel will complain if it cannot find the add-in workbook.

Appendix 1

Good Modelling Practice

THE PRINCIPLE OF ERROR REDUCTION

The Principle of Error Reduction accepts that errors are inevitable. Some techniques are more prone to error than others. We reduce the risk of error by using alternative techniques and a consistent methodology that serves to enhance the detection of errors when they occur. This is basis for the quality assurance process.

The Feedback Principle

In the absence of apparent error, how do we ensure that we are right? The Feedback Principle is the first element of quality control – we *actively* seek to test and validate our work continuously throughout the model development process.

The Top-Down Principle

This principle helps us make sense of the complexities of the modelling environment. Rather than becoming immersed in immense amounts of detail (bottom-up), we retain a view of the model's overall purpose and results.

MODEL RISK FACTORS AND THE RISK ASSESSMENT

The following checks should form part of the overall risk assessment of a model and the results should be recorded on the audit sheet, if there is one. Note that risk assessment must take into account the justification for the use of a particular technique or feature – the use of iteration by an experienced analyst following the methodology set out in Chapter 5 should provide some reassurance. The use of iteration by a graduate recruit with an Excel Level 3 course certificate should give rise to grave concern!

This list is not comprehensive or in any particular order. All of these risk factors are described and explained elsewhere in this book.

- Iteration and the presence of circular code
- Linked files
- Macros
- User-defined functions
- Excel add-ins
- Array formulas
- R1C1 notation
- Calculation – manual, automatic except tables
- Precision as displayed
- Hidden sheets
- Hidden rows/columns
- Merged cells
- AutoComplete
- Extend list formats and formulas
- Accept labels in formulas
- 1904 date system
- Error values
- Range names
- Location of inputs
- Hard-coded values
- References to blank cells
- Left-to-right inconsistency consistency
- 3-D or cross-sheet calculations
- Protection – cells or sheets

THE RULES OF GOOD MODELLING

The 'rules' and statements in this section are derived from various sections of this book where they are discussed in detail. I summarise them here to offer a stimulus for discussion. If you also refer to the FAST standard and to the SMART and BPM modelling methodologies you will see that there is overwhelming agreement on what constitutes good – and bad – modelling practice.

Structure: General

- Building models: design the output first.
- Using models: identify the outputs first.
- Separate inputs from workings and outputs.
- Use the same sheet layout throughout the model (each column has the same function on each sheet).
- Use cell comments.
- Use colour consistently.
- Use colour for incomplete/temporary formulas.

- Create a 'hard edge' for the right-hand edge of the model.
- Document your work.
- Make navigation simple and straightforward.
- Garbage in, garbage out.

Inputs Sheet

- Numbers only – no formulas (except data tables).
- Range names should have the suffix '...In' or similar, to indicate their origin.
- Document the sources of your assumptions – especially any 'plug' numbers.
- Cross-check your inputs against your data sources.
- Keep numbers in the same units that are given in the documentation.
- The input sheet drives the timing of events in the forecast period.
- Multiple inputs sheets are acceptable.
- If using file links, use a separate input sheet for each file.

Workings Sheet

- Only one workings (calculations) sheet.
- Formulas only – no numbers.
- Use links to bring the data from the inputs sheet(s).
- Left-to-right consistency – formulas should be the same across the whole forecast period.
- Use the base column to preserve the rule of left-to-right consistency.
- No 3-D (cross-sheet) calculations – no calculations which include references to other sheets.
- A general increase in complexity from top to bottom.
- Use basic number formatting.
- Keep formulas simple and short.
- Sign – liabilities should be positive.
- Use group and outline techniques to keep the workings manageable.

Outputs Sheets

- Contains links to workings sheet.
- No links to other output sheets.
- Summary formulas only.
- No values.
- Use appropriate number formatting.
- Use consistent sign convention.
- Use graphs to 'tell the story'.

Range Names

- The principle of range names is the natural language formula.
- Use consistent and meaningful names.
- Remember that many people do not like and distrust names.

Audit Sheet

- A rule-based methodology can only work if you have the techniques to detect and locate exceptions (Chapter 2 and 3).
- 3-D (cross-sheet) audit calculations are acceptable – audit check formulas are *about* the model, not part of it.
- Cross-check workings calculations with the equivalent summary formulas on the outputs sheets.
- Cross-check output sheets with each other.
- Use past experience – if something has gone wrong before, think of an audit check which might have identified it and use it in your future models.
- Don't move on from a piece of modelling unless all audit checks are satisfied.
- 'Stress test' the model – use extreme values.
- Predictive outcomes – use values which generate known results.
- Use ratios as rationality checks.

Printing

- Set up the page layouts as early as possible.
- Be ready to print at any stage.
- Complete the outputs as you go.

Saving

- Save frequently and rename/renumber after major steps.
- Don't save multiple copies of the same model.
- Don't distribute copies of your model.
- Keep track of the versions.

Formulas

- Avoid long formulas.
- Keep formulas short.
- Break complex logic into simple steps.
- If today you can't immediately understand a formula which you wrote last week, it is too complex.
- Avoid IFs: consider using the masking techniques from Chapters 5 and 6.
- Avoid OFFSET: use INDEX and MATCH functionality.
- Clarify sign switching using = 0-.
- Avoid circular formulas; if you really have to, use iteration but make sure it is controlled with a switch.
- Use range names and enjoy the benefit of natural language formulas.
- Do not use 3-D (cross-sheet) calculations.
- Do not prefix formulas with +. Use =.

File Links

- Don't link to other files; if you have to, put your file link formulas on an input (link) sheet.

Macros

- Avoid using macros; if you have to, make sure they are documented, simple to use and thoroughly tested.
- Don't produce 'black boxes'.

Problems with Excel Commands

Under certain conditions, you may find that Excel doesn't appear to work properly. Menu commands and other tools may not be available if:

- The workbook is protected.
- Group mode is active.
- File, Options, Advanced, For objects, show: All is off.
- Page Layout mode is on.
- The window is frozen.
- Edit mode is active.
- The Alt or F10 keys have been pressed.

Appendix 2

Keyboard Shortcuts

This is a list of the keyboard shortcuts which I think are most useful for routine modelling. This is not a comprehensive list of all Excel shortcuts; refer to Excel Help for a full list, using 'keyboard shortcut' as the search string, or read the Using Shortcut Keys topic in the Contents of Help.

THE RIBBON

The tools on the Ribbon are accessed by pressing the Alt key, followed by the letter corresponding to the relevant tab, followed by the letter for the tool or command. For example, to decrease one decimal place use Alt+H, then 9. Some of the shortcuts use letter pairs, so to use the Page Setup dialog box press Alt+P, then S and P in the quick succession.

Press Esc to back up or return to the worksheet.

These Excel 2013 shortcuts work in both Excel 2003 and Excel 2007 with UK/US keyboard layouts.

Non-Ribbon Commands

General

Ctrl+Z	Undo
Ctrl+Y	Redo
F2	Edit cell
F4	Repeat last action
Ctrl+R	Fill right
Ctrl+S	Save
F12	Save as
Alt+=	AutoSum
F11	Create chart (chart sheet)
Alt+F1	Create chart (in worksheet)
Ctrl+Shift+"	Copy cell above
Ctrl+;	Insert date
Ctrl+Shift+:	Insert time
Shift+F10	Shortcut menu

Selection

Ctrl+A	Select sheet
Shift+Space	Select row
Ctrl+Space	Select column
Shift+arrow	Select in direction
Shift+End+Enter	Select to end of row
Ctrl+*	Select current region

Navigation

F5	Go to/Go back
Ctrl+PgUp	Previous sheet
Ctrl+PgDn	Next sheet
Ctrl+Home	Go to A1/top left of sheet
Ctrl+End	Go to bottom right of working area
Alt+PgUp	Screen left
Alt+PgDn	Screen right

Auditing

Ctrl+[	Select precedents
Ctrl+]	Select dependents
Ctrl+'	View formulas (toggle on/off)

Formatting

Ctrl+Shift+1	Comma, two decimals
Ctrl+Shift+4	Currency, two decimals
Ctrl+Shift+5	Percentage, no decimals
Ctrl+Shift+~	General number format
Ctrl+#	Date format
Ctrl+B	Bold
Ctrl+I	Italic

Group and Outline

Alt+Shift+right arrow	Group rows (or columns)
Alt+Shift+left arrow	Ungroup rows (or columns)
Ctrl+8 (not number keypad)	Display or hide outline symbols
Ctrl+9 (not number keypad)	Hide rows
Ctrl+Shift+(	Unhide selected rows
Ctrl+O (not number keypad)	Hide columns
Ctrl+Shift+)	Unhide columns

Names

F3	Paste names
Ctrl+Shift+F3	Create names
Ctrl+F3	Name manager

Index

Note: Page numbers followed by "f" and "t" indicate figures and tables respectively.

A

ABS function, 47
Absolute reference, 101–102
Access control, 207
Alteration errors, 21
Arithmetical checks
  ABS function, 47
  audit check formula, 48, 48f
  errors, 46–47
  inputs–workings–outputs structure, 46–47
  project cash flow check, 47, 47f
  ROUND function, 48
  SUM function, 47–48
  #VALUE! error, 48
Arithmetic mean, 252
Array formulas, 154–156, 154f–155f,
    236–238
Audit sheet, 286
  checking types, 32
  control sheet, 77
  inspection and validation regimes, 32
  layout, 33–35, 34f–35f
  modelling methodologies, 32
  MUT, 33, 64f
  risk assessment exercise, 32
  risk factors, 33
Audit tools and techniques
  Ctrl+[and F5 combination, 24
  Evaluate formula dialog box, 25, 26f
  Excel's error checking tools, 26–27
  Excel's protection, 22
  F9, 23, 23f
  F2 and F5 combination, 24
  F2 edit cell, 23
  Formula Auditing Ribbon group,
    24–25, 25f
  green error indicator triangle, 27
  trace precedents, 23
  View Formulas, 24, 25f
  Watch window, 26, 26f

Audit workbook
  delta sheet, 62, 63f–64f, 64
  F5 Go To, Special, 62, 63f
  financial statements, 56–57
  IRR
    discrepancy, 59–60, 61f
    formula, 59, 60f
    reconstruction, 60, 61f
  key results sheet, 59, 60f
  layout, 57
  model audit firms and forms, 56
  sensitivity testing, 62
  timeline alignment, 57–59, 59f
AutoFill click-and-drag technique, 42
Automation
  assigning macros, 261–263
    Excel ribbon, 263, 264f
    keyboard shortcuts, 261–262
    workbook buttons, 262–263, 262f
  debt sculpting, 269–275
    macro, 274–275, 274t–275t
    workbook formulas, 270–274, 270f–271f,
      273f–274f
  debugging, 275–278
    breakpoint technique, 276–277, 277f
    immediate window, 277–278, 278f
    locals window, 277
    step mode, 276, 276f
  error handling, 268–269, 269f
  macro security settings, 256, 256f
  quarterly/annual macro, 267–268, 268t
  recorded macros, 257–261, 258f
    Iteration macro, 258–261, 259f
  UDF, 278–282, 279f
    local range names, 281–282
    management, 282
    tax calculator, 279–281, 280f
  written macros, 264–267, 265f
    branching, 265–266
    writing, 266–267, 266t

B

Basel II requirements, 5
Bid models/projects, 15
BODMAS, 132
Bottom-up approach, 69
BPM methodology, 9–10, 17, 32, 73, 284
Break-and-make technique, 30, 117
British Department for Transport (DfT), 3–4
Budgeting model, 68–69, 79
Button button, 262, 262f

C

Calculation errors, 21
Cell reference formulas, 101
Change checks, 53–54
Change control, 208
Charting
    F11 and Alt+F1, 229, 230f
    updating charts, 230
CHOOSE function, 240–242, 241f
Circularities and iteration, 149, 150f
    circular formula, 144
    Circular References tracking tool, 146, 146f
    circular warning, 145, 145f
    error tracking, 147–149, 147f–148f
    interest-earning cash account, 149, 149f
    iteration command and constraints,
        150, 151f
    profit and loss statement, 152
    sensitivity analysis, 152–153
    switch mechanism, 151, 152f
    TRUE/FALSE response, 153
Coercion, 139
Combo box, 216–218, 217f–218f
Commercial bank loan, 165, 166f
    finished repayment mask, 168, 170f
    loan corkscrew, 165, 166f
    loan drawdown flag, 168, 171f
    repayments, period identification, 172, 173f
    revising the counter, 165–168, 169f
    simple repayment mask, 165, 167f
Commission errors, 20
Compare and contrast approach, 9–10
Competence errors, 21–22
Conditional formatting, 219–223, 219f–222f
    problems with, 222–223
Corkscrew, 124, 135–136, 136f–137f, 141,
    172, 270, 272
Counters, 139–140, 140f–141f
Ctrl+A function arguments, 157, 158f
Custom formatting, 223–229, 224f–226f
    conditional format, type of, 228–229
    currency, 228

reporting, 228
    styles, 227, 227f
Custom validation, 214–215

D

Data inputs
    custom validation, 214–215
    data validation, 214
    drop-down lists, 215–216, 216f
    list and combo boxes, 216–218, 217f–218f
    validation, problems with, 215
Data tables
    observations, 236
    one-way, 235–236, 237f
    risk analysis using, 254
    table recalculation, 236–238
    two-way, 236, 237f
Data validation, 214
Dates
    Ctrl+#, 193
    DATE (Year, Month, Day), 194–196,
        195f–196f
    date series, 196
    NOW(), 193–194
    risk factor, 193
Debt sculpting, 269–275
    macro, 274–275, 274t–275t
    workbook formulas, 270–274, 270f–271f,
        273f–274f
Debt service cover ratio (DSCR), 271
Define Names dialog box, 112, 112f
Delta sheets, 248–250, 249f–250f
Documented modelling methodology, 17
Domain errors, 22
Drop-down lists, 215–216, 216f

E

EDATE function, 194, 196f
Environmental checks
    file links, 37–38, 37f–38f
    iteration status, 36–37
    R1C1 reference style, 38
    technical settings, 35, 36f
    time stamping, 35, 36f
Error handling, 268–269
    debt cover ratio, 158
    #DIV/0! error value, 158
    error identification functions, 158
    good old IF
        empty quotes "" technique, 161
        format, 160
        IF formulas, 159
        test condition operators, 160

IFERROR and IFNA, 159
ISERROR function, 159
MAX/MIN solution, 161–162
AND and OR, 161
Error recognition, 22
Error values
    break-and-make technique, 30
    diagnostic tools, 27
    #DIV/0!, 28–29
    #N/A, 29
    #NAME?, 28
    #NUM!, 29
    printing without errors, 29
    #REF!, 28
    Trace Error tool, 29
    #VALUE!, 27–28
European Spreadsheet Risks Interest Group
    (EuSpRIG), 6
Excel Undo, 269

F
Feedback principle, 283
Financial checks
    Audit Chart, 53
    balance sheet, 49–50, 50f
    cash flow, 50
    domain knowledge, 49
    income statement, 50
    IRR, 52, 52f
    ratio analysis, 51–52
    Reserve accounts, 51
Financial functions, 196
    concatenation, 203
        INT and MOD, 204–205
        TEXT, 204
    ISTEXT, 201–203
    LARGE and SMALL functions,
        200–201, 202f
    net present value (NPV), 196–197,
        197f
        arithmetic NPV version 1,
            197, 198f
        arithmetic NPV version 2,
            197, 198f
    N/number function, 203
    RAND, 201
    XNPV, 197–200, 200f
Flags, 138, 139f
Flexible, appropriate, structured and
    transparent (FAST) document, 9–10
Formula AutoComplete, 157
Function Arguments dialog
    box, 157

G
Good modelling practice
    audit sheet, 286
    error reduction, 283
    excel commands, 287
    file links, 287
    formulas, 286
    inputs sheet, 285
    macros, 287
    outputs sheets, 285
    printing, 286
    range names, 285
    risk assessment, 283
    risk factors, 284
    rules, 284–287
    saving, 286
    structure, 284–285
    workings sheet, 285
Grouping, 211–212, 213f

H
HLOOKUP function, 175

I
INDEX function, 243, 243f
Input control, 207
Input errors, 20
Insert Function dialog box, 157
Institute of Chartered Accountants of England
    and Wales (ICAEW), 5
    ICAEW's 20 principles, 8–9
Intellectual challenge approach, 131
Internal rate of return (IRR), 199
    discrepancy, 59–60, 61f
    formula, 59, 60f
    reconstruction, 60, 61f
Iteration macro, 264

K
Keyboard shortcuts, 289–290

L
Laidlaw Enquiry, 3–4
Late binding functions, 157–158
List box, 216–218
Logical/Boolean operators, 162
Logical mask
    combined mask, 164, 165f
    depreciation formula, 163
    simple depreciation mask,
        164, 164f

LOOKUP function, 242, 242f
Lookup table, 177, 177f
LOOKUP without using LOOKUPS
  INDEX, 180, 180f
    cash flow forecast, 178, 179f
    cash flow minimum value, 178, 179f
    look-ahead counter, 180, 181f
    look-back counter, 180–182, 181f
  MATCH, 182, 183f
  nested INDEX/MATCH, 182, 184, 184f

M

Macpherson report, 3–4, 7–8
Macros
  assigning, 261–263
    Excel ribbon, 263, 264f
    keyboard shortcuts, 261–262
    workbook buttons, 262–263, 262f
  debt sculpting, 274–275, 274t–275t
  macro security settings, 256, 256f
  quarterly/annual macro, 267–268, 268t
  recorded macros, 257–261, 258f
    Iteration macro, 258–261, 259f
  written macros, 264–267, 265f
    branching, 265–266
    writing, 266–267, 266t
Masks technique, 137–138, 138f
Microsoft Backstage, 81–83, 82f–83f
Model interrogation, 231–233, 234f
Modelling Compliance Officer, 12–13
Model structure
  accuracy, 72
  agreed model structure, 69–70
  audit/control sheet, 77
  bottom-up approach, 69
  budgeting model, 68–69
  custom views, 89
  database application, 67–68
  documentation, 80
  edge effects, 71–72
  error reduction, 68
  feedback, 68
  File Properties
    Advanced Properties dialog box, 84, 84f
    Contents, 85
    General, 84
    metadata, 83–84
    Statistics, 84
    workbook Properties, 85–86
  fit to page, 87
  forecast period duration, 72
  group mode, 87

headers and footers, 87–88
inputs/assumptions sheet,
  73f, 74
key information, 78f, 81
Microsoft Backstage
  Document Inspector, 82f, 83
  Document Inspector results,
    83, 83f
  Info Backstage view, 81, 82f
model development
  AutoComplete feature, 91–92
  cell comments, 92
  data entry, 92
  fill right, 92
  grouping, 90
  layout, 90–91
  new file, 90
  number formatting, 91
  printing, 92
  saving, 90
  sign conventions, 93
  units and base columns, 91
navigation
  Alt+PgUp/Alt+PgDn, 89f, 93
  Ctrl+[, 96–97
  Ctrl+arrow, 95
  Ctrl+End, 94–95
  Ctrl+PgUp/Ctrl+PgDn, 93
  F6, 95
  Go to and Go back, 94f, 95
  Home/Ctrl+Home, 94
  Hyperlinks, 96f, 97–98
  Name Box, 95, 96f
  Right-Click Scroll Tab buttons, 94
outputs, 76–77, 76f–77f
page setup, 87
print area, 86–87
Print Titles, 85f, 88
quality assurance framework, 67
report generation, 88
robust model structure, 70
rule-based methodology, 67
sensitivity and scenario analysis,
  68–69
spreadsheet colour, 72
timesheeting system, 68–69
top-down approach, 68, 86
variations
  budgeting model, 79
  consolidation model, 79–80
  straightforward inputs–workings–outputs
    structure, 78
  timesheeting system, 79

version control, 71
workbook structure, 73–74,
    73f, 97f
workings/calculations sheet. *See* Workings/
    calculations sheet
MUT, 33, 64f

N

Name Manager, 112–113, 113f
Names creation
    Create Names command, 110–111, 110f
    #VALUE! error, 111, 111f
National Audit Office (NAO), 4
Natural Language Formulas (NLF), 104–105
Net present value (NPV), 196–197, 197f
    arithmetic NPV version 1, 197, 198f
    arithmetic NPV version 2, 197, 198f

O

Omission errors, 20
Outlining, 211–212

P

Password protection, 210–211, 211f
PEMDAS, 132
Periodicity change
    quarterly to annual, 140–141, 141f
    relative sum technique, 143, 144f
    rolling total, 141–143, 142f–143f
Personal.xlsb, 257
Phantom file links, 130
Pointing errors, 19–20
Pool concept
    completed pool, 186, 187f
    counter addition, 186, 187f
    details addition, 184, 185f
    fixed schedules
        CapexHappening event, 189
        completed depreciation routine, 189, 191f
        depreciation schedule, 188, 188f
        depreciation schedule counters and masks,
            189, 190f
        OFFSET, 189–193, 192f
        ScheduleCheck, 189
    loan pool, 184, 185f
    mask technique, 184
    PoolAdditions, 186
    PoolCf/AssetLife, 188
    PoolCf/Term, 184
    PoolCounter, 186
    PoolRemovals formula, 186

tax losses, 188
#VALUE! errors, 186
Project Finance Sector, 4–5
Public Accounts Committee report, 3–4
Public–private partnership (PPP), 4–5

Q

Quality assurance
    access control, 16
    Basel II requirements, 5
    bid models/projects, 15
    British Department for Transport
        (DfT), 3–4
    change control, 17
    code review, 16
    compare and contrast approach, 9–10
    cost/benefit analysis, 16
    documented modelling methodology, 17
    end-user computing, 6
    European Spreadsheet Risks Interest Group
        (EuSpRIG), 6
        modelling methodologies, 10
    flexible, appropriate, structured and
        transparent (FAST) document, 9–10
    formal model audit, 14
    ICAEW's 20 principles, 8–9
    in-house methodology, 9–10
    input control, 17
    Institute of Chartered Accountants of
        England and Wales (ICAEW), 5
    Laidlaw Enquiry, 3–4
    Macpherson report, 3–4, 7–8
    model audit and review, 13, 14f
    Modelling Compliance Officer, 12–13
    modelling culture and environment, 13
    National Audit Office (NAO), 4
    peer review process, 13–14
    project documentation, 15
    Project Finance Sector, 4–5
    Public Accounts Committee
        report, 3–4
    quality requirements, 10–11
    risk assessment, 16
    risk management, 6
    Sarbanes–Oxley Act (2002)
        (SOX), 5
    Senior Responsible Owner
        (SRO), 12
    spreadsheet governance, 5–6
    training/modelling standards, 6
    UK regulatory environment, 5
    version control, 17

Quality control
    alteration errors, 21
    arithmetical checks. *See* Arithmetical checks
    audit sheet, 56. *See also* Audit sheet
    audit tools and techniques. *See* Audit tools
        and techniques
    audit workbook. *See* Audit workbook
    calculation errors, 21
    change checks, 53–54
    commission errors, 20
    competence errors, 21–22
    domain errors, 22
    environmental checks. *See* Environmental
        checks
    error recognition, 22
    error reduction, 19
    error values. *See* Error values
    financial checks. *See* Financial checks
    input errors, 20
    model map
        conditional formatting, 54, 55f
        graphical view and components, 54
        hard-coded values, logic values, 54, 55f
    model reviewer and review plan
        formulas audit, 30
        printing, 31
        reporting issues, 31–32
        spreadsheet navigation, 30
        time and resource management, 31
    omission errors, 20
    pointing errors, 19–20
    spreadsheet error, 19
    structural checks. *See* Structural checks
    taxonomies, 19
    third party model audit tools, 64–65
    timing errors, 21

R

Range names, 285
    applying names, 115–116, 116f
    benefits, 109
    break and make technique, 117
    cell reference version, 125
    combination names, 121
    Create Names technique, 116
    Ctrl- and Shift-clicking techniques, 117
    dynamic range names, 127–128
    empty ranges, 129
    extending ranges, 119, 119f
    external name references, 130
    FAST Viewpoint, 106–107
    Formula AutoComplete, 115, 115f

    geographical precision, 105
    individually named cells, 114
    intersection formulas, 121–122
    listing names, 128–129
    local/sheet level name, 109,
        122–123, 123f
    logical and consistent approach, 109
    misspelled/redundant range names
        deletion, 117
    mixed reference range name, 126, 126f
    multiple names, 129–130, 130f
    named ranges movement, 119
    #NAME? error value, 117
    Name Manager, 117
    names and functions, 120–121
    naming convention, 107
    naming formulas, 127
    naming values, 126, 127f
    natural language approach, 107
    Natural Language Formulas
        (NLF), 104–105
    now-redundant global range names, 122
    one *vs.* two dimension, 110
    Paste Name, 115
    Phantom file links, 130
    poor range names, 108, 108f
    principle, 107
    relative reference, 113–114
    removing names, 117–119, 118f–119f
    research participants, 104
    reusable code, 109
    row headings, 105, 106f
    Rule of Thumb, 106
    speed, 105
    three-dimensional/cross-sheet names,
        123–124, 124f
    #VALUE! error, 114
    Visual Basic for Applications (VBA)
        macros, 110
R1C1 referencing, 38, 103, 103f
    functions, 102
    Name Manager, 104
    workbook, 102, 102f
Relative referencing, 101
Revolving credit
    cash cascade concept, 175
    completed revolver, 175, 176f
    loan facility, 172
    revolver setting, 172, 174f
Risk
    analysis, 250–254
        data tables, 254, 254f
            Monte Carlo simulation, 252–253, 252f

controls
   access, 207
   change, 208
   input, 207
   version, 208
ROUND function, 48

S

Sarbanes–Oxley Act (2002) (SOX), 5
Scenario analysis, 238–248
   cell reference method, 244–245
   function approach, issues with, 243
   multiple input sheets, 244, 246
   printing scenarios, 247–248
   range name method, 245–246, 245f
   Scenario Manager, 239–240, 240f
      CHOOSE function, 240–242, 241f
      INDEX function, 243, 243f
      LOOKUP function, 242, 242f
   Solver, 250
Senior Responsible Owner (SRO), 12
Sensitivity analysis
   data tables, 235
   Goal Seek tool, 233–235, 235f
   one-way data table, 235–236, 237f
   two-way data table, 236, 237f
Sheet protection, 208–210, 209f
SMART methodology, 9–10, 17, 32, 73, 284
Standard deviation, 253
Stream of consciousness approach, 69
Stress testing, 231–232
Structural checks
   array formulas, 45–46, 46f
   blank cells reference, 41
   3-D/cross-sheet calculations, 42–43
   Go To, Special command, 43
   hard-coded values, 39–40, 40f
   hidden columns and rows, 44
   hidden sheets, 44, 45f
   input values location, Go To Special,
      39, 40f
   left-to-right consistency, 41–42
   merged cells, 44–45
   Name Manager dialog box, 44

SUM function, 47–48
Switches, 138–139

T

Table recalculation, 236–238
Third party model audit tools, 64–65
Timesheeting system, 68–69, 79
Timing errors, 21
Timing management
   base column, 134–135, 134f–135f
   corkscrew
      accumulated depreciation corkscrew, 136,
         137f
      cardinal modelling rule, 135
      profit and loss and cash flow items, 136,
         136f
      Trace Dependents tool, 135, 136f
   left-to-right consistency, 133–134
   multiple periodicities, 132–133
   time dependency and independency, 133
Toolbars, keyboard shortcuts, 289–290
Top-down approach, 68, 86, 283
Trust Center, 256, 256f

U

User-defined functions (UDF), 278–282, 279f

V

Version control, 208
Visual Basic for Applications (VBA), 110,
   255–256
VLOOKUP function, 175, 177–178

W

West Coast Rail Link, 3–4
Workbook protection, 210, 210f
Workings/calculations sheet
   error reduction, 74–75
   inputs sheet, 74f, 75
   logic cascade, 75
   sheet size, 75
   workings formulas, 75

Printed in the United States
By Bookmasters